ALEXANDER REVISITED

Contemplation & Criticism

1979 – 2014

Ron Dennis

Posturality Press
Atlanta

ALEXANDER REVISITED
Contemplation & Criticism, 1979–2014

ISBN 978-0-9882525-1-6

Published by
    Alexander Technique of Atlanta/Posturality Press
    Ronald J. Dennis, Proprietor
    Websites: www.posturecounts.com
              www.posturality.com
    Email: rondennis@compuserve.com

Cover Photo Credits:

F. M. Alexander, courtesy of Jeroen Staring Collection (originally published in *Who*, September 1941).

Ron Dennis, candid shot by George Eckard, 1993.

To F. Matthias Alexander (1869–1955)

Affectionately,

"It was you that broke the new wood,
Now is a time for carving."

From "A Pact" by Ezra Pound

"a Book is a Person, not a Thing"
W. N. P. Barbellion
The Journal of a Disappointed Man

Author's Foreword

When, in 1977, I left my enviable position as Principal Clarinet of The Saint Paul Chamber Orchestra to train in Alexander, I was often asked why. The reply I developed that seemed sufficiently correct as well as brief was, "Because I had an intuition that I would have more to say as an Alexander teacher than as a clarinetist." At the time, so far as I knew, I was speaking figuratively, but now, almost 40 years later, it seems that it was literally as well. The present volume spans 35 years, from just before I was certified in 1979, to now$_{2014}$, with the last piece still "in press." Which is not to say that I've written my last, but that a line must be drawn somewhere, and here seems realistic, all things considered.

Naturally in this foreword to my collected Alexandrian writings, many of which were previously self-published as separate booklets, I would like to say just the right things to explain or justify them, but essentially in vain: there they be, set down with whatever ability, and for whatever worth, as readers may determine. Nevertheless, as my intellectual children—no others—left to this world, I fondly wish them well.

Thanks especially to Claire Rechnitzer, an Alexander teacher who found that my work brought to hers a new clarity and who generously agreed to provide the General Introduction to this volume. She is that "solitary individual," hopefully to be multiplied, whom both Kierkegaard and I "call with joy and gratitude my reader."

A small corpus of my writings, the editorial columns of *The Alexandrian*, this country's first periodical of the

Technique established and edited by me from 1981–1985, is not included in the present collection. For the most part consisting of topical introductions to the articles of each issue, these pieces published here would lack much meaningful context. On the other hand, through 13 issues, *The Alexandrian* did present to its audience many substantial articles of lasting value, at a time when serious periodical writing on the Technique was relatively rare. I thus am including as Appendix II the complete contents of *The Alexandrian,* deservedly to memorialize these writings and their authors, as well as to document my own literary efforts in the Technique. Reviewing this historic array, I confess I'm impressed, and, for interested potential readers, these materials remain in the archives of the American Center for the Alexander Technique, now2025 digitized and available at www.acatnyc.org. Appendix I contains my "Whither NASTAT" of 1994, a controversial and still-relevant piece which didn't fit conveniently in the collection's main divisions but which really couldn't be left out.

Because the contents of this book span such a period of time and have appeared in such different formats, it has been a labor to reconcile the texts in terms of layout, cross-reference, and index. But in passing my eyes many times over these pages I think to have come pretty close to the mark—in any case essential meaning should be clear enough. I do cringe a little when encountering inevitable anomalies of time, place, or circumstance, but for the most part have left them unremarked unless detrimental to fact or substance.

I welcome any such corrections, to be included along with subsequent writings—Lord willing—in a future printing or edition.

General Introduction

By Claire Rechnitzer

Whenever I chance to meet veteran Alexander Technique teachers, in person or through their writing, I am always eager to observe their style, learn about their particular research and special applications, hear stories about their lineage, and measure my own understanding and interpretation of the Technique against theirs. Having encountered Ron Dennis as both author and hands-on teacher, I can affirm that this collection of his thoughts offers plenty of opportunity for all of the above. But particularly in terms of my own evolving conception of our work, I am grateful and not just a little awed.

Ron's take on the practice and principles of the Technique is exceptionally thoughtful, clear, and grounded, yet he never expects his views to be taken at face value. In these collected writings, he explains his reasoning with patience and humor, anticipating his readers' questions and answering them. While many practitioners may tell you what the Technique is like, or what it is not, Ron's writing proves, through careful definition of terms and avoidance of jargon, that it is possible to talk about the Technique without resorting to metaphors or *via negativa* descriptions. "Every analogy," he says, "breaks down under the reality of comparative objective conditions" (p. 210), and a common thread through his writing is his insistence that we can and should find language that could serve the Alexander Technique professionally for the benefit of all.

When I exchange work with my peers, I seek an atmosphere that allows for differences or mistakes with care and kindness. When experimenting on my own, I hope to avoid second-guessing myself or blindly deferring to those with more experience. There are a number of pieces in this collection that are shining examples of what can be gained through reflection, feedback, learning from experience, and getting past false starts. Collectively, these writings suggest *an approach* to the honing of skills, and show, in the manner of Nobel Laureate Nikolaas Tinbergen and science generally, that the best way to learn something useful is by asking purposeful questions.

Read "Teacher, Heal Thyself" (see p. 134) and see how Ron's method of inquiry is strikingly similar to F. M. Alexander's account of his own "Evolution of a Technique" in *The Use of the Self*. Peruse his research and technical studies and note how they go beyond the applications of popular Alexander Technique "how to's"—singing, exercise, birth, etc.—to seek insight, corroboration, or amendments vis-à-vis the basic working assumptions and principles of the Technique. Address with him the physiological, philosophical, and even ethical implications for, and of, the Technique in "A Modern Theory of Coordination and Its Implications for the Alexander Technique" (especially the last paragraph, p. 175). In all of his writing Ron treats his sources with generosity and respect through detailed footnoting and cross-references.

When I teach, I try to put my students at ease by letting them know how I am teaching them. As I gleaned through reading him, and confirmed in working with him, Ron has a way of describing—what he's looking for, what he sees, what and how he hears, feels and thinks—that is all the more impressive for its basis in observation, as well as from the intuition expected in Alexander teachers. His tone, though perhaps lofty, is never patronizing or impatient. He is *judicial*—in the sense of "inclined to make or give judgments; critical; discriminating"—but he carries that quality with grace and a sense of humor that does indeed put readers or hearers at ease.

Ron's determination to find language that members of our young profession can agree upon is born from a sincere—though not blind—belief that the Technique is timeless and can help people from all walks of life. Far from accepting—though not without entertaining a possibility—that the Technique is either passé, ahead-of-its time, or elitist, he rather thinks that we have not well-communicated its worldly message, and that, to that end, we need to put our minds to clearing up what he considers "basic *mis*-understandings of the Technique within our own Alexandrian community" (see p. 239). I find Ron's efforts on that front particularly useful for our collective understanding, but have also found that paying attention to him has helped me think *for myself* with greater clarity and ease.

I hope that people will read this collection with care, perhaps repeatedly, for what Bruce Kodish dubs its "inestimable service to the community of AT teachers" (see p. 15). I hope they will find several "polished miniatures" that speak to them, and also read between the lines to discover the thought-provoking ideas introduced, as Phyllis Richmond says, "almost under the radar" (see p. 82). And I hope the book will be read not just by those Robert Britton identifies as "anyone who is on the path of investigating the phenomena of being a living, standing and moving human" (see p. 160), but surely by Alexander Technique teachers.

Indeed, I hope that teachers especially will read this book, and read it with their colleagues, so that we may begin together to address more effectively the predicament of the "underperformance of the Alexander Technique in the human potential and wellness marketplaces" (see p. 239).

I hope they recommend it to their trainees in order to prevent what David Langstroth calls the critical "muddle of understanding" (see p. 39), which he suspects "can be traced back to the way Alexander Technique teachers are trained." Finally, I hope teachers will introduce at least parts of this collection to curious students who want to know what Alexander Technique teachers know, to help facilitate a correct and professional conversation between student and teacher, and to help recruit the next generation of Teachers of the Alexander Technique.

Having appeared in various publications over the course of many years, all the articles and essays in this collection would have been very difficult to track down individually even by those aware of their existence. The collection and organization of these pieces into a book not only makes them accessible to new readers, but brings to readers both new and old a special value that is decisively greater than the sum of its parts.

December 1, 2014
Cincinnati, Ohio

Table of Contents

(Contents listed separately for each Book)

Book I

Conceptual Foundations

Contents

Introduction

By Bruce Kodish

Big things sometimes do come in small packages. The modest booklet that you hold in your hands, written [with the exception of David Langstroth's article] by veteran Alexander Technique (AT) teacher Ron Dennis, provides the basis for a modern (2005) reformulation of the form of cognitive-kinesthetic education* known as the "Alexander Technique".

Although the articles herein have been published separately, their appearance here where they can be read together and repeatedly—I suggest at least 2 or 3 times— does an inestimable service to the community of AT teachers.

For one thing, careful reading leaves little doubt that every AT teacher has a theory of what he or she is doing and why. Mr. Alexander did. And so do you. The question remains, what *kind* of theory do you have? Hopefully, in a profession based on the constructive application of conscious thought, you do not have a mainly unconscious one. You'll be able to remedy that as you contend with these articles—whether or not you agree with any, all, or none of Ron's formulations.

Ron's writing also makes clear that, whatever else it consists of, the Alexander Technique involves a system of related formulations. Ron's reconsideration and reformulation of "Primary Control" requires similar treatment of other foundational notions such as "Use" as well as a new

---

*A term coined by Ron and cited in my *Back Pain Solutions* (Pasadena: Extensional Publishing, 2001), pp. 14, 271.

formulation, that of "Correlative Control." This involves in turn re-defining the Alexander Technique. (I hope that he expands the treatment of "Direction," "Inhibition," etc. in future writings.)

Ron demonstrates herein that scholarship in our discipline requires adequately and accurately referring to the views of F.M. Alexander without giving them undue deference. Ron is not afraid to challenge and go beyond Alexander and in doing so, as a fellow explorer, gives him the best honor that anyone can.

In this regard, I do have a small 'bone' to pick with Ron. In his response to David Langstroth, he agrees that Alexander himself did not talk about "primary control" in terms of a neurological mechanism. Not so. Check the references to Magnus in *The Use of the Self* and *The Universal Constant of Living*. For example, in *The Use of the Self*, Alexander referred to "This primary control, called by the late Professor Magnus of Utrecht, the 'central control', ..." (p. 441 in *The Books of F. Matthias Alexander*, New York: IRDEAT, 1997) Alexander not only defined "Primary Control" vaguely and reified it in some of his writings/statements but also definitely described it, at times, in terms of neurological mechanisms (reflexes) favored in his time.

Ron's work will challenge AT teachers who continue to follow Alexander in discussing "Primary Control" and related notions in a similar manner. Any up-to-date discussion of Alexander Technique in terms of 2005 neuroscience requires a more system-based approach that includes both involuntary, i.e., reflexive, and voluntary, i.e., skill-based, aspects. Ron refers to this, and especially to the significance of skill in understanding our work. In my opinion, the importance of skill cannot be emphasized too much.

"There is nothing more practical than a good theory."
Your skill as an AT teacher—and the skills of your students in refining their Use—can benefit in manifold ways by working with the theoretical-practical issues that Ron Dennis addresses in these pages.

Preface

Naturally an author—certainly one who addresses matters of import to professional colleagues—wishes the work to be at least read if not always accepted, and, in some degree at least, to go on. Hence this more accessible and durable form of my articles on the conceptual foundations of the Alexander Technique that appeared in *AmSAT News* and on the Web from 1999–2005. Included is David Langstroth's "Reply to Ron Dennis [etc.]" not only as a prerequisite, as it were, to my own "Reply to a Reply," but on its intrinsic merit, and for its valuable references.

On the subject of references, and because my writing is so full of them, I've converted the original endnotes to footnotes in order to encourage you to read them integrally with the text; especially the commentaries (in contrast to the purely source notes). To me, some of Alexander's most provocative notions are found in his footnotes, such as, for example, "In this connexion I wish it to be understood that throughout this book [*CCCI*] I use the term conscious guidance and control to indicate, primarily, a plane to be reached rather than the method of reaching it [!]." Whether any of mine are on a par with that you may judge, but as an example you could take a look at Note 1 in "The 'Other Half' of Primary Control" (p. 60).

On reviewing these pieces as a set, I'm pleased to say that I found movement in their progression. In "Reply to a Reply," for example, responding to the external stimulus of Langstroth's criticism, I really needed to expand my treatment of theory, not only to answer him but also to clarify the whole matter of theory and practice in the Technique. Less obvious but not less important was the inner-generated change from "secondary level" within voluntary movement behavior ("Defining Primary Control") to "collateral control" within Use ("The 'Other Half' of

Primary Control"). But perhaps the greatest movement as such was from my initial and trenchant criticism (which was not a total rejection) of the concept of Primary Control, on the one hand, to the full acceptance of it—howbeit through radical re-definition—on the other.

It would be an error to say that I found nothing that I would change in these pieces, but with two large exceptions, any such changes would be more in the realm of style than of substance. The first of these exceptions is the point brought to light by Bruce Kodish in his Introduction, i.e., FMA's explicit reference to Primary Control as a discrete neurological mechanism. The second is a citation that by rights I should have given on Korzybski's General Semantics, to which I referred in "Reply to a Reply." General Semantics, an "Alexander Technique" of verbal communication as it were, should be far better known among us, and our own Bruce Kodish, together with his wife Susan Presby Kodish, both internationally recognized authorities in this field, have written an excellent book on the subject.[1] Otherwise, the set as a whole well represents my thought on the Technique as it is now, and, given my stage of life and the relative stability of the subject matter, as it is likely to remain.

One last clarification is that, because writing for a professional audience, I freely abbreviate the titles of F. M. Alexander's four books, known to all. For the record, however, *MSI* is *Man's Supreme Inheritance* (1910, 1918); *CCCI* is *Constructive Conscious Control of the Individual* (1923); *US* is *The Use of the Self* (1932, 1943, 1946); *UCL* is *The Universal Constant in Living* (1941).

---

[1] *Drive Yourself Sane: Using the Uncommon Sense of General Semantics*, Rev. 2nd Ed. (Pasadena: Extensional Publishing, 2001).

This booklet was printed directly from Microsoft Word files using a very slick software package called *ClickBook 8* (www.bluesquirrel.com).

Thanks to *AmSAT News,* in particular to Michael Protzel and Phyllis Richmond, for initial publication of my articles, and to David Langstroth for kind permission to reprint his Reply (to which the copyright notice on this book is not intended to apply). A very special thanks to Bruce Kodish for contributing the present Introduction.

Ron Dennis
Atlanta, October 2005

Primary Control and the Crisis in Alexander Technique Theory

AmSAT News 45, Summer 1999

To speak of crisis in that aspect of our work relegated by FMA himself to second place or worse—"the practice and theory of my work,"[1] "mere theorizing,"[2] as he was wont to say—may seem less than earthshaking to my staunch Alexandrian audience, yet there are firm grounds for doing so. In practical terms because of the increased visibility and demand for information about the Technique occasioned by the expansion in alternative health and regulatory issues, these grounds encompass no less the ongoing quest for truth. Specifically, I will argue that the concept of "primary control" (hereafter, PC), as articulated by FMA in *The Use of the Self* (1932) and as constantly touted since, is not credible as a conceptual foundation of the Technique, and that this "primary noncredibility," at such a late historical juncture, *indeed constitutes a crisis* in the Technique's self- and consequently public image.[3]

---

[1] *UCL*, "Introductory."

[2] *US*, Chap. 1.

[3] More so, I submit, than the issues of plagiarism, eugenicism, and racism as maintained by Jeroen Staring in his *The First 43 Years of the Life of F. Matthias Alexander* (Vols. I & II, self-published, Nijmegen, The Netherlands, 1996 & 1997) and elsewhere. While surely relevant to any full assessment of FMA, these issues were clearly tangential to the development and transmission of his practical work, as indeed evidenced by present day AT teachers' widespread ignorance of them, while primary control clearly was not, as evidenced by its general acceptance today as a defining element of the AT.

Let us immediately see a basic structural problem with this concept.[1] As a word, "control" functions either as a noun or as a verb. To control-as-verb something, for example an automobile, is totally different from a control-as-noun something, such as a thermostat: the one is a process, the other a thing. Such lurking ambiguity in the meaning of a word makes it ill-suited for the clear communication of fundamental ideas, which is the explicit purpose of theory. At the level of ultimate reality we apparently must, with Heisenberg, accept uncertainty, but at the level of verbal communication, both with others and ourselves, about the AT, we should not continue to accept unnecessary confusion.

Virtually uncommented upon in the AT literature to date is the fact that FMA's famous *account* of PC ("Evolution of a Technique," in *US*) came some 35 years after the alleged discovery itself. Neither has anybody seemed to notice—truly amazing—that FMA wrote two prior and major expositions of his work (*MSI* and *CCCI*) without mentioning PC once! And yet it was perfectly clear to Eric David McCormack in his 1958 Ph.D. dissertation that "This new principle of the 'primary control' then, *which represents the outcome of his experimental observations* [emphasis added], may be taken to be the centre or core of Alexander's entire system."[2] Frank Pierce Jones advanced the explanation that "The doctrine of a 'primary control,' whether or not it was the same control as the one demonstrated by Magnus, provided Alexander with a parsimonious explanation for his findings, and he continued to use

---

[1] See my "Afterthoughts on Breath as Postural Process, *NASTAT News,* No. 16 , p. 203.

[2] University of Toronto, pp 26-27.

it, along with 'inhibition' and 'use,' when talking or writing about his technique."[1]

I submit that an unbiased observer, in possession of the above facts, would be hard pressed to conclude other than that PC was not, strictly speaking, what FMA actually discovered, whatever that might have been,[2] but a label attached retroactively to it. But the distinction is no mere quibble, for "speaking strictly" is what theory— *good* theory—is all about. A parsimonious explanation for the Master doesn't automatically make good theory for the Work.

Following FMA's lead, PC—"that relativity in the use of the head, neck, and other parts"[3] as he succinctly if loosely characterized it—has been taken up almost universally by the AT community. Here are some examples from the literature:

1. Aldous Huxley: "Alexander's fundamental discovery was this: there exists in man, as in all the other vertebrates, a primary control conditioning the proper use of the total organism. When the head is in a certain relation to the neck, and the neck in a certain relation to the trunk, then (it is a matter of brute empirical fact) the entire psychophysical organism is functioning to the best of its natural capacity."[4]

---

[1] *Body Awareness in Action*, p. 48.

[2] I tend to agree with Dart in this regard: "The basic discovery Alexander made from 1888 onwards was the practice of deliberate conscious inhibition." Alexander Murray (ed.), *Skill and Poise: A Selection from the Writings of Raymond Arthur Dart*, paperback, n.d., p. 93.

[3] *US*, 3rd ed. (Re-Educational Publications Ltd., 1955) p. 9.

[4] *Saturday Review of Literature*, Oct. 1941.

2. Patrick MacDonald: "One of Alexander's discoveries and one which has immense significance in the learning of the Technique is what he called 'The Primary Control.' This is a master reflex of the body, so that by organizing it one can modify all the postural relationships throughout the body."[1]

3. Giora Pinkas: "So to me, what F.M.A. emphasized is not an aspect, but the core, the central control mechanism, located in the brain, and related to the spinal cord. Being primary, by its natural hierarchical function, it governs other, secondary patterns, down the line, to the fingers and toes."[2]

4. Alexander Murray: "When this [starting on the toes] is done with the assistance of a skilled teacher, the primary control is activated and the whole system is tonified."[3]

5. Missy Vineyard: "But we claim to enhance in students something we call the primary control, and we claim that

---

[1] *The Alexander Technique As I See It*, p. 6.
[2] *NASTAT News*, No. 5, p. 6.
[3] Alexander Murray (ed.), *Skill and Poise: A Selection from the Writings of Raymond Arthur Dart*, paperback, n.d., p. 73.

this is a physiological mechanism rooted in a reflex system that all possess."[1]

6. Freyda Epstein: "Primary Control: Rediscovering our built in reflex which governs poise and posture."[2]

Not that the chorus has been totally harmonious. A faint cautionary note:

7. Eleanor Rosenthal: "Attempts have been made to explain the primary control in neuromuscular terms; I don't find them entirely satisfactory. Nevertheless, I do know that if I use Alexander's model, and work on the hypothesis that there is a primary control that can be activated by improving the relationship between the head, neck, and torso, I will get results reassuringly similar to Alexander's."[3]

Audible skepticism:

8. Wilfred Barlow: "Few people would find it helpful nowadays to talk about a 'primary control,' although in the past the phrase did emphasize the prime importance of a proper USE of the head and neck, at a time when anatomists and physiologists had no very clear account to give of the factors underlying balance."[4]

And patent discord:

---

[1] *NASTAT News*, No. 24, p. 15.
[2] Workshop advertisement, n.d., author's possession.
[3] *Medical Problems of Performing Artists*, June 1987, p. 54.
[4] *The Alexander Technique*, p. 16.

9. Frank Meulendijks & Loes Bredius: "Primary Control Can Not Be Located."[1]

In Nos. 1-6 can be clearly seen the tendency toward elaboration and particularly toward *reification*—"regarding or treating an abstraction or idea as if it had concrete or material existence"—of FMA's original notion. *It is this reification of primary control, via the uncritical appropriation of 'control' in its sense as a noun, that is the most damaging consequence of FMA's belated and actually specious introduction of primary control into the Alexandrian canon.* A reified primary control puts the AT community in the embarrassing and ultimately untenable position of having to explain a neural mechanism that has no evident basis in empirical research. I personally have looked at a fair amount of movement science literature since I began doctoral work in 1984, and have found nothing to indicate the kind of overarching mechanism implied by primary control.[2] At the 1996 NASTAT AGM I publicly asked Chris Stevens, the Ph.D. physicist-AT teacher-researcher, if there were any way in which he would be prepared to explain primary control to a neurologist. He replied, with only the briefest pause to consider, "No." Deborah Caplan, who could attest to this exchange because she later commented to me on it, does not men-

---

[1] *NASTAT News*, No. 30, p. 4. This perceptive article may be read with profit both on its own terms and for its relations, too complex for further comment here, to the present text. See also in the same issue "The Primary Control: A New Look at Alexander's Discovery" by Chris Stevens and Ariane Hesse, pp. 7-9.

[2] Lest I be hoist with my own petard, there is in fact just one instance in my scientific reading of an hypothesis suggestive of primary control, although clearly offered by N. Bernstein, the eminent Soviet movement scientist, as speculation about the role of tonus of the neck and trunk musculature in organizing movements. See my "A Modern Theory of Coordination and Its Significance for the Alexander Technique," *The Alexandrian*, Vol. II, No. 2 (p. 169).

tion primary control at all in her book.[1] Even FMA himself eventually saw this huge problem with reification, admitting in a post-1940 letter to Frank Pierce Jones, "There really isn't a primary control as such. It becomes a something in the sphere of relativity."[2]

How FMA could put forward, so late and without qualification, primary control as *the* discovery upon which his technique was based, is a serious question, and certainly one that all Alexandrians should reflect upon. Jeroen Staring's voluminous research leaves little doubt that FMA was less than forthcoming in matters relating to early sources and influences on his work.[3] In conversation with Staring, Walter Carrington has acknowledged that FMA was, with regard to the revision in later years of certain of his texts, "lazy."[4] All things considered, it is difficult not to see a decided tendency toward loose linguistic behavior on FMA's part.

Hopefully contributing to a broader understanding of this vexing issue is a remarkable notion brought out by Lawrence A. Cremin (an educator who, incidentally, was a student of Dewey's) in his book *Public Education*.[5] Cremin is discussing James Olney's theory of autobiography as applied to educational biographies, in particular the concept of "metaphors of self." I follow Cremin in quoting Olney at length: Metaphors, Olney says

---

[1] *Back Trouble: A New Approach to Prevention and Recovery.*

[2] In response to Jones' first published article on the AT ("The Work of F.M. Alexander as an Introduction to Dewey's Philosophy of Education," *School and Society*, No. 1462, 1943). Cited by Marian Goldberg, *NASTAT News*, No. 4, p. 7, copy of original letter in possession of Alexander Murray.

[3] Staring, *The First 43 Years of the Life of F. Matthias Alexander.*

[4] "Objectionable Remarks", *Direction* (Vol. I, No. 6), p. 234.

[5] New York: Basic Books, 1976, pp. 42-43.

are something known and of our making, or at least of our choosing, that we put to stand for, and so help us understand, something unknown and not of our making; they are that by which the lonely subjective consciousness gives order not only to itself but to as much of the objective reality as it is capable of formalizing and of controlling.[1]

Cremin goes on to point out that "such metaphors as they appear in autobiographies are ordinarily retrospective and hence far more *clear, simple, and certain* [emphasis added] than what Olney refers to as the 'objective reality' of the life." Certainly, FMA's "Evolution of a Technique" is nothing if not an educational autobiography. Certain was his need to put the story down in *some* coherent and manageable fashion, and certain as well the events and effects of many, many intervening years. We may profitably inquire with Cremin, I think, "What metaphors of self' did the subject seem to choose or *come to believe* [emphasis added]?" Surely in this light primary control appears more plausible as retrospective metaphor than as primordial discovery.

Needing to be made clear at this juncture is that criticism of FMA's later theory, rooted so doggedly in primary control, by no means implies criticism of his work as a whole. "Fortunately the 'primary control' hypothesis did not hold up the development of Alexander's practical teaching methods," Wilfred Barlow said.[2] "Talk is cheap, it takes money to buy whiskey," the old woman said.[3] There can be little doubt that all the people who paid FMA's

---

[1] *Metaphors of Self: The Meaning of Autobiography*, Princeton Univ. Press, 1972, p. 30.

[2] Barlow, *The Alexander Technique*, p. 16.

[3] Franklin A. Brainerd, *Raingatherer*, Minnesota Writers' Publishing House, 1973, p. 22.

fees—including the present writer, by proxy so to speak—(1) were not totally gullible and (2) cared more for his hands and the practical help he gave them than for his current theoretical notions. In their likewise sharp criticism of Freud, Daniel Yankelovich and William Barrett observe pointedly, "Contradictions of this sort do not mark the end of the road for any discipline; on the contrary, they can be immensely productive, calling as they do for a basic shift in thinking."[1] What FMA actually gave the world was a sustained, forceful, and—yes—beautiful example of effective hands-on work for personal psychophysical change. Now, in the present historical moment, in a world dominated by the critical/scientific outlook, it surely behooves us his self-chosen heirs to raise the level of the theory to that of the practice. Which brings us to the question, what then if not primary control? But first a few words, not from our sponsor (who is our sponsor, anyway?), but about theory.

The word 'theory,' though it lacks the sharp noun/verb dualism of 'control,' nevertheless has distinctions in meaning that need to be clarified and borne in mind. The ancient Greek *theoria* meant "witnessing," in the sense of "participation in the delegation sent to a festival for the sake of honoring the gods."[2] Such a delegate would naturally expect faithfully to report to his constituency what he saw, heard, and otherwise experienced. As Gadamer further points out, in this primitive sense *theoria* in no way implied separation and abstraction, but rather proximity and affinity vis-a-vis the subject. It is no doubt the particularly medieval sense of theory as abstract speculation, the revolt against which was the genesis of modern

---

[1] *Ego and Instinct*, Random House, 1970, p. 88.
[2] Hans Georg Gadamer, *Reason in the Age of Science*, MIT Press, 1986, p. 17.

science, of which FMA and the modern mind in general were and are so suspicious. Even in the critical discourse of today, theory has two senses not always distinguished, the one *predictive* and the other *descriptive*. Predictive theory tells us what will *likely* happen based on a limited but relevant number of observations: "If Germ X is present, Disease Y occurs," etc. The quality of a predictive theory is its success rate. Descriptive theory, on the other hand, tells us more or less systematically what something is: "A major scale consists of two conjunct tetrachords," etc. Only by a fundamental misunderstanding could we say something like, "If two tetrachords come into conjunction, a major scale occurs." The quality of a descriptive theory is its understandability relative to its accuracy and its completeness. Closer to *theoria* than to predictive theory, descriptive theory can never tell the whole story completely accurately, but the conscientious witness does her best. (In the courts, the opposing attorney actively helps her to do her best.) It is also important to realize that while predictive theories may and probably must have descriptive aspects, the converse is not necessarily true. So much for theory in general.

Regarding AT theory in particular, I am of course aware that the Technique finds ultimate definition not in any theory, however cogent, but only within "that solitary individual's"[1] unique and ongoing experience. That said, would anyone seriously disagree that the only ground

---

[1] Kierkegaard, *Purity of Heart Is To Will One Thing*, "Preface."

upon which a profession can be solidly built is conceptual agreement on basic premises?[1] Or that the public can be reliably informed of our purposes and methods only in terms meeting general standards of rigorous discourse? Theory-wise, these terms need not be based solely or even primarily in empirical research, but they do need to reflect established knowledge to the extent that such knowledge bears upon, illuminates, and helps to communicate our work. That is to say, *good descriptive theory* will fill the bill. I note with pleasure "On Defining the Alexander Technique" by Joe Armstrong,[2] who has carefully framed ten Alexander hypotheses that generally meet the standard of discourse described above and that, significantly, do not do so in terms of primary control (hallelujah, nowhere to be seen!). That I would take substantial issue with Mr. Armstrong on specific points as well as on the assumption that AT theory need be "based on what Alexander himself claimed it to be" must remain for another discussion, in view of my need to bring the present one to a close.

What then if not primary control? In a word, skill. Skill the rubric, the unifying concept, under which is comprised everything the Alexander teacher and student are seeking to accomplish both mutually and individually: skill in bodily support and movement, skill in thinking,

---

[1] Curiously, Walter Carrington, always eloquent in his elucidations of the Technique, appears to disclaim having any conceptual basis for it. Sean Carey: "You don't have a 'formal' doctrine of change, then?" Carrington: "No, not a bit. If I had one, that would mean I had a conceptual basis for the Technique, wouldn't it?" Walter Carrington in Discussion with Sean Carey [exact title?], galley copy without title page in author's possession, n.d., p. 64.

[2] *NASTAT News*, No. 42, p. 20.

skill in the always mutual employment of both. Our Alexandrian practice is eminently describable in terms of skill, which has an extensive literature of its own waiting to be mined for corroborative findings and insights. It is astonishing to me how little the skill of the student—as contrasted with that of the teacher—is discussed or even mentioned in conventional AT texts. A model of skill acquisition establishes the continuity of our Alexandrian learning process to all the practical and fine arts, as well as to that of the conventional classroom. All the foregoing is not to say that the concept of skill is a panacea for the many communicational challenges attending the AT, but it is to say that, in terms of theory, the *terra firma* of skill is far more secure than the foggy marshes of primary control.

After all this fulmination against primary control, I want to close in acknowledgement that it can remain an important concept, *skillfully used*, for our Alexandrian practice if not for our theory. The crux of the matter lies in (1) knowledge of the term's noun-verb duality, (2) reflection on that fact in terms of real situations, and (3) practice in using this reflectively-modified knowledge in action. For example, in teaching there are times when it is appropriate to return a student to a global from a more focal awareness. On such occasions, a direction such as "Coming back to primary control ... ," accompanied by a hand at head/neck, is a succinct reminder of the primariness of a lengthening response to the omnipresent gravitational challenge as well as to the specific task at hand. Knowledge, Reflection, Practice, the elements of skill regardless of the activity to which applied. Let us hear once more these words of the founder: *"There really isn't a primary control as such. It becomes a something in the sphere of relativity."* That something, I submit, is skill, skill in that ultimate art of the use of the self.

Reply to Ron Dennis' article "Primary Control and the Crisis in Alexander Technique Theory"

By David Langstroth

http://alexandertechnique.com/ats/pcdavid (2000)

I would like to start by saying that I believe Ron Dennis has justified the use of the term "crisis". However, it is apparent from his article that the crisis lies, not in "Alexander Technique theory", but in the failure of many well educated and trained members of the Alexander community to understand it. Ron Dennis gives us a list of quotes on the primary control from various people, some well known and some more obscure, which reveal more about their idiosyncratic ideas than about any aspect of "Alexander Technique theory".

The issue is really a lot simpler than Ron makes it out to be. The Alexander Technique is based on the observation that maintaining a certain relationship between head, neck, torso and limbs establishes a standard of general co-ordination which is beneficial for functioning and manner of reaction. It is how Alexander solved his vocal problems, and improved his general health. It is what he taught to his pupils in Australia, and later in London and America.

Now, contrary to Ron's article, I do not believe that this is compromised in any way because Alexander coined the term "Primary Control" to describe this phenomenon later in his career. The fact is that from the very beginning he taught pupils to maintain this relationship of parts, and the results justified him in doing so. My own experience confirms it. When I maintain this relationship of parts in activity, I experience an improvement in co-ordination which affects a variety of particular symptoms.

Ron talks about the embarrassing position of having to explain a neural mechanism that has no evident basis in empirical research. What neural mechanism is he talking about? Alexander never described the primary control as a neural mechanism. If Ron has the idea that he has to defend some notion of a neural mechanism then I well understand his embarrassment. The primary control is defined by Alexander (who, after all coined the term) in the following way:

"I discovered that a certain use of the head in relation to the neck, and of the head and neck in relation to the torso and other parts of the organism, if consciously and continuously employed, ensures, as was shown in my own case, the establishment of a manner of use of the self as a whole which provides the best conditions for raising the standard of the functioning of the various mechanisms, organs, and systems. I found that in practice this use of the parts, beginning with the use of the head in relation to the neck, constituted a primary control of the mechanisms as a whole, involving control in process right through the organism, and that when I interfered with the employment of the primary control of my manner of use this was always associated with a lowering of the standard of my general functioning."

So all this worry about the absence of a neural mechanism, or some sort of little black box that the anatomists have never been able to find, is unnecessary. Anyone who describes the primary control in this way ought simply to be corrected.

Ron claims to have looked at a fair amount of movement science literature since 1984 and has never found anything to indicate the primary control. Perhaps Ron has been looking for the wrong thing (a neural mechanism?), or perhaps he has not looked as extensively as he thinks he has. I will make a few suggestions.

In 1989 the second International Union of Physiological Sciences Conference was held at Fontainebleu near Paris. There, a satellite symposium met to specifically consider head movement control. It resulted in the joint publication of 115 technical papers under title The Head-Neck Sensory Motor System (Berthoz et al, 1992). Running throughout these papers is the recognition of the primary importance of the head and neck to the behaviour of the whole animal. In the preface the editors state,

"The need for a thorough analysis of all aspects of head movement control is all the more important because head movements are a core element of orienting behavior involving a number of interactive sensory and motor systems." (Berthoz et al, 1992, p.xv)

The following are a few excerpts from these papers. In a paper on head position and posture in new-born infants Jouen (1992) describes both how neck reflexes affect the limbs, and how breathing is modified by posture. Bland and Boushey (1992) describe the cervical (neck) spine as being the most complicated articular system in the body. What is most interesting is their report that either awake or in sleep the neck moves over 600 times an hour. No other part of the musculoskeletal system is in such constant motion. This discovery makes sense in the light of Alexander's discovery of its primary role in the co-ordination of activity. Benson and Brown (1992), Wilson (1992) and Pompeiano (1992) all contributed papers confirming the role of proprioceptors in the neck in controlling posture. Pompeiano described this process as a complex co-ordination of excitation and inhibition. Taylor (1992) pointed out the loss of motor co-ordination that results from the disruption of the activity of the neck in postural reflexes, similar to Alexander's concept of interfering with the primary control. She goes on to emphasise how the perception of the relationship between head and body is vital for successful interaction with the environment. Gurfinkel et al (1992) asserted that in man the neck reflexes were likely controlled by some higher structure of the central nervous system than they were in animals, and suggested that a system of internal representation played a part in the correct working of these reflexes. This supports the idea that conscious cognitive processes, such as directions, would be effective in controlling this relationship of parts. Straube et al (1992) and Zangemeister et al (1992) asserted, like Alexander 100 years previously, that pulling the head back and down increased postural instability and interfered with the smooth coordination of walking. Brown (1992) linked imbalance arising from the neck with conditions of tension, irritability, vertigo, loss of concentration, headache, numbness and poor memory.

This is by no means an extensive list of research, but should illustrate that there is a scientific recognition of the primary importance of the head and neck in controlling animal (including human) behaviour.

Ron recounts a question he put to Chris Stevens about how to explain the primary control to a neurologist. Chris Stevens was reputedly unable to answer. Well, this anecdote, interesting as it might be, hardly constitutes a crisis. The question he put to Chris Stevens is in fact rather an odd one. For the description of the primary control is the same whether you are describing it to a neurologist or a milkman. However, it was probably interpreted by Stevens as meaning, "What is the underlying neural mechanism?" Here we come back again to that persistent fallacy that this is about a neural mechanism (Who started this anyway?). The maintenance of a certain relationship of parts, starting with the head and the neck obviously involves neurology (like any other action), but where does the assumption come from that this implies a dedicated neural mechanism?

At a certain point Ron diverges to consider the origins of the term "theory", and to explain the different types of theory. While this is very interesting, his academic preoccupation with the theory of theory is a bit of a dead end. For Ron has construed the relationship between theory and practice in the Alexander Technique completely back to front. And this in spite of the fact that in his very first sentence he reminds us that Alexander put practice before theory. Let me explain this with a little digression of my own. Take the example of a new method of mine (entirely fictitious for the purposes of this posting). I will call it the Langstroth Technique. The Langstroth Technique is based on the idea that the colour blue has positive energies. This is my theory (please don't take this seriously, it's only an example). Using my theory, I can devise a practice which involves shining blue lights on people. Now this is an instance in which theory comes before practice. The effectiveness of my practice depends entirely on the truth of my theory. If someone can show that I am wrong about the positive energies of blue light then the practice is rendered worthless. Many practices are in fact just like this, that is, based on assumptions or theories which themselves are not proven. The Alexander Technique however is the other way round. Alexander started by discovering something that works and then later coined a term to describe it. It is completely wrong of Ron to claim that the technique is founded on the concept of the primary control. In fact, the concept of the primary control is founded on the practice of the Technique.

Ron also attempts to support his argument by the claim that "Evolution of a Technique" was written many years after the events it describes, and that it is a natural tendency of the autobiographical writer to make things appear in retrospect much more simple and clear than they actually were at the time. Ron is probably right about this, and we have no way to really know how clear or fuzzy Alexander's thinking was at the time. Ron's worst case scenario might actually be true: Alexander might have actually figured out the thinking for all those events only years later. But whether he did or didn't is irrelevant. He found a practical procedure that worked. It doesn't really matter if he finally decided to call it the primary control some years later.

The final point I want to address in Ron's article is his quote from a letter written by Alexander to Frank Pierce Jones after 1940: "There really isn't a primary control as such. It becomes a something in the sphere of relativity." I'm sure I don't need to point out to Ron Dennis, with his academic qualifications, that a snippet removed from personal correspondence and quoted out of context is of questionable value in trying to support a particular point. We don't know from this what the understanding was between Alexander and Jones, or what particular interpretation we ought to put on it. It is just as likely that Alexander was refuting the idea that the primary control was some sort of anatomical entity (like a neural mechanism). He may have been asserting that it is about maintaining the relationship of parts in activity.

If I've gone on at some length and bored you all, you can wake up now, for I shall come to the main point. Alexander discovered that a certain relationship of parts, if maintained in activity has a co-ordinating influence on the organism as a whole. He eventually decided to call this the primary control. If this is shown not to be the case, then there is no Alexander Technique. Yet it can be tested by anyone, and so far the evidence is overwhelming that Alexander was right. He found it to be true, I find it to be true, and a great many others have found the same thing. It is a practical point not a theoretical one. It cannot be decided by the ebb and flow of the carefully constructed arguments of academics.

Dissent may be an interesting theoretical position, but let us be clear about the implications. If you do not agree, then when someone comes to you with a knee problem, for example, there is no reason to spend any time with the head and neck. Simply focus on the knee and work on it. Thus, you become a teacher of a collection of specific practices, not one general one. And in doing so, you might call yourself a coach, a physiotherapist, or some other title, but you will not be an Alexander Technique Teacher.

But maybe someone can satisfy my curiosity. Do Alexander Teachers who claim to disagree with the "concept of the primary control" still work with the head and neck? Or do they just work in specific ways with specific to try to solve specific problems?

As I said at the beginning the real crisis here is a muddle of understanding. This can probably be traced back to the way Alexander Teachers are trained, particularly to the lack of rigorous standards for training, either academic or practical. Here, I believe that Alexander did set a bad example, but that is another story for another time.

References:

Bland, J. H. and Boushey, D. R. (1992) `The Cervical Spine, from Anatomy and Physiology to Clinical Care', in Berthoz, A., Vidal, P. P. and Graf, W. (eds) (1992).

Benson, A. J. and Brown, S. F. (1992) Perception of Liminal and Supraliminal Whole- Body Angular Motion', in Berthoz, A., Vidal, P. P. and Graf, W. (eds) (1992).

Berthoz, A., Vidal.. P. P. and Graf. W. (eds) (1992) The Head-Neck Sensory Motor System, Oxford, Oxford University Press.

Gurfinkel, V. S., Lebedev, M. A. and Levick, Y. S. (1992) `What about the So-Called Neck Reflexes in Humans?', in Berthoz, A., Vidal, P. P. and Graf, W. (eds) (1992).

Jouen, F. (1992) Head Position and Posture in Newborn Infants', in Berthoz, A., Vidal, P. P. and Graf, W. (eds) (1992).

Pompeiano, O. (1992) `Excitatory and Inhibitory Mechanisms Involved in the Dynamic Control of Posture during the Cervicospinal Reflexes', in Berthoz, A., Vidal, P. P. and Graf, W. (eds) (1992).

Straube, A. Paulus, W. and Brandt, T. (1992) "Do Head Position and Active Head Movements Influence Postural Stability?', in Berthoz, A., Vidal, P.and Graf, W. (eds) (1992).

Wilson, V. J. (1992) ' Physiologic Properties and Central Actions of Neck Muscle Spindles', in Berthoz, A., Vidal, P. P. and Graf, W. (eds) (1992).

Zangemeister, W. H., Bulgheroni, M. V. and Pedotti, A. (1992) 'Differential Influence of Vertical Head Posture During Walking', in Berthoz. A., Vidal, P. P. and Graf, W. (eds) (1992).

Reply to a Reply

www.unique-technique.com/Folder1/reply.htm (2000)

David Langstroth's reply to my Primary Control article makes it clear that I need to say more, not only in response to points raised by DL but also regarding my own treatment of theory, not, I see in retrospect, adequately addressed in my paper. For convenience both in composition and cross-reference, I follow the general order of DL's Reply, and take this opportunity to thank him and others for their contributions to an important discussion.

DL begins by claiming that FMA coined the term primary control to describe the practice not only that he had employed to solve his own vocal problems but also that he had taught his pupils "from the very beginning." I point out that this claim can only be based on FMA's own testimony in *US*, Chap. 1 (and presumably orally), which is precisely the testimony at issue relative to primary control. Thus, there is no independent evidence, in FMA's writings or elsewhere, for this claim. Certainly in the early writings through *MSI*, there is no assertion of "a certain relationship between head, neck, torso and limbs." I and my trainee have read aloud completely through the 1,000-odd pages of Jeroen Staring's two-volume *The First 43 Years of the Life of F. Matthias Alexander,* which, one might say, goes rather thoroughly over the ground up to 1912. Via a painstaking comparison of the writings of FMA, Scanes Spicer, and others, Staring argues convincingly, if not conclusively, that the posture/movement aspect of FMA's teaching, in contrast to the respiratory, became dominant only after 1910. Staring also shows, and conclusively, that FMA's concepts of inhibition, direction, sensory appreciation, and even aspects of the manual technique, were all anticipated in mid- to late-19th-century therapeutic literature. This is said not at all to detract from FMA's work, which, unlike the others, has indeed survived. But it is abundantly clear that any meaningful discussion of the Technique's origins is now impossible without assimilating either Staring's work *or* all of its source material.

DL's next point concerns primary control as a neural mechanism; he says that FMA never described primary control thus. That is true, and neither did I say that he did, but that is not really the point [But see Bruce Kodish's Introduction, p.16, my error]. The point is that others *have* so described or characterized it, and continue to do so, the "master reflex" notion advanced by Patrick MacDonald, a very influential teacher, being perhaps the most obvious instance. DL implies that I am worried about the absence of a neural mechanism. For the record, I am not. Clearly there are neural mechanisms, those studies cited by DL being welcome recent additions to a long train of investigation. What I *am* worried about is not only the Technique's being represented by a simplistic model of movement control in particular and human behavior in general, but also the effect upon teaching practice of such a model. FMA's error was less in intro-ducing the term than in doing so in such a vague manner as to lend itself so readily to the confusion and misunder-standing acknowledged even by DL. I must say I find rather naive the suggestion that those of contrary opin-ions on primary control "ought simply to be corrected." After all, we're talking about strong-minded and intelli-gent Alexander folk here, not naughty puppies.

DL's account of the "Langstroth Technique" brings us to the issue of theory, seen by him as a diversion in my paper. That was hardly my intent, but, as indicated above, I have only belatedly seen my error. For the prob-lem was in saying too little too vaguely about theory, rather like FMA's treatment of primary control. In my paper I was thinking of "theory" implicitly in several senses while using it explicitly in only two. A device of Korzybski's General Semantics, in which the different senses of a word are identified by numerical subscripts, is an elegant way to bring clarity to the matter. In common usage, then, at least the following meanings of "theory" can be distinguished (the order of subscripting is arbitrary):

Theory$_1$, formal predictive theory, as in my paper.

Theory$_2$, formal descriptive theory, the same.

Theory$_3$, informal predictive theory, as in hunches, intuitions ("My theory about the race tomorrow is ...").

Theory$_4$, informal descriptive theory, as in talking about, explanations ("His theory on the Technique is ...")

Theory$_5$, formal speculative theory, as in Plato's theory of the good.

Theory$_6$, informal speculative theory, as in opinions ("Her theory regarding the case is ... .")

Now we are in a position to lay to rest this question about theory and practice in the AT in general and in FMA's working out of it in particular.

First of all, the title of my paper should now read "Primary Control and the Crisis in Alexander Technique Theory$_{2,4}$." My chief concern in this side of our work is how we conceive and thus describe it, both formally and informally. I maintain that our language in this usage should be as precise and relevant as the use of our hands, and have given reasons why I think "primary control" is not the best language for this purpose. On the other hand, we all make use of theory$_3$ in the daily use of ourselves, including our teaching, *as did FMA in working out the Technique*: " 'Is it not fair, then,' I asked him [his doctor], 'to conclude that it was *something I was doing that evening in using my voice that was the cause of the trouble?'"* (The fact that I cite FMA from a source previously called into question [*US*] means only that I accept—as in the Bible—some things more than others.) What is practice after all but the increasing refinement of an ongoing "hunch and trial" process? So no, I have not "construed the relationship between theory and practice in the Alexander Technique completely back to front," as DL asserts, although my error was serious enough in treating the term "theory" simultaneously in both a broader and a more specific sense than did, for example, FMA, who only meant theory$_5$ when he spoke of "mere theory" and probably theory$_2$ in referring to "the practice and theory of my technique."

In passing, I note that, in referring to my "academic preoccupation with the theory of theory," DL seems (theory$_6$) to be intimating something beyond the mere fact of my status as a Degreed Person. He seems to resent, or at least take exception to, my daring to talk seriously about theoretical matters relative to a technique so eminently and obviously practical as ours (yes, mine too). He as much as says that such matters of theory are, in effect, self-evident. However, judging from the volume of thoughtful response to my paper, this is clearly not the case. What *is* the case is that coy locutions such as "academic preoccupation" do not serve either communication or collegiality.

The question of context regarding FMA's comment to Jones about there not being a "primary control as such" is fair enough, and I confess to not having read the entire letter [I since *have* seen it, with no prejudice to my citation of this sentence. see p. 245]. But, as the unequivocalness of some utterances makes less pressing the usual burden of contextual reference, my confidence that FMA's letter actually existed and that the material was quoted as written (Note 20 of my paper) seemed to me at the time sufficient to the scholarly task. Nonetheless, the point is well taken. I have, however, reviewed Jones' *School and Society* article, which I published in "The Frank Pierce Jones Memorial Issue" of *The Alexandrian* in 1982. The sentences to which FMA was probably responding most likely were these:

1. "The primary control of the mechanism, which consists in the preservation of a certain relativity between the head and the neck, they [Magnus and his school] described as the 'tonic neck reflexes.'"

2. "When he [FMA] had succeeded [in inhibiting the impulse to pull his head down], a new use (the tonic neck reflexes of Magnus) took its place; and this proved to be the mechanism conditioning all other reflexes and thus controlling psycho-physical activity." Thus I agree with DL that FMA probably "was refuting the idea that the primary control was some sort of anatomical entity," but (again), that's not the main point. The main point is that others (including Jones[1943] we now see) did (and do) so conceive and propagate this notion of an anatomically more-or-less discrete primary control. Perhaps the foregoing will help answer DL's indignant question about who started this "persistent fallacy" anyway (I do not mean to imply that it was only Jones).

It remains to respond to DL's brief but potent closing comments regarding dissent from primary control orthodoxy (the p.c. of pc?) on the one hand, and authenticity as an Alexander teacher on the other. To quote him, "Do Alexander Teachers who claim to disagree with the concept of the primary control still work with the head and neck? Or do they just work in specific ways with specific [sic] to try to solve specific problems?" Of course I can, and will, speak only for myself, but first there is an assumption of DL's to be exposed. This assumption is that (1) working with the head and neck and (2) working with other parts of the anatomy are mutually exclusive. I do not believe this to be so, but rather, as is often the case in such apparently "either-or" matters, a question of emphasis and priority. Thus, I find it not only desirable but also eminently possible to give a focal direction such as to aim the knees forward in walking, in the general context of lengthening the stature and all else that "neck free" implies. I have helped the possessors of several pairs of ailing knees in this way, so DL's example is nicely apposite. The whole matter is very much like acquiring skill on a musical instrument; one is always playing the whole instrument all the time, yet at different phases different aspects of the process are selected for particular attention—rhythm, tone quality, physical technique, phrasing—all the while the total performance being guided by its *primary control*, in this instance, necessarily to be sure by the mechanisms of hearing but sufficiently only by *conscious musical listening*. No analogy is perfect, but this one is very close, and, I trust, obvious enough not to require further pursuit.

So, as long as the "control" in primary control is understood first and foremost as a verb (coordinative process) and not as a noun (neural mechanism), I have no conceptual problem with it, the objections voiced in my paper notwithstanding. A better term, however, and hence a better conception (or vice-versa) would be "primary coordination," or even "primary relationship" (if emphasizing the postural over the motional aspect of use), both of which I employ regularly. Truth be told, "primary response" would add to the postural and motional the necessary *ethical* dimension of the concept of the use of the self, but that must be another story for another time.

Defining Primary Control

AmSAT News 64, Summer 2004

In my "Primary Control and the Crisis in Alexander Technique Theory"[1] I argued that "primary control" (PC), despite its venerable place in the Alexandrian canon, has serious limitations as a conceptual foundation for the Alexander Technique. My purpose here is to show how PC can actually *become* the solid base that it has always purported to *be.*

Appearances perhaps to the contrary, this is not a complete about-face on my part: in my previous writing I have suggested that the problem lay less in the concept itself than both in FMA's initial characterization of it and in the multiple understandings of it by his successors. Moreover, beyond this admitted ambivalence on my part, I have found pressing and positive reasons why PC should be conceptually rehabilitated, among them its historical status, its elegance, and particularly its importance, not only to our profession but to humanity in general, when adequately defined. The solution to the problem lies in a definition that can be both accepted by the Alexander Technique profession and intelligible to the informed laity. I am of course aware that no aspect of the Technique can

---

[1]*AmSAT News*, Summer 1999; also at www.unique-technique.com/Folder1/crisis.htm. To this assault there was a predictable critical reaction, most substantially in David Langstroth's "Reply to Ron Dennis's article ..." (www.alexandertechnique.com/ats/pcdavid). I responded with "Reply to a Reply" (www.unique-technique.com/Folder1/reply.htm), answering Langstroth at length as well as expanding on aspects of my original paper. These three papers (there was no further response from Langstroth) form a desirable though not necessary background for the present one.

be understood solely in verbal terms: ongoing experience and idea meet and ineffably blend in each unique "empersonment" of the Technique. However, that which *can* be said, i.e., theory, need be articulated as comprehensively, as clearly, and as accurately as possible—as much so as we strive to use our hands—and that is what I now attempt.

The first order of business is to come to terms (literally) with "definition." Soltis makes a useful distinction among three types: *stipulative, programmatic, descriptive.*[1] A stipulative definition means what the definer stipulates, or says, it will mean: "For my purposes, x *will be* ... ." A programmatic definition projects upon the thing defined the fulfillment of an expectation or plan: "X *should be* ... ." A descriptive definition claims sufficiently to characterize the reality or nature of that which is defined: "X *is* ... ." Disagreement may arise over a stipulative definition, but this is less problematic than the muddle that often obtains between programmatic and descriptive ones. Much of our past difficulty with PC has resulted from differing ideas about what it *should be,* its "program," as it were, rather than what, by common agreement, it *is.*[2]

---

[1] Jonas F. Soltis, *An Introduction to the Analysis of Educational Concepts* (2d ed.; Addison-Wesley Publ. Co., 1978), pp. 7-11.

[2] FMA's own definition is clearly programmatic: "... that relativity in the use of the head, neck, and other parts which proved to be a primary control of the general use of the self." At this point, like FMA, "I [too] break my story here to call attention to a very curious fact ..." (*US*, Centerline Press Edition, p. 15), namely, that between the First (Dutton,1932) and Third (Integral Press or Re-Educational Publ.,1946) Editions of *US*, there is a change in this text referring to PC. In the First Edition, the text reads, "As is shewn by what follows, this [putting the head forward and up] proved to be the primary control of my use in all my activities." The Third Edition has, "The experiences which followed my awareness of this [putting the head

Because the definition of PC offered here claims sufficiently to characterize a reality in nature, it is descriptive in type: *Primary Control—the process, as primary task, of bodily adjustment to gravity.* This definition does *not* tell us where PC might be located, what it should look or feel like, how it works, or how to get it—those are the province of further theoretical work—but it *does* distinguish non-trivially that which is defined from everything else.[1] And although this definition of PC ultimately must stand alone—the sign, commonly understood, pointing to the thing—like many definitions of complex phenomena it requires further explanation to become meaningful. I thus proceed by first enlarging, in a Webster's-based gloss, upon each of its substantives, and by then giving a briefer note such as might be used in a commentary.

"Process," defined in part by Webster as "a series of actions, motions, or operations definitely conducing to an end, whether voluntary or involuntary," immediately implies that the "control" in PC is verbal and not nounal.[2]

---

forward and up] were *forerunners* [italics mine] of a recognition of that relativity in the use of the head, neck and other parts which proved to be *a* [italics mine] primary control of the general use of the self." In this later text FMA seems less categorical in his conception of PC; he also appears, at least obliquely, to acknowledge what I claimed in "Crisis," that "primary control" was a later interpretation of his earlier experience.

[1] An extreme example of a trivial definition would be "PC is two English words"; less so would be, "PC is a basic idea of the Alexander Technique." More will be said later about the full significance, in contrast to the mere non-triviality, of the concept of PC. It might be objected that my definition, too, is programmatic, as it projects an intention on PC relative to how it should be understood. I will only venture at this point that whatever my "program," it is so general as to amount to sufficient description of PC at any relevant level of consideration. See also note 11.

[2] All references are to *Webster's New International Dictionary* (Second Edition, Unabridged, 1934).

The lexical noun/verb duality of "control" makes it problematic as a conveyor of precise meaning and has no doubt abetted the differing conceptions of PC that I documented in "Crisis." But in the present definition this problematic aspect of "control" is obviated by the precision and proximity of "process." As indicated by Webster, "process" is neutral with regard to origin and execution of action, reflex or willed. In the past, dominated by reductionistic science, too much effort has been spent in attempts to establish PC as a discrete mechanism.[1] With Dart, we need to see the issue as one of integrating the voluntary and involuntary contributions to behavior.[2] In practical discourse, we need to say not, "We *have a* ... " (as a mechanism) but rather, "We *exercise* ..." (as integrative process) "Primary Control."

In "primary task" we have the concept pointing to a reality that is crucial, and yet generally not recognized: the reality that, regardless of whatever else we are doing, we are priorly, ongoingly, and actively managing ourselves in a gravitational environment. In the present definition, "primary" carries mainly Webster's sense "Of the first order in successive divisions, combinations, or ramifications"; it also connotes "firsthand, fundamental, radical." In understanding, with Webster, "task" as "Labor or study

––––––––––––––––––––

[1] For example, Frank Pierce Jones' Chapter 13 of *Body Awareness in Action*, "What Is the Mechanism?". Also, Jones, "The Work of F. M. Alexander as an Introduction to Dewey's Philosophy of Education," (*School & Society*, Jan. 2, 1943; reprinted in *The Alexandrian*, Spring/Summer 1982) and cited by me in "Reply to A Reply."

[2] Raymond A. Dart, "The Attainment of Poise," (*S. A. Medical Journal*, Feb. 8, 1947), p. 78: "The prime fact about human body movement is that it entails the co-operation or integration of both conscious and unconscious mechanisms." Recent movement science has tended toward the concept of "contributions" over "mechanisms" to allow for the possibility and inclusion of non-mechanical, or at least non-observable, influences on higher-level behavior.

imposed by another, ... anything imposed on one by duty or necessity," we may be invited to whimsical speculations about the work vis-à-vis gravity that Mother Nature has assigned to us. In any case, "primary task" allows us to see that everything usually thought of as accomplishment in the world is possible only secondarily as a function of primarily responding to the unending gravitational task.

"Every person has a body, or more properly is a body."[1] In this terse sentence is forcefully conveyed the idea that the body, considered inferior relative to the mind by centuries of religious and philosophical doctrine, is a primary datum and desideratum, here and now, of our being. This necessary recasting, argued by FMA himself,[2] of traditional dualistic thought, is not to assert that "mind" is solely a function of brain, nor, for that matter, that FMA was inconsistent to speak of "the Directive Agent of the sphere of consciousness."[3] But it is to assert that "bodily" in the present definition keeps us squarely in the arena of observable fact (without excluding, however, at least for oneself, observable thought). Webster on "adjustment" needs, I think, no further comment: "to bring into proper relations; as, to *adjust* a garment to the body, or behavior to circumstances, or oneself or another to an environment."

And finally, "gravity." For present purposes "gravity" will mean (stipulative definition!) not seriousness or solemni-

---

[1] *Atlas of Human Anatomy*, Explanatory Text by Jesse Feiring Williams, MD (Allen & Unwin, 1952), p. 7.

[2] US, Chap. 1, "Evolution of a Technique." See also, and particularly, Ellen J. Langer, *Mindfulness* (Addison-Wesley, 1989).

[3] "Re-Education of the Kinesthetic Systems Concerned With The Development of Robust Physical Well Being." In *MSI*, Centerline Press Ed., p. 60.

ty, but rather that which makes things fall down. Into the actual physics of things we need not, and indeed cannot, go.[1]

Summarizing and synthesizing the foregoing:

Voluntary movement behavior (use) takes place simultaneously on two levels. The more obvious level is that of the specific willed activity: standing, walking, speaking, typing, swinging a golf club, whatever. The less obvious is that of the general response to the challenge of terrestrial life in general, and bipedal stance and locomotion in particular, in a gravitational environment. The more obvious level is *secondary* and the less obvious *primary* because the former depends upon the latter. Both levels involve involuntary (reflex) and voluntary (willed) contributions, and both levels involve, or have involved, learning. Quality of performance, a function of learning and a given criterion of the secondary level, is no less one of the primary, though there much less recognized: many if not most people have little or no idea of quality issues at the primary level.[2] However, both experience and increasing evidence show that subnormal performance at this level (commonly referred to in "postural" terms) not only exists but also exerts an influence on health, work, and living in general. *Quality of performance at the primary level—demonstrably a function of acquired as well as innate psychophysical control—thus is a factor of real-world importance*; "primary control" is the concept that captures

---

[1] However, in response to an early reader of this paper, Mr. Bryan Niblett (to whom thanks), I consider that this definition holds as well under conditions of zero-gravity.

[2] Not even Hans Selye, MD, great elucidator of the stress concept in medicine, could see either the fact or the implications of gravity as a stressor of the human body! See his *The Stress of Life* (rev. ed., McGraw-Hill, 1966), Chap. 17, "The Stressors of Daily Life."

this complex idea for our employment and ultimate benefit.[1]

My concern about this definition as it finally emerged was mainly that it was too general and thus too removed from orthodox Alexandrian thinking.[2] After all, I reflected, with this definition PC won't be unique to us anymore; I've taken it right out of the Alexander Technique per se and given it to whomever wants it, free for the asking! For if PC becomes "the process, as primary task, of bodily adjustment to gravity," and remains no longer "… that relativity in the use of the head, neck, and other parts …," then anybody with whatever kind of notion about it can do with it just as they please. Unsettling notions, these.

But, I thought on, isn't the universality of PC something that has always been harped on in the Technique, "Everybody has a Primary Control, but not everybody uses it," or some such? And if it's universal, then shouldn't a proper definition reflect that universality in such a way that anybody can see it without limiting it in particular terms, like a peak that becomes visible as the cloud lifts?

---

[1] Perhaps not the earliest with this insight, FMA was certainly, like Freud with the unconscious, the first to take "clinical possession of the new continent." See Daniel Yankelovich and William Barrett, *Ego and Instinct* (Random House, 1970), p. 9.

[2] This process of "emergence," to some extent a movement from the overly- to the sufficiently- descriptive, is at least partially documented by these successive versions of the definition as I jotted them down on an envelope over a couple days at my studio between lessons:
1. "process by which human beings as primarily terrestrial physicalities adjust their posture and movement to gravity as primary terrestrial force."
2. "process by which humans as physical beings adjust themselves to gravity as a primary physical force."
3. "process by which a person adjusts the body in its specifically mechanical function to the demands of a gravitational environment."
4. "process, as primary task, of bodily adjustment to gravity."

And won't that heightened visibility lead to more interest in it and concern about it, and ultimately to those who possess and demonstrate knowledge of it? Obviously what I've written in this paper indicates that my answer to these questions was Yes. Henceforth, it would behoove us to relinquish our parochial claim to this brilliant if flawed coinage of the Founder. That, in turn, would mean pursuing and justifying our particular approaches to Primary Control, both as a profession and as individual teachers, outside, as it were, of the definition itself. In return, through agreement on this conceptual foundation of our work, we advance in knowledge and in professional unity, and hence in our aspiration to true professional status. We also present to the world a concept of great importance, and that is a rare thing indeed.

The "Other Half" of Primary Control

AmSAT News 66, Winter 2004

In my "Defining Primary Control"[1] I argued that this potential conceptual foundation of the Alexander Technique would best be served by the definition "the process, as primary task, of bodily adjustment to gravity." I realized at the time of that writing, without taking the necessary thought to do it, and also not wanting to overcomplicate the issue, that the whole story hadn't been told, that part referring to whatever it is to which Primary Control[2] indeed relates *as* "primary."

Clearly, what I will for now simply refer to as the "goal-oriented"[3] aspect of Use[4] is not identical to that of bodily adjustment to gravity. The violinist playing a concerto and the programmer at her computer both exercise Primary Control relative to gravity but other control relative to the specific activity. An adequate theory of Use requires a concept for this "other control" commensurate with that of Primary Control. "Secondary," however, the most usual term paired with "primary" and the one I used in "Defining [PC]" to characterize the "more-obvious" level within Use, is lacking for the necessary refinement of theory because goals in the normal process of living are not really subordinate or secondary to bodily adjustment to

---

[1] *AmSAT News* (Summer 2004), p. 14.

[2] I capitalize "primary control" to indicate its status as a technical term of the Technique.

[3] Discussed more fully below.

[4] Although an elegant and accurate concept when understood in the Alexandrian sense, "use" presents problems in writing, even for a professional audience, because it is identical in appearance with both the noun and the verb of common use (!). I therefore either capitalize it or enclose in italics when using in the technical Alexandrian sense.

gravity.[1] Another possibility would be "contributory," as in the distinction between or among causes of death. Here, the sense of subordination is less than with "secondary," but still present. A third among the ready options would be "general," as in the distinction between types of elections. FMA thus, in his own characterization, linked Primary Control with "general use of the self."[2] However, in this notion there is no specific accounting for that which in Use may be considered as other-than-primary.

Casting the conceptual net more widely, I came up with "collateral," "complementary" and "correlative." Comparing dictionary definitions for each,[3] we see that "collateral" means "situated or running side by side;" "complement" (as noun) has the sense of "something that completes, makes up a whole, or brings to perfection"; while "correlation" implies "a causal, complementary, parallel, or reciprocal relationship, *especially a structural, functional, or qualitative correspondence* between two comparable entities" [italics added]. Obviously the three terms are close in meaning, but it is particularly the italicized portion of the definition for "correlation" that makes it the more accurate choice: "collateral" emphasizes separate things in tandem; "complementary" completes without implying the degree of contribution;[4] but "correlative" has the strong sense of reciprocity needed to balance "primary" as something "firsthand, fundamental, radical."[5] We come thus to a concept and definition that

---

[1] Indeed, it is our goals, considered both as ends and also as the sub-goals that constitute means, that generally inform and define our normal consciousness and awareness.

[2] *US*, Third Edition (Integral Press or Re-Educational Publ., 1946), p. 9.

[3] *American Heritage Dictionary of the English Language*, 1969.

[4] As in 10° + 80° and 45° + 45° both equal 90°.

[5] See "Defining Primary Control."

conjointly stands with and at the same time over against Primary Control in a theory of Use: *Correlative Control—the process of bodily organization in the goal-oriented aspect of activity.*

As noted above, "goal-oriented" seems to be this definition's only substantive needing fuller treatment, either as not previously discussed (in "Defining [PC]") or reasonably obvious. This aspect of activity is variously characterized in psychological literature as "goal-directed," "intentional," "purposive" (or "apparently purposive"), "conscious," or "voluntary." The common thread of meaning running through them testifies to our *feeling* that we do freely at least some of what we do. The present discussion will certainly not undertake the hoary issue of whether that feeling is reliable (although our experience in the Technique should at least lead us to question it), but rather how best to conceptualize that "other half" of Use.

In terms of overall human activity, FMA himself broadly distinguished between "use" on the one hand and "functioning" on the other, corresponding to the more usual (at the time) distinction between willed and reflex behavior. Although over-simplified, this is a useful distinction in the practical pursuit of our work, as it tells us what we may and may not deal with *directly* in our professional capacity: essentially, posture and movement (Use) we may deal with, digestion and the like (functioning) we may not. In terms of Use, however, FMA only distinguished between Primary Control on the one hand and "general use of the self" on the other. Alternatively, my schema divides Use into Primary and Correlative Controls, as a more specific, yet not overly-technical, way in which to think about and act upon issues within our professional purview. As to choosing among the terms cited above, "goal-oriented" seems the most fully comprehensive, descriptive and specific, and on that basis I use it in the definition of Correlative Control.[1]

It remains to give an example of this kind of thinking in operation. If we consider the harried programmer at her workstation, we observe that her whole spine is flexed forward and her head retroflexed on her neck in a postural compensation allowing her to see the screen: the classic "back-and-down" slump. This is an issue of Primary Control. Correcting it will reduce strain on the system and very probably gradually improve in process her comfort, job performance, and overall sense of well being. What we don't immediately observe, however, is that her "mouse-arm" is unduly tensed, via an isometric contraction of biceps and triceps. It is only after her report of discomfort in the arm that we analyze more closely and identify this misuse, not directly related to bodily adjustment to gravity per se, but rather to goal-orientation in her present activity. This is an issue (an example easily multiplied) of Correlative Control. Correcting it may well end the specific problem in relatively short order. Needing to make a decision about how to proceed, the Alexander Teacher alert to Primary/Correlative Control issues might well begin, not with the usual head-neck-back, but with arm, not that the one approach in any way precludes the other: it's simply a question of "what's next." After all, as

---

[1] The revealing of Correlative Control allows at least tentative closure of a problem touched on—somewhat arbitrarily, I confess—but not resolved in "Defining [PC]" (Note 11), namely, that of the role of Primary Control in the unusual (but not hypothetical) conditions of zero- or near-zero gravity. We now see that in such an environment, there *is no* Primary Control, Use (but not functioning!) in these conditions being solely (or virtually) a matter of Correlative Control.

The Man said, "our work is made up of seeing people and trying to help them."[1]

I want to emphasize that, as concepts, Primary Control and Correlative Control are constructs and not concrete things: even though they point to realities in nature, in the actual person there is only Certain Ongoing Stuff commonly referred to as "life." Also, these constructs represent a continuum and not a dichotomy in thought, and they do not represent the only way, however potentially helpful, of conceptualizing Use.[2] It is most important for us to bear in mind FMA's statement in a late letter to Frank Pierce Jones: "There really isn't a primary control as such. It becomes a something in the sphere of

---

[1] "Bedford Physical Training College Lecture," in Jean M. O. Fischer, ed., *Articles and Lectures* (Mouritz, 1985), p.169.

[2] An important and seminal paper in this regard is George B. Whatmore and Daniel R. Kohli, "Dysponesis: A Neurophysiologic Factor in Functional Disorders" (*Behavioral Science*, 13, March 1968), pp. 102-124. These authors, whose work Michael Gelb characterized rather cavalierly in his *Body Learning* as an "electronic Alexander Technique" (p. 146), call "dysponesis" what we call "misuse" (Gr. "dys," bad or faulty," "ponesis," effort or work). Dysponesis is manifested in terms of four kinds of "misdirected efforts": performing efforts, bracing (or postural) efforts, representing (or imagining) efforts, and attention efforts. The approach to therapy involved both increasing the patient's awareness of misdirected efforts and direct practice in reducing them via bio-feedback. Of special interest for us should be the authors' premise of potential misdirected efforts in the psychic processes of representing and paying attention, both of which are, or certainly can be, factors in Alexandrian Inhibition and Direction. These few remarks hardly do justice to the rich content and implications of this paper; it was the subject of my first piece of writing on the Technique, "Dysponesis, Or, Misuse Revisited," to which Dr. Whatmore, a psychiatrist, responded congenially. AmSAT would do well to investigate re-printing Whatmore and Kolhi's paper, a perfect example of relevant and useful collateral knowledge.

relativity."[1] As I pointed out in "Crisis,"[2] *reification*—the regarding or treating an abstraction or idea as if it had concrete or material existence—is an occupational hazard of thinking and to be guarded against. Further, I'm definitely not advocating any kind of piecemeal, symptom-relieving, or otherwise end-gaining approach to the Technique; nor would I for a moment diminish the importance of working with traditional issues in the traditional manner. But I do think we need to gain clarity in the conceptual grounds of our discipline, and to be open to modifications to practice when so indicated; FMA in his last book remarked of his own lifetime work that "the knowledge gained is but a beginning."[3] Apropos, I recently chanced upon a passage that expresses a particular truth for us in the Technique and that bears full quotation in closing:

The history of science is full of examples of incomplete theoretical systems which persisted for long periods of time because of their association with practical techniques of proven value [emphasis added]. *In all such cases, theoretical advances were retarded by this association, and in every case the theoretical advance, when it finally came, helped to refine and improve existing techniques.*[4]

---

[1] In response to Jones' first published article on the Technique ("The Work of F. M. Alexander as an Introduction to Dewey's Philosophy of Education," *School and Society*, No. 1462, 1943). Cited by Marian Goldberg, *NASTAT News*, No. 4, p. 7, copy of original letter in possession of Alexander Murray.

[2] "Primary Control and the Crisis in Alexander Technique Theory," *AmSAT News* (Summer, 1999).

[3] *UCL* (Dutton, 1941), p. xlii.

[4] Stanley R. Palombo, M.D., *Dreaming and Memory: A New Information-Processing Model* (Basic Books, 1978), p. 24.

Defining the Alexander Technique

AmSAT News 68, Fall 2005

If words are not precise, they cannot be followed out, or completed in action according to specifications. Confucius[1]

Over the past few years in several articles I've been working to frame definitions for basic concepts of the Alexander Technique that are both rigorous and potentially understandable at least within and hopefully without the Alexander professional community.[2] In particular, I've sought definitions that are not only descriptive but also non-dualistic,[3] in the spirit of FMA's declaration in *The Use of the Self*, "that the so-called 'mental' and 'physical' are not separate entities" and "that all training ... must be based upon the indivisible unity of the human organism."[4] Thus far, the labor has yielded a new definition for an existing concept—Primary Control—and a new concept and definition for the "other half" of Primary Control, Correlative Control. Now it is time to offer up a definition of the Technique itself:

---

[1] *The Analects*. In *Confucius*, Ezra Pound, trans. (New Directions Paperbook, 1969) p. 249.

[2] "Primary Control and the Crisis in Alexander Technique Theory," *AmSAT News*, Summer 1999; "Reply to a Reply" (www.unique-technique.com/Folder1/reply.htm), January 2000; "Defining Primary Control," *AmSAT News*, Spring 2004; "The 'Other Half' of Primary Control," *AmSAT News* (Winter 2004).

[3] See my "Defining Primary Control" for a fuller discussion of definition types.

[4] *US*, Third Edition (Integral Press or Re-Educational Publ., 1946), pp. 2, 3.

The Alexander Technique is the teaching that imparts the meaning of *the use of the self*.

It must be immediately noted that this definition is not as self-explanatory (so to speak) as one would hope, because it employs a technical (one could justifiably say, an *esoteric*[1]) term, i.e., the phrase in italics. This problem, regrettable from the perspective of ready communication, I believe to be unavoidable, and it is important here at the outset to understand why.

Quoting Michael Polanyi from his pivotal work *Personal Knowledge*:

> To the extent to which a discoverer has committed himself to a new vision of reality, he has separated himself from others who still think along the same lines. ... Formal operations [in the present case, verbal communication] relying on *one* framework of interpretation cannot demonstrate a proposition to persons who rely on *another* framework. ... [Acceptance of the new vision by some] produces disciples forming a school, the members of which are separated for the time being by a logical gap from those outside it. They think differently, speak a different language, [and] live in a different world ... .[2]

Surely FMA's work was and is a new vision of reality. And who of us as Alexander teachers has not felt this "logical gap" between us and our non-Alexandrian fellows, a gap that seems only to widen with time as our own experience deepens, and as we continue to struggle to say *really* what it is that we believe and do? And yet, how can those

---

[1] In the sense of "understood only by a small group" (*American Heritage Dictionary*).

[2] University of Chicago Press, 1968, p. 151.

others, without this experience, *really* comprehend us? Obviously for the most part they can't, in any full sense of the term. However, the cognitive dimension of understanding can be cultivated to some extent apart from the sensory-motor, and, in the measure that we can understand and communicate our own ideas clearly, then with Polanyi we may hope that "those who listen sympathetically will discover for themselves what they otherwise would never have understood."[1]

It is the concept of "the use of the self" that I think is most central and most radical in Alexander's thought. Only this concept—at once 1) a vision at odds with still-pervasive mind-body dualism, as well as 2) the contribution to knowledge belonging uniquely to FMA—allows us to frame a truly *descriptive* definition of the Technique, i.e., one that non-trivially distinguishes it from everything else. Otherwise, we resort to programmatic definitions that may serve a particular purpose but do not express the defining characteristic(s) of the work.[2] Because all definitions imply an understanding of the defining terms,

---

[1] *Ibid*

[2] An example of the programmatic type of definition is that appearing on the address page of the last few issues of *AmSAT News*: "The Alexander Technique is an educational discipline cultivating psychophysical coordination in everyday living." The problem with this definition is that it does not describe *one* thing, but potentially many. Indeed, one could substitute for "The Alexander Technique" any of several current "bodyworks" as well as certain martial arts together with various hybrids and still have a valid if vague statement.

I proceed, as in my previous essays, by enlarging upon the substantives of the definition announced above.

The *American Heritage Dictionary* defines the noun "teaching" briefly as "a precept, or doctrine." I would go beyond that to say that a teaching is a set of values associated with certain principles and practices. Teachings—Christianity, Psychoanalysis, the Alexander Technique, among others—imply an approach to the conduct of life through the insights of individuals; they are based and promulgated more on privately-experienced than on publicly-observable things. By their nature teachings remain outside the realm of scientific law or theory, being validated only by individual persons, and not by the experimental method. Indeed, "method" is a term frequently used in defining the Technique, but it seems to me that "method" suggests a degree of orderly and systematic approach to procedure—and also of emotional detachment—that is neither possible, desirable, nor typical in our work. Other terms seen in this definitional capacity are "means" and even "technique" itself, the latter being painfully redundant and the former simply vague.

"Impart" need not detain us long; Webster tells us that it carries the felicitous threefold sense of "to bestow a share or portion of," "to allow another to partake in," and "to communicate the knowledge of."[1] (As an aside, I've begun to consider the possibility of calling myself an Imparter of the Alexander Technique!)

----

[1] Webster's New International Dictionary of the English Language, Second Edition.

"Meaning," by contrast, is a term quite full of itself. Under Webster's Entry 1 we have "intent, purpose, aim, object." Entry 2 invites us to consider "that which one intends to convey by an act or, esp., by language," while Entry 3 offers "'sense, signification." Entries 4 and 5 add the notions of "remembrance," "knowledge; understanding." Entry 6 fruitfully supplies "the psychological context of anything" and "the body of habitually associated ideas." Finally, Entry 7 informs us that, in Logic, "meaning" is "that which a correct definition exhibits" (!). After going through a process of substituting these various dimensions of meaning for "meaning" in my definition of the Technique, I would suggest that it is the amalgamation of Entries 1, 2 (esp. in the sense of "convey by an act"), and 6 (esp. "body of habitually associated ideas") that gives to the term the required psycho-physical unity. Readers are encouraged to perform similar thought experiments for themselves.

Turning to the crux of the matter, "the use of the self," the great significance of this concept is that it obviates the mind-body and posture-movement dichotomies almost universally present, explicitly or implicitly, in conventional thought on such matters. Apparently, the most specific treatment FMA gave to the notion of "use" per se was in a footnote of *US*;[1] beyond that, he seemed to consider it self-explanatory in context, and to be undeterred by the lack of exact definitions of "use" and "self" as he understood them. In *UCL*, for example, he said, "Instead [of using terms such as "postures," "body mechanics," etc.] I prefer to call the psycho-physical organism simply 'the self,' and to write of it as something 'in use,' which 'functions' and 'reacts.'"[2] With few exceptions the writers

---

[1] P. 2.
[2] *UCL* (Dutton, 1941), p. xxxvi.

who followed him in the main took or take the same approach.[1]

The definition of "use" that I offer as sufficient to the need is this: *Use is that waking activity that is assessable in terms of kinematics and kinetics.* "Kinematics" refers to the *dynamic shape* of movements—linear and angular displacements, velocities, and accelerations; "kinetics" refers to the *forces*, ultimately those of muscular action and gravity, involved in producing movements.[2] "Assessable" I define as "susceptible of judgment as to quality." Vision and touch yield respectively kinematic and kinetic information, while hearing also becomes involved in making inferences about the kinematics and kinetics of vocal Use.[3] As *teachers*, of course, we have a primary

---

[1] Two exceptions were Wilfred Barlow and Frank Pierce Jones. Barlow defined it thus: "USE [*sic*] means the way we use our bodies as we live from moment to moment." Aside from the obvious circularity of defining a concept in terms of itself, the very use (!) of "use our bodies" maintains the duality FMA strove so mightily to overcome. Jones put it this way: "The term 'use' covers the total pattern that characterizes a person's responses to stimuli." Here Jones avoids circularity and duality but nevertheless projects the overly-general "total pattern" concept onto his definition. For example, one could have a certain visceral response to the stimulus, say, of an unliked food, and, while part of the individual's "total pattern," such a response would seem to belong to Functioning and not Use. Of Jones however I hasten to add that from my own reading experience it was he who most clearly saw and explicitly treated the radical change in thought implied by the concept of Use (see various references in *Body Awareness in Action*, esp. p. 58).

[2] David A. Winter, *Biomechanics of Human Movement* (John Wiley & Sons, 1979), p. 7.

[3] I don't mean to imply that an Alexander teacher's studio should be an "instrumentarium" for the recording and measurement, as opposed to the real-time assessment, of movement. What I have in mind is what Alexander teachers traditionally and actually do, i.e., transform acquired knowledge, experience, and current perceptions— hopefully as increasingly guided by valid theory—into practical help

concern with the processes—including Alexandrian Inhibition and Direction—by which Use is modified, but this concern belongs more to the domain of pedagogy than to the definition of Use.[1] Indeed, in our assessment of Use per se outside a specific instructional situation we function much like art critics or livestock judges:[2] what counts for us is that which we directly perceive, and whether or to what extent our criteria are met, rather than what we infer about the particular processes through that which we perceive has come to be.[3]

But what about "posture"? Although we may sometimes find it useful to distinguish between the postural and motional aspects of Use, in terms of rigorous theory there is no need, indeed, it is misleading, to do so. On this

---

for students. This model of "thinking in activity" is articulated at a more general level in Donald A. Schön's *The Reflective Practitioner: How Professionals Think in Action* (Basic Books, 1983).

[1] Inhibition I define as the interception of an habitual response; Direction is the organization of a modified response. These concepts are eminently discussable in terms of their application, but their definitions in Alexandrian terms, it seems to me, are relatively straightforward. See esp. Michael Protzel's penetrating analyses in "Why Do We Tense Our Necks," *AmSAT News* (No. 62, Winter 2003) pp. 17-19 and also "Alexander's Error," *AmSAT News* (No. 67, Spring 2005), p. 14 ff. Additionally it must be noted that "direction" also contains spatial and proprioceptive meanings in the Alexander Technique, but this phenomenon of *condensation of meaning* must await another discussion. See G. Spencer Brown, *Laws of Form* (Julian Press, 1972) p. 81.

[2] I.e., those who appraise individual specimens relative to a breed standard.

[3] Each of us, of course, is Thinker as well as Mover; as such, our waking thoughts and thought processes are "susceptible of judgment as to quality," and belong in the fullest sense to our Use. Thus, while maintaining a clear professional perspective as Alexander teachers, at some level we must deal with those aspects of the Technique leading necessarily toward psychology and philosophy, both in practical work with students as well as within ourselves.

point we have the authority of T. D. M. Roberts, a leading neurophysiologist, who sees what most people would call "posture" simply as "background activity":

> Accordingly, because this background activity is essential to the successful performance of the voluntary movement itself and has to be co-ordinated with it, there are advantages in treating the whole process *as a unity* [italics added].[1]

The unity thus posited is that which is pointed to by the concept of Use!

Needing fuller treatment is my restriction of "use" to "waking activity." In *UCL,* Chapter 1, FMA explicitly recognizes the "faulty and often harmful manner in which we use ourselves in our daily activities *and even during sleep*" [italics added].[2] I accept FMA's hypothesis that aspects of habitual Use (waking activity) may continue into sleep, but I think that such activity should be considered as Functioning and not Use. As I pointed out in "The 'Other Half' of Primary Control," without this distinction (which does not imply a hard-and-fast line) between Use and Functioning, we lose our conceptual way in determining what we properly deal with and what we don't in our professional capacity. Sleep is unconscious behavior and therefore nonconducive to conscious Inhibition and Direction, the explicitly Alexandrian means whereby Use is changed.

We come finally to "self." Among the several works consulted that discuss or define "self" explicitly, I found no single expression of this concept that was adequate to my

---

[1] *Neurophysiology of Postural Mechanisms*, Second Edition (Butterworths, 1978), p. 9.
[2] P. 3

intuition of it in Alexandrian terms. For instance, from
The Evolving Self : A Psychology for the Third Millenium by
Mihaly Csikszentmihalyi:

> While this [the self conceived as a homunculus] is not
> literally true, there *is* something in our mind that is
> more than the sum of the individual neurons that
> make up the brain. This something is the self, the
> brain's awareness of its own form of organizing infor-
> mation.[1]

Surely far from FMA's conception of "the self," this notion
is also a fair example of the kind of dualism (and vague-
ness to boot) referred to earlier in this essay. To make
short a story that for me has been a long reflection on
this matter, I found the key to the unified conception I
was seeking in Hubert L. Dreyfus' *What Computers Can't
Do: The Limits of Artificial Intelligence*. There, in the last
chapter called "The Situation as a Function of Human
Needs," was this sentence:

> People have begun to think of themselves as objects
> able to fit into the inflexible calculations of disembodied
> machines; machines for which the human form-of-life
> must be analyzed into meaningless facts, rather than *a
> field of concern organized by sensory-motor skills* [italics
> added].

Voilà! By combining this last idea with constructs from
Heidegger (*Being and Time*) and the Book of Exodus, I
finally discovered the definition that did full justice to all I
had thought about "the self" over the years: *The self is
that I-am whose being-in-the-world comprises a field of
concern organized by sensory-motor skills.* Here—granted

---

[1] Harper Collins Publ., 1993, p. 217.

a certain loftiness of language—nonetheless remain no vestige of a mind-body split and no values, perceptions, and actions apart from continuous situational flow.

Two parting observations: 1. The second instance of the definite article in my definition of the Technique is not exchangeable for the indefinite "a"; for it is precisely *this* teaching in all its particularity and exclusivity relative to "the use of the self" that makes the definition necessarily descriptive rather than contingently programmatic. 2. It is only our own full acceptance and consistent employment of the non-dualistic concept of "the use of the self" in our professional discourse at all levels that may eventually allow the capitalization, quotation marks, or italics to be removed, in acknowledgment that the idea has finally passed into common understanding.

In each of my previous articles I've given an example of how the theoretical ideas discussed could be applied in a practical way. I was surprised that such an application for this definition of the Alexander Technique came up so quickly, even before the article was finished. What happened was that I realized when recently renewing my professional liability insurance that I had become lax in getting from my students an "understanding and agreement" relative to the scope of practice of the Technique. I knew I needed something to this effect in writing, but wanted it to be as brief and non-legalistic as possible. This is what came out, ultimately printed on a 4 by 6 card, along with the student's basic contact information:

> I understand and agree that the Alexander Technique is the teaching that imparts the meaning of *the use of the self*, and that, as such, it should not be construed as a substitute for medical examination, diagnosis, and treatment. I further understand and agree that I am well-advised to consult with a physician relative to any symptoms that I have now or subsequently become aware of. I agree to keep Ron Dennis

informed about any unexpected changes in my experience relative to the Alexander Technique while I am his student.

For what it's worth, this is the first time I feel comfortable with language about the Technique in such a context, and have had no negative or questioning reactions from students completing the form.

This paper completes at least the first stage of the task I set myself a few years ago to write down my considered beliefs about the foundations of our work. Having reached in 2002 my 30th year in the Technique as well as the 65th in my life, I felt that both I and the time were ripe, and have pressed on with it. I wish it understood that, while I often enough take a critical stance toward FMA, I count myself second to none in respect for his achievement. But among Alexandrians, in my experience, remains a tendency toward adulation of his person and uncritical acceptance of his thought. To me, we not only do the founder highest honor, but also best advance our profession, by bringing to his rich and fundamental insights not only the practical expertise, but also the theoretical clarity, that they surely deserve.

Lastnotes

1. Page 50, Line 7: Better to say "theoretical/practical."

2. Page 53, Note 1: Bryan Niblett resides in Abingdon, Oxon, UK.

3. Page 68, Note 3: Each of us, of course, is *Feeler* as well as Thinker and Mover. Relative to the Alexander Technique, "feeling" (psychologically, the affective or emotional domain) belongs to Functioning rather than to Use.

4. Page 27, Note 2: According to Jean M. O. Fischer (personal communication, May 2006), transcribing from FMA's original letter to Jones, the last word of this quotation is "relationship" and not "relativity," as given by Goldberg. Later in the letter "relativity" is used in characterizing primary control as "... that relativity of the head to the neck and the head and neck to the body at a given time ... ." It is embarrassing to be party to the furtherance of an inaccuracy in quotation, but in this case the change of wording does not affect my argument. [Contrariwise, I now$_{2014}$ have in my possession of what I am told by John Nicholls is an actual copy of the letter that FMA sent to Jones in which the controversial last word is indeed "relativity" (letter with copy enclosed to me from John Nichols, 6-11-2006).

Book II

Atlanta Alexander News

Selections

18 Issues 1990-1994

Contents

Atlanta Alexander News

Price $1.00
No. 18
Fall 1994

Fourth Anniversary Issue   Newsletter of Alexander Technique of Atlanta

"So Long For Awhile ...

... That's all the songs for awhile." Those of a certain age (as the French so delicately put it) may hear again in memory the theme song of old radio's "Your Hit Parade." Or maybe not. In any case, the sentiment was ready to mind as I began contemplating this piece and seems appropriate for the occasion of announcing my decision to move from regular to occasional publication of the *Atlanta Alexander News*.

A few factors have brought me to this. One is that I feel I've said, for the time being and in terms of newsletter format at least, most of what I needed to say. Appearances perhaps to contrary, my writing energies are less than overflowing, and what there are of them seem more and more drawn toward the broader themes of theory and practice in the Alexander Technique itself—my statement, as it were.

Another thing is that I've invested in a production-quality video camera in order to begin an exploration of this medium in both actually working with students and documenting aspects of my own teaching practice. I feel about this somewhat as I did in getting my first computer, just ten years ago, very excited about the prospects but daunted by the efforts involved, both technical and creative.

Some further factors are my new commitment in teacher-training (12 hours per week in clock time alone), the ongoing cultivation of my private clientele, and of course, my music. As the be-bopper said (on the sidewalks of New York) when asked how to get to Carnegie Hall, "Practice, man, practice"! All the aforementioned require me to make some space in my life, psychological as well as temporal.

So, having done *AAN* for four years and 18 issues now, it's feeling like time to move on. Many thanks to my contributors, both financial and literary, to those who sent or spoke words of encouragement and appreciation, and to my dear Zouzy, who helped fold, seal, and stamp many a copy. Bye for now.

What we need is an education for our bodies that shall be, on the bodily plane, liberal and not merely technical and narrowly specific. The awareness that our bodies need is the knowledge of some general principle of right integration and along with it, a knowledge of the proper way to apply that principle in every phase of practical activity. ... What is needed is a practical morality working at every level from the bodily to the intellectual. ... So far as I am aware the only system of physical education which fulfils all these conditions is the system developed by F. M. Alexander.

                              Aldous Huxley, *Ends and Means*

An Alexander Carol

(Tune: "Deck the Halls")

First, we let the neck be free, Fa la la la la, la la, la, la!
Poise the head, just let it be, Fa la etc.
Easy back, hips, knees, and ankles, Fa la etc.
Letting go all cares and rankles! Fa la etc.

Next we practice inhibition,
It's against all intuition,
'Tis the story need be told,
Seek the new by stopping old!

Now we're giving the directions,
Joining in our predilections,
Choosing ease for self and others,
Alexander sisters, brothers!
Fa la la la la, la la, la, la!

Credo

Among the more prestigious students of the Alexander Technique over the years was the brilliant Raymond A. Dart, professor of anatomy in the University of Witwatersrand, Johannesburg. Dart was introduced to the Technique in South Africa around 1940, and subsequently became a staunch and articulate advocate of Alexander's work.

In 1981, in launching the first Alexander periodical in this country, (*The Alexandrian*, edited by myself and published by the American Center for the Alexander Technique), I quoted the last sentence of Dart's "An Anatomist's Tribute to F. Matthias Alexander" as follows:

It is a reasonable inference that each individual's part in the totality of human social behaviour is not confined in its effectiveness to the skill we succeed in attaining bodily and mentally in our use of ourselves but extends far beyond our daily acts and thoughts to our becoming as skilled as possible, as Alexander himself did, in communicating our knowledge about that better usage to others by the human practices of recording, of speaking and also of writing thereupon.

This is the spirit that to this point has animated my communicational endeavors in the Technique, and that I trust will continue to do so.

> If you apply the principle to the carrying out of one evolution, you have learned the lot.   FMA

Published quarterly at 1819 Brookhaven Circle, Atlanta, GA 30319 (404) 841-0386 ● 1994

Preface

As related in the Preface to my 1st Series (*Conceptual Foundations*), my aim in these compilations is to extend and hopefully to make more useful the life of my Alexandrian writings to a wider-than-original audience. Most of my production over the years has taken the form of shorter pieces in periodical or occasional publications and thus is already lost to many potential readers, from my standpoint an unfortunate situation. Actual readers, of course, will make their own judgments.

After moving from New York City to Atlanta in 1990 and settling in, I found myself with time on my hands and a teaching practice to promote, thus the *Atlanta Alexander News*. Mostly it was distributed among various local contacts and a growing student base, but there was also a small national mailing list. Altogether I produced 18 single-sheet issues over four years, ending in 1994. Each number contained, in addition to news snippets, an article or two by me—collected in this booklet—together with occasional pieces by students past and present. Early on these articles had an overt marketing thrust—"A Quality Investment," for example—but later became more philosophical and thus more reflective of my natural bent.

Preparing this compilation—scanning the original newsletters into files and then proofing them—forced me to read all the articles again word-for-word, such that I can report that they remain, with one exception detailed below, factually accurate. Beyond "just the facts," I'm gratified to find my thought still timely and in one case actually prophetic: in my last issue (Fall 1994) I wrote, "Appearances perhaps to contrary, my writing energies are less than overflowing, and what there are of them seem more and more drawn toward the broader themes of theory and practice in the Alexander Technique itself—my statement, as it were." It was subsequently in 1999 that "Primary Control and the Crisis in Alexander Technique Theory," the first of five articles in my *Conceptual Foundations* series, came out in *AmSAT News*.

The exception referred to above occurs in Part II of "An Overview of Alexander Politics" (p. 24). This article, to my knowledge the first and only one ever to deal with this aspect of the Technique's history, was reprinted in full in the Autumn 1992 *NASTAT News*, and from that exposure drew some corrective and critical response from Eleanor Rosenthal of San Francisco. Eleanor pointed out (*NASTAT News*, Autumn 1994, p. 6), whereas I had claimed in Part II that, in the 1960's, "... none of the recognized teachers here [Marjorie Barstow, Lulie Westfeldt, Frank Pierce Jones] who could have done so took the crucial step of establishing a training program," that Lulie Westfeldt had in fact started such a program "however short-lived." In the same letter Eleanor also challenged aspects of my characterization of the New York Alexander scene in the 80's, to which I responded next issue (Winter 1995, p. 4). I pointed out that my observations were based only on the period when I was actually there (1977-1990) rather than on an earlier period of Eleanor's personal presence and experience on the scene. Not unduly to re-hash "ancient history," as it were, suffice it here to say that perceptions do vary, and that (reader beware!) *all* history involves not only a selection of facts—in itself an interpretation—but also, to greater or lesser degree, an explicit interpretation of them.

In every issue but one I included a quotation or two that I thought appropriate for the subject at hand; these are set in italics at the end of each section and unless otherwise noted are FMA's. In going through the file I also found a few notes of appreciation and encouragement— "thoughtful and thought-provoking newsletter," "particularly enjoyed reading 'A Quality Investment,'" "thoroughly enjoyed your newsletter," "always enlightening, interesting and to the point"—balm indeed to the solitary writer and thanks again to Joan Frost, Pamela Blanc, Sally Bennett (wherever she be), and Lyn Charlsen for sending them!

Again I mention *ClickBook 8.0*, the software program by Blue Squirrel (www.bluesquirrel.com) that has so facilitated production of this work; it takes a group of word-processed files and automatically creates a booklet from them—incredible!

Very special thanks to Phyllis Richmond, *AmSAT News* Editor, who provided the Introduction to this 2nd Series compilation.

Ron Dennis
Atlanta, February 2006

Introduction

By Phyllis G. Richmond
Editor, *AmSAT News*

Ron Dennis has been writing about the Alexander Technique for almost 30 years. Before I became acquainted with these short pieces, I knew his writing only through his recent scholarly essays concerned with defining the Technique. Those pieces were published in *AmSAT News* and later compiled as "Conceptual Foundations." The 24 short pieces you hold in your hands predate that scholarly work and show us another aspect of his thinking.

These brief essays were written from 1990 to 1994 for a one-page newsletter Ron produced with the intention of presenting the Technique to new and prospective students. They display the rational thought and careful attention to word choice that are the hallmark of everything he writes. His approach is practical, straightforward, and full of good sense. He explains concepts in clear language, with a touch of understated wit, relating the Technique to the world in which we live. It requires great thoughtfulness and care to write like this—not too complex, not too theoretical, not too esoteric—finding the right balance for a new student.

These short pieces also provide Alexander Technique teachers with food for thought. How do we explain concepts to a lay audience? How do we present our ideas about what we do? There is much to mull over, much to be learned from studying how Ron goes about it. I appreciate and admire his skill in introducing thought-provoking ideas almost under the radar, in an unpretentious and practical way.

Ron went on to devote his writing energies to parsing the language and theory of the Alexander Technique, producing pieces for readers well-versed in Alexander's writings. These little pieces intended for the Alexander novice have lasting value, not only as precursors to his better known writing, but especially for the polished miniatures they are in themselves.

F. M. Alexander: The Unlikely Prophet

Edward Maisel, a former director of the American Physical
Fitness Institute, called F. M. Alexander "a unique and
seminal genius of the twentieth century" as well as "the
true father in Western culture of the sensory awareness
movement and the nonverbal humanities." Yet today, not
one person in a thousand has heard Alexander's name, or
knows of the technique for mind-body wholeness he
brought full-blown to London from Australia in 1904,
when Freud's psychoanalysis was still in its infancy as
were physical therapy and chiropractic, and the origina-
tors of some latter-day bodyworks, such as Rolf and
Feldenkrais, were yet children. A glimpse of Alexander's
life will help us understand how he became the pioneer
that he authentically was.

Frederick Matthias Alexander was born on January 20th,
1869, in Tasmania, an island off the southeastern coast
of Australia. A sickly child, he was privately educated,
and never attended public school or university. By the age
of sixteen he had left home for Melbourne, where he
worked for a time in various commercial occupations,
among them tea tasting. But he was nursing a love for
Shakespeare and for acting, and before long was having
some success as an elocutionist, giving one-man public
recitations, in an era and locale where such shows could
still draw respectable audiences. Thus was Alexander led
to adopt the stage as his profession.

All went well for a few years, until in his early twenties
the young reciter began to experience recurrent severe
hoarseness, calamitous in its implications for his career.
Things came to a head—or, let us say, to a throat—when,
after resting his voice on the advice of his doctor for two

weeks before a crucial engagement, Alexander was barely able to finish the performance, his voice virtually gone. Having found no help in medical counsel and treatment, he faced the thoroughly unattractive dilemma of either giving up his chosen career, or else attempting, with no professional or personal preparation, to cure himself.

By temperament and circumstance unable to accept the former course, Alexander doggedly chose the latter, and over the next several years carried out a truly amazing self analysis, his only resources his own reasoning ability together with a set of multiple mirrors, in which he learned to observe with minute detail his postures and movements. He came to see that in all of his activities and not just in speaking alone, he was compromising his potential for ease and flexibility by unconsciously over-tensing virtually every muscle in his body. As he gradually learned to "un-do" these faulty habits—the "use" of himself—the vocal problem improved and eventually ceased, in combination with striking improvements in general health and sense of well-being.

Free to return to the stage, Alexander instead devoted the rest of his life to the technique he had developed in working through his problem. He originated a method of teaching this technique through the use of his hands to convey kinesthetic information. By guiding his students in common movements, such as sitting and standing, he was often able to facilitate a direct sensory experience of efficiency in movement that contrasted vividly with the habitual. In London, where he had been encouraged to emigrate by a Melbourne doctor, he taught many of the leading actors of the day, as well as George Bernard Shaw, Aldous Huxley, and other notables. In the United States he worked with prominent members of the New York intellectual community, including John Dewey, who wrote introductions to three of Alexander's four books:

Man's Supreme Inheritance (1918), *Constructive Conscious Control of the Individual* (1923), and *The Use of the Self* (1932). *The Universal Constant in Living* appeared in 1941 with a foreword by the eminent biologist, George Coghill. In 1930, Alexander founded a training course for intending teachers, with which he was associated until his death, and from which is descended the present population of about 1,000 certified teachers of the Alexander Technique world-wide.

Alexander died on October 10th, 1955, in his eighty-seventh year. Perhaps the most elegant tribute to his achievement was made by Professor Nikolaas Tinbergen, co-winner of the 1973 Nobel Prize in Physiology/Medicine, himself a student of the technique, in his acceptance oration of which half was devoted to Alexander's work:

> *This story, of perceptiveness, of intelligence, and of persistence, shown by a man without medical training, is one of the true epics of medical research and practice.*

Indeed, an unlikely prophet.

A Letter to the Editor
Note: The following letter was declined for publication.

It is incredible to me that, in the whole of *The Atlanta Constitution's* recent "Aching Back" series, [10/29-30/90] the word "posture" or a derivative therefrom occurs NOT ONCE. Yet, not only the commonest of common sense, but also accepted medical authority, tell us that the body's habitual stance—subject to gravitational law no less than the tallest skyscraper—exerts a profound influence on all its parts, not least the back. Why do we suppose that Somebody always told us to stand up straight? I quote Dr. René Cailliet; whose series of clinical hand-books on musculoskeletal pain has been in print for over 25 years: "Posture, the 'static' spine, cannot be overemphasized in its clinical significance."

The problem is that efficient upright posture is not our inviolate birthright by virtue of inherited reflexes, but is to a large degree a learned skill. One reason among others that we do not acquire and maintain this skill as we mature is that our culture places no value upon it. We are rewarded for learning to balance our bank accounts rather than our postural patterns, eventual depletion of the former being the all-too-frequent consequence of deterioration of the latter. The sad truth is that if we erected our buildings as mindlessly as most erect their bodies, the landscape would soon be littered with ruins, since inanimate structures lack the ability, which we possess for better and for worse, of compensating for defects in alignment through muscular tension.

Again to quote Dr. Cailliet, "Regaining good posture should be a primary objective of anyone who wants to reverse the effects of the aging process, functionally as well as cosmetically." This, unfortunately, is not so simple as "stand up straight" and be done with it—neither the spirit nor the flesh nor both in concert are capable of immediately following such a directive after a lifetime, however long, of going their own way. Nor can one's untutored notion of "straight" have nearly the requisite precision, based as it must be, if improvement is being sought, on faulty prior experience. No, one must approach the gaining of postural skill in the same way as playing golf, the piano, or any other complex activity: through analysis, reflection, and above all, through having an adequate model upon which to base one's practice.

A Quality Investment

Regarding Alexander study, perhaps the second most frequent question asked me, after "What is your fee?", is "How many lessons does it take?" At this point, I always imagine the inquirer's mental computer ready to whip out a cost-benefit analysis that is not the less decisive for its lack of basis in experience. It is natural enough, especially in troubled economic times, to think of the outlay for lessons in terms of "cost." Here, however, I want to suggest that it might more productively be viewed as a quality investment.

The nature of a cost is that as soon as whatever has been bought has been used up, it has to be bought again. Food is a cost, as is an automobile. By contrast, a return, or increase in value, is expected of an investment, of which houses and education are examples. Since the Alexander Technique is education in learning to use one's body to its best advantage, it clearly qualifies as an investment. Why is it one of such quality?

The main answer to this question is that one's health—irrespective of coverage by insurance—truly is one's wealth, and that the proper use of the body is a major factor in health. And here I'm not talking just about freedom from pain and tension, important though that be, but about the full, co-ordinated, long-term functioning of the whole body. The crux of the matter is stated by Joel E. Goldthwait, M.D., who himself lived to 95 years, in *Essentials of Body Mechanics in Health and Disease* (Fifth Edition, J. B. Lippincott Co., 1952):

> An individual is in the best health only when the body is so used that there is no strain on say of its parts. This means

that, when standing, the body is held fully erect, with no strain on the joints, the bones, the ligaments, the muscles or any other structures. There should be adequate room for all the viscera, so that their function can be performed normally unless there be some congenital defect.

Alexander expressed the same thing more broadly, if less clinically, in his saying "Use affects functioning," which comprehends the notion of the use or employment of the total self—body, mind, spirit—in all activity and in rest.

Returning to the question of "how many lessons," the only real answer is, as with how much water to drink or money to make, "Enough." Enough to satisfy the individual's needs, whether they be freedom from discomfort or the pursuit of a whole Alexander life-style or something in-between. More concretely, enough so that the change in the individual's thinking and behavior implied by "education" is operative and stable. The student alone ultimately determines how much feels like enough. It should be remembered though, as often demonstrated in lessons, that what one "feels" isn't necessarily what's actually going on. Thus, a certain provisional attitude toward the "feelings," which is one outcome of effective Alexander lessons, is potentially a part of the process of coming to sense how much formal study is enough. This process isn't always clear-cut or simple—but hey, how many important ones are?

Another Unpublished Letter

The Editors, *Creative Loafing*: [an Atlanta alternative newspaper]

The Atlanta Constitution has declined to print the enclosed [my letter of 10/31, published in the Nov 90 issue of this newsletter], and so in my conviction that the subject matter deserves public airing I am sending it along to you. Since the area of postural education in general and the Alexander Technique in particular may be unfamiliar, I also include a piece by Jane Brody [*NY Times*, 6/21/90] for your reference. Lots of people know that their backs hurt, and spend lots of money looking for relief, but how many know, for example, that in the kinder and gentler year of 1932, the Subcommittee on Orthopedics and Body Mechanics of the White House Conference on Child Health and Protection reported on the basis of considerable empirical data, that perhaps 75 per cent of the country's youth, both boys and girls, exhibited subnormal and potentially symptom-producing grades of body mechanics (roughly equivalent to "posture" for present purposes), and called for widespread instruction in body mechanics at virtually every level of public and private education, from medical schools to kindergartens?

I, of course, have a vested interest in this matter because of my profession, and realize that Letters to the Editor cannot be a venue for special pleading. On the other hand, if the problem of back pain warrants a two-part series in a major metropolitan newspaper, then the public deserves not to be deprived of awareness of an important dimension of this problem.

Gaining control in the simple psycho-physical evolutions during lessons means sooner or later gaining control in the practical spheres of daily life.

No. 3, March 1991

Review of *MINDFULNESS* by Ellen J. Langer

234 pp. A Merloyd Lawrence Book $6.95

Every now and then a book appears that is broadly perceived to embrace the principles of the Alexander Technique from a totally different perspective, and hence to open another avenue of understanding for and communication about our discipline. Such a book was *Zen and the Art of Archery* by Eugen Herrigel, known by many Alexander teachers and students, and such a book is, or should be, *Mindfulness* by Ellen J. Langer.

Dr. Langer's credentials are impeccable: at Harvard, Professor of Psychology, Chair of the Social Psychology Program, and member of the Division on Aging of the Faculty of Medicine. Her research of 15 years, of which the current book is both summary and synthesis, has been widely reported in scholarly articles. Her writing admirably satisfies the not-always compatible demands of rigor and grace. Her achievement has been to illuminate, within the Western scientific perspective, the operational core of many traditional disciplines East and West: the practice of being present to oneself, or "mindfulness."

At the outset, her conception of mindfulness is deftly conveyed through its lack in mind*less*ness [italics added], "when the light's on and nobody's home." Certainly this is the essential situation of many people bound up in habit and routine. Tracing the roots of mindlessness both in repetition and in a form of inappropriate mindset called "premature cognitive commitments," Langer goes on to show its costs in terms of narrowness of self-image, unintended cruelty, loss of control, learned helplessness, and stunted potential. Readers sympathetic with Alexander's concepts of end-gaining and means-whereby surely will note with satisfaction her analysis of "education for outcome" as a root of mindlessness: "From kindergarten on, the focus of schooling is usually on goals rather than on the process by which they are achieved."

Shifting to the positive aspect, Langer identifies three key qualities of mindfulness as (1) creation of new categories, (2) openness to new information, and (3) awareness of more than one perspective. The net potential effect of these for the individual is to open the possibility for reflection, choice, and responsibility. The story of the Birdman of Alcatraz is recounted as an example of the principle of "control over context"—the power of new constructs to modify behavior, and presumably experience, dramatically for the better.

Succeeding chapters deal with mindfulness in aging, creativity, education, and of particular interest, in health. In this latter, Langer vigorously attacks the notion of mind-body dualism, ". . . one of our strongest mindsets, a dangerous premature cognitive commitment." Cited here is the extreme example of a psychiatric patient living in the "hopeless ward" of an institution. Moved because of renovations to a ward where patients usually improved, the patient also improved. Upon being subsequently returned to his former "hopeless" environment, he died immediately, from no apparent physical cause. Langer also challenges the common dualism that sees thought and feeling as separate, or at most, as simply related to each other. "Viewing them instead as part of one total simultaneous reaction, a reaction that may be measured in many different ways, may be more clarifying," she suggests.

It should be emphasized that, while Langer is advocating the benefits of becoming more mindful, she is doing so not only from theory but also from data. Her research designs illustrate beautifully how a concept can (and must) be operationally defined in order to serve as an experimental variable. For example, "mindfulness" in one striking experiment consisted of giving each of one group of residents in a nursing home a choice of houseplants to care for and also some responsibility in making small decisions about their daily routines. A similar group was not given these choices and responsibilities. A year and a half later, the people in the "mindful" group were not only more cheerful, active, and alert, but also many more were still alive compared to the others. In all, Langer has based her conclusions on the results of over 50 similar-ly-innovative and rigorous studies.

"Because rigidly following set rules and being mindful are, by definition, incompatible, this book will not offer pre-scriptions." Thus does researcher Langer mindfully and properly eschew the role of guru, though perhaps without due recognition of yet another lurking dualism, that between "rigidly following set rules" and "being mindful." For the distinction would seem to be softened in consider-ing the vast area of human practice—the area of "meth-od"—devoted to structure in moving from one mode of being toward another.

Method implies that getting from here to there generally requires a route. A route isn't always a fixed, open road. In the wilderness, a route is more often a direction, with possibly some hint of previous use—indeed, a mindful predecessor might even have left some marks. One can seldom follow such a route rigidly—a landslide may have obscured the trail, or a stream may be high. Or, scenery of interest to the present traveler may suggest a side-jaunt. But one is generally content and wise to return to the trail. Getting lost is uncomfortable and quite likely dangerous. Selecting a route, if there is a choice, is a matter of information and preference. Staying on a route, if an alternative becomes available, is a matter of information and judgment. Without pressing the analogy further, I wish mainly to remind that more is required of the individual in becoming mindful than intellectually digesting this profound and excellent book, as I have little doubt the author would agree.

One way, of course, was revealed by F. M. Alexander. In becoming mindful of habitual patterns in the use of himself, in methodically articulating his process, and in laboring lifelong to communicate it, he not only created his own path but also blazed it for others. That we can now, thanks to Ellen Langer, conceive his work addition-ally as "mindfulness in daily movement" is truly an en-richment of it.

There is no such thing as a right position, but there is such a thing as a right direction.

Taking a Stand on Postural Journalism

This month's issue (May 1991) of *American Health* magazine, published by the Reader's Digest Association, fea-
tures an article called "Taking A Stand On Posture" by
Howard Muson, a former editor of *Psychology Today*. My
colleague Gene King of New York (to whom thanks and
greetings) brought it to my attention, particularly in that
a physician whose postural views I generally respect,
René Cailliet, MD, was one of the authorities cited. Media
attention to posture always makes my Alexan-
der-teacher's heart beat a little faster, anyway, so I
rushed out to buy a copy. Sad to report, the article is a
prime example of a lot that's lacking in popular writing in
this area, so much that I feel moved to comment at
length.

There is, initially, the question of graphics—the first, and
perhaps strongest, impression such a piece makes. Fac-
ing the title page, we see a color photograph taking up the
full length and more than half the width of the page. This
pictures a yuppie-type male in his skivvies, with dress
shoes and socks and a motorcycle-style helmet. The
helmet has fore-and-aft straps under jaw and occiput,
and an eye-bolt screwed into the top with attached cable
leading up. The figure is posed in an energetic looking
stride, with gut in, chest out, and shoulders back. The
whole display is obviously a media-hyped version of the
old postural adage to carry oneself as though having a
string attached to the top of the head pulling one up. Its
dubious postural value aside, I found the image a real
turn-off, more ridiculous than cute, and certainly not an
inducement to practice the virtues the article attempts to
preach.

As a check against my own bias, I showed the picture, without reference to its context, to my Alexander Technique class in the Theater/Dance Department at the University of Alabama in Birmingham. I asked them two questions: (1) solely as an image, do you find this positive, negative, or neutral? (2) in your current understanding of good posture, do you find this positive, negative, or neutral? To question (1) the response was 3 positive, 11 negative, 3 neutral. Question (2) yielded 2 positive, 11 negative, 4 neutral. Not to claim a whit of generalizability for this result, I would hope at least that it might prompt the article's author, editor, and publisher to consider more carefully their means relative to their ends.

Then there is the question of the article's content. We read, for example, "When the lower back is curved, the vertebrae supported by the pelvic bone tilt and pull on the surrounding muscle tissue, possibly squeezing out the protective disc material between them and pinching nerves." Curved in what direction and to what degree? Are we to make efforts to "straighten out" the normal lordotic curve of the lumbar spine that absorbs shock and directs the discs protectively away from the vulnerable nerve roots located near the lateral posterior aspect of the vertebral bodies? The quoted statement sounds a note of authority through its facile recital of anatomical terms, but really amounts to a cavalier account of the body mechanics involved that poses a positive menace in its implication that any curve in the lower back is bad.

Another incompletely-presented notion is that postural traits seem to run in families. Dr. Cailliet is quoted as saying, "The son has rounded shoulders, the father has rounded shoulders, the grandfather had rounded shoulders. We don't know why this is so, but some of it is clearly genetic." The problem with this observation is that it virtually ignores the role of learning in the acquisition of postural habits. Of course, we all come into the world with a specific biological inheritance and associated traits and tendencies, but the fact remains that, as human infants, we necessarily learn the skills of upright stance and locomotion in the presence of human models; as in any other form of learning, imperfect models result in imperfect copies. In later life we sometimes have a choice in our selection of models, as in taking up golf or the piano. But in the case of our basic motor skills, the model is forced upon us by the very nature of human nurture. Small wonder that daughter rounds her shoulders, as did mother and grandmother before her!

The article's greater failing, however, is less in what it does say than in what it doesn't. It is fine that some common notions of "good posture," such as the military brace, are criticized, and that some manifestations of "poor posture," such as Dr. Cailliet's "forward head," are pointed out. But nowhere—either in the author or in his cited authorities—do we find any expression of, or get a contextual sense for, the inadequacy of "posture" itself as a concept. A concept adequate to the complexities of human movement behavior must reflect the essential unity of what we habitually and uncritically distinguish both as "posture" and "movement," and as "mental" and "physical," in all of our motor acts. As the great physiologist C. S. Sherrington put it, "To take a step is an affair not of this or that limb solely but of *the total neuromuscular activity of the moment* [emphasis added]—not least of head and neck."[1]

To date, the ideas put forth that most adequately encompass the vast conceptual scope of "total neuromuscular activity of the moment" are F. M. Alexander's *use of the self* and R. A. Dart's *poise*.

Alexander, whose teaching dates from ca. 1900, summarized his view thusly: "If the reader will remember that the subject of my study has been, and is, the living psycho-physical organism, which is *the sum of a complex of unified processes* [emphasis added], he will understand why I refrain as far as is possible from using such terms as 'postures,' 'mental states,' 'psychological complexes,' 'body mechanics,' 'subconscious,' or any of the thousand and one labelled concepts, which have like barnacles, become attached to the complicated idea we have of ourselves owing to the kind of education to which we have been subjected. Instead I prefer to call the psycho-physical organism simply 'the self,' and to write of it as something 'in use,' which 'functions' and 'reacts.'"

Professor Dart, anatomist and distinguished paleontologist, wrote, "Terminological failure to distinguish the static symbolism of posture from the dynamic plasticity of poise has thus been responsible for a great deal of confusion both in the nomenclature of, and medical thought concerning, movement."

According to the Russian movement-physiologist N. Bernstein, whose basic research is cited in many texts, "The motor activity of organisms is of *enormous biological significance* [emphasis added]—it is practically the only way in which the organism not only interacts with the surrounding environment, but also operates on this environment, altering it with respect to particular purposes."[4] With the evidence of faulty motor activity in humans piling up on all sides—the back-pain statistics alone bear witness—we need the best thinking tools available for this problem. That the profound conceptions of Alexander and Dart, together with associated practical experience, remain unfathomed by writers like Mr. Muson and magazines like *American Health* imposes a baleful limitation on the quality of communication that can be made on the crucial matter of poise in the use of ourselves.

---

[1]The Endeavor of Jean Fernel, Cambridge Univ. Press, 1946.
[2]The Universal Constant in Living, E. P. Dutton, 1941.
[3]"The Attainment of Poise," S. A. Medical Journal, Feb. 8, 1947.
[4] The Co-ordination and Regulation of Movements, Pergamon Press, 1967.

The vast majority of mankind are unacquainted with poise, *either physical or psychical.*

R. A. Dart

No. 5, July 1991

Reports from the Front

This past Spring 1 taught a for-credit Alexander workshop in the Department of Theatre/Dance at the University of Alabama in Birmingham. Special thanks to Chairman Karma Ibsen and Professor Melanie Grebel for their parts in making this successful. As part of the course requirements, participants wrote a summary of their experience, three of which 1 am pleased to publish here. Thanks to Deborah Daws, Victor McCoy, and Brent Smith, who have kindly given permission to share their work.

DEBORAH - The Alexander Technique class has taught me more about myself than I ever could have imagined. When the class first began I didn't believe that anything, especially this, could change the way I feel about my 'self' but it did. Throughout the course—each meeting—I felt certain changes in my self, not only my body but my being. I really learned a good way to relax that could be used in every aspect of my life. The best part about Alexander is that it doesn't require any special equipment and there is no pressure. I have come to learn that Alexander is all of the things we know we should do for our bodies—we just don't for one reason or another.

VICTOR - When I first went to the Alexander Technique class, I really had no idea what to expect. All I knew was it was a movement class of sorts. I had noticed it was being offered as a theatre or dance class, so I reasoned it would be less actor oriented than most movement classes. I liked that idea. I've known for some time that I misuse my body, and the thought of a more essential study of movement intrigued me ... I began to wonder just how "out there" the Alexander business was, but soon I began to make discoveries that changed my mind.

100

The first discovery was allowing the knee joint to initiate movement in walking. I realized that left to my own habits my foot instigated the movement of walking, causing strain in my butt and my back. But by allowing the knee to lead, the foot follows naturally and the strain was gone. It also curbed my tendency to plod around heavily on my feet.

The second and most important discovery came some time later. Through session work I found out I sink my torso down into my hips. This creates a massive weight from the tops of my legs, pressing down into the floor. This tendency is the main factor that causes me to smash my heels against the floor when I walk.

The last discovery I made is also the hardest one to deal with. The fact that being aware doesn't fix it has been a harsh reality for me. Don't get me wrong, I appreciate being aware, but oftentimes it's very frustrating. It stands to reason that if you are aware of something that causes you unnecessary pain, you could stop it. Monitor it, yes. Stop it, no. So now, I'm living with the double-edged sword of the awareness of self.

I try to congratulate myself when I'm thinking about it, and not to be too hard on myself when I'm not. And to keep in mind these are very gradual, very slow and not impossible changes. I realize it's a lifelong process that can't be much more than just comprehended in nine or ten weeks. But in the short time I have been associated with it I can notice a visible difference within myself.

BRENT - If I had known exactly what this course was about before I registered for it, I probably would have taken it anyway under the assumption that it would be a very easy class, considering that I already had pretty good control of my posture and I was already somewhat in touch with my body. I maybe would have said something like, "All right, let's see this Dennis guy fix something that's not broken." But, not knowing exactly what to expect, I was fortunate enough to begin the class with a clean slate, open mind.

I have to admit that at first, I was a bit wary of the language. "You are now in the process of allowing your neck to be free to let your head lead your spine in a lengthening direction while allowing your back to widen." It seemed like a very roundabout way of saying "stand up straight." Needless to say, I did not stay disillusioned for long as Ron explained that no one ever really stands up straight. He also explained that in order to fully experience and appreciate action or movement, or anything for that matter, one must be aware of not just the end result, but also of the means required to accomplish the end. Therefore, instead of just standing erect, one should begin the process of standing erect by allowing the neck to be free to let the head lead the spine, etc. ...

My biggest revelation in this class came to me a few weeks after Ron worked with my group on individual projects. I didn't have anything specific to work on, so we just took a look at the way I stand. The main adjustment Ron found was to move my shoulders forward a few inches. For a while, I acknowledged this only as moving my shoulders forward a few inches. That is until one day when it dawned on me that this was in fact the physical effect of widening my torso. By widening my torso, this resulted in moving my shoulders forward (and out). This intrigued me, because I had not, until that point, really understood the idea of widening. I mean, since muscles only contract, how could you "push" your shoulders away from your center. Upon my revelation, I discovered, or rather, rediscovered my habit of throwing my shoulders back slightly. This meant that really, muscles in my back were actually pulling my shoulders back. Therefore, the key was to release in order to allow my torso to widen.

All of this brought back memories of how when I was much younger, I was aware of this habit with my shoulders. I'm not quite sure when this started but I am pretty positive that this was not always present. This led me to believe that it might have been a sort of unconscious decision at some point in my life that subsequently became habit. This eventually seemed so natural that [it] began to feel right.

So now I am faced, or rather given a concrete, tangible example of something that feels right, but isn't. From this course I've learned that the main objective is to have what is right to feel right. In order to accomplish this I have been and will be using the tools that I have attained through Alexander. This means remembering to inhibit the impulse to contract my shoulder muscles whenever I become aware of it. I also find it beneficial to focus at least some of my attention on my upper torso when I do my self-work on the floor.

Since I began this process I've become to feel more and more comfortable and at ease with what I think of as a corrected, lengthened, widened, and freed-neck stature. I realize that the Alexander Technique is a long and possibly never-ending journey, but I am secure in the knowledge that I have taken the first steps and am guaranteed progress as long as I use what I have learned to not only improve myself in the areas that I know need improvements, but also to find other areas that need attention.

Everyone is always teaching one what to do, leaving us still doing the things we shouldn't do.

Impressions of the Third International Congress

Any talk of the Third International Congress on the F. M. Alexander Technique—held in Engelberg, Switzerland, August 13-19, 1991—must certainly begin with a tribute to certified teacher Michael Frederick, the Ojai, California-based originator and impresario of the first three of these conclaves. No one unfamiliar with the tangled history of the Technique as it has developed both in and out of England in the 35 years since Alexander's death can appreciate the full significance of the congress idea and its first realization in Stony Brook, New York in 1986. In these few lines, it must suffice to say that the opportunity afforded by these congresses for dialog among Alexander teachers world-wide is not only a positive but very likely a crucial factor in the future development of the profession. Michael has announced that the Engelberg Congress is the last he will be organizing, and all of us are indebted to him, and to Lena Frederick, also a certified teacher and Michael's co-operative, for their incredible efforts in realizing this vision.

Speaking of Engelberg, I mustn't simply mention it in passing without saying how much this unique place contributed to the overall experience and success of the Third Congress. The train ride from Zürich, the final ascent to Engelberg by cog-rail, the quaint and intimate village itself, the supremely reserved and competent Swiss people, the natural scene commanded by snow-capped peaks, the wonderful breakfasts in the hotels, the rambles in Alpine meadows to symphonies of cowbells, the restaurants and sidewalk cafés—all told, a venue unlikely to be surpassed (though it certainly should be emulated) in its very special *gemütlichkeit.*

The general format of this Congress was similar to the first two—plenary sessions first thing in the morning, followed by rotating master classes with the Technique's most senior teachers and many special presentations. Because of the manner of scheduling, one could select only two of 17 different "specials," a restriction that I and many others found frustrating. On the other hand, it was certainly better to have too much rather than too little to choose from, and the Steering Committee is to be commended on their composition of this far-ranging menu.

A moving tribute to Patrick Macdonald was prepared by several of his students and delivered by Yehuda Kuperman of Basel. Macdonald, now retired from active teaching, is a graduate of Alexander's very first training class whose powerful personality and teaching style have created virtually a separate school within the Technique. Characterizing his mentor as "the great Romantic of the Technique," Kuperman was heartfelt without undue sentimentality, and Macdonald's special force came through on the accompanying videos, despite some unfortunate technical glitches that required all the audience's indulgence.

If Macdonald has been the Technique's great romantic, certainly Marjorie Barstow of Lincoln, Nebraska, also a graduate of the first training and now past 90, represents its classical pole. As spare in her persona as in her words and the superb use of her hands, Marjorie too has attracted a large group of disciples devoted to her special vision of the work. Marjorie's presence at Engelberg was a poignant reminder of her unique contribution to the Alexander work in America, both in terms of introducing the Technique to hundreds of people in her workshops and, for many, many years, of maintaining a staunch if solitary Alexander outpost in the nation's Heartland.

Most of the presentations and events that I witnessed came off almost too predictably, but the same cannot be said for that of certified teacher and training-course director Neal Katz of Boston. Neal's topic, "Generations of Habit: A Family Systems Perspective on the Alexander World," dealt with the sensitive issue of F. M. Alexander's own family life, in particular the alleged alcoholism of his father, and how this may have affected Alexander both personally and professionally. Not that the phenomenon is by any means confined to the Alexander movement, but the tendency toward factionalism that has seemed to characterize the Technique, with possible roots in aspects of the founder's own personality, suggests a potentially important avenue of understanding for the Congress's stated theme of "Developing the Profession."

Among these impressions of presence at the Third International Congress was one, unmistakably, of a great absence: Judith Leibowitz. Judy—"Mother of American Alexander Work"—who was to have been the Congress's keynote speaker, succumbed to cancer in New York in late 1990. Her life and contributions to the Alexander Technique were recalled in a special memorial session by colleagues and friends Deborah Caplan, Eleanor Rosenthal, Tommy Thompson, and Walter Carrington. Among Judy's many talents and accomplishments, it has always seemed to me that one of the greatest was a conspicuous generosity of spirit, in all of life as well as in her outlook on the Alexander Technique. It was this, I believe, coupled with her incomparable skill, that drew so many to her, both as teacher and as trainer. Having witnessed this largesse on countless occasions and been its personal beneficiary, I can think of no more fitting tribute to Judy—as we leave Engelberg in anticipation of the 1994 Centennial Congress in Sydney—than its ongoing practice by us all.

An Overview of Alexander Politics

Part I

Every movement, whether outwardly concerned with governance or not, acquires a political and worldly dimension. As Mahatma Gandhi once wryly remarked (at least in the film), "It takes a lot of money to keep me in poverty." Having devoted this issue's lead article to the Third Congress, with its inevitable political overtones, it seems appropriate to keep these matters in perspective through a fuller discussion. Ultimately, they are related to both historical and contemporary concerns about the training, qualification, and certification of Alexander teachers.

Frederick Matthias Alexander began teaching in London in 1904, after having developed the Technique on his own in Australia during the previous dozen-or-so years. Early on, F. M. (as he is commonly referred to in Alexander circles) brought his brother A. R. (Albert Redden) Alexander into partnership, and for many years the two brothers were the only sources for instruction. Before 1930, however, F. M. had also qualified at least two early students and associates, Irene Tasker (who, incidentally, was a pioneer of Montessori education in England) and Ethel Webb, his long-time personal secretary.

It was not until 1930 that Alexander opened the first formal training course, when he felt some confidence—after 40 years of experience—that the necessary skills could be learned in such a setting and that there would be a demand for trained teachers. The duration of the London course was set at three years, with a total time investment, considering the days and hours of classes, of about 1600 hours. This was the basic, and indeed, virtually the only arrangement for becoming certified until

Alexander's death in 1955, although a few teachers were certified in America during the war years, when Alexander and his school for children found sanctuary in Stowe, MA, at a facility provided by the American Unitarian Association.

The issue of a democratically-organized professional society to protect and propagate the technique had come up in F. M.'s lifetime, but he had vetoed it on the basis that he personally could be overruled by a majority. Appearances perhaps to the contrary, Alexander's decision in this case seems not entirely self-serving, as possibly only the individual who has uniquely created something of value can fully appreciate. But in any case, within a few years of Alexander's death, and for the above-mentioned purposes, the certified teachers in London had organized the Society of Teachers of the Alexander Technique (STAT).

Clarification from Walter Carringon

Letter to *NASTAT NEWS*, No. 19 (Winter 1993)

"... in Ron Dennis' fascinating 'Overview of Alexander Politics' he states that FM had vetoed the setting up of a professional society 'on the basis that he personally could be overruled by a majority.' This was not the case. In fact FM said that we should arrange what we thought was best and that he would agree to it. But most of us at the meeting considered that it would be entirely inappropriate for FM, as the originator of our work, to be placed in a position where his judgment could be overruled. We therefore rejected the proposal. As a result the Society was not formed at that time."

We must learn to distinguish between the variations of a teacher's art and the principles of the teaching technique which is being employed.

108

An Overview of Alexander Politics

Part II

The main motivation behind the founding of STAT (Society of Teachers of the Alexander Technique, London) was
defining and maintaining standards, now that the founder was gone, for the training and certification of new
teachers of the Alexander Technique. Witnesses relate
that controversy ran high, as is often the case in succes-
sional situations, and that in the end, aside from establishing the administrative machinery of the new society,
all that could be agreed upon was that trainings must
consist of at least 1600 training hours over three years.
Teachers approved to conduct programs under these
standards submitted their graduates to STAT, which duly
conferred membership and a credential, the STAT certificate. From its inception in the late 50's until the
mid-80's, STAT considered itself the sole source of an
Alexander teacher's legitimacy, short of recognition by F.
M. Alexander himself.

In the U. S., meanwhile, teaching had been going on since
the mid-30's. Two graduates of Alexander's first training
class, which had finished in 1934, were Americans who
returned here to work, Marjorie Barstow in Boston (with
A. R. Alexander) and Lincoln, [Nebraska] her home, and
Lulie Westfeldt in New York. Westfeldt was joined later in
the 30's by Alma Frank, a New Yorker returning from
London where she had gone to train with Alexander.
Before 1950, however, virtually the only other active
American teacher was Frank Pierce Jones of Cambridge,
who had been trained by Alexander during the latter's
war-time sojourn in Stowe, Massachusetts (see Part 1).

We can now note that by 1960, the technique's having experienced a quarter-century of steady if gradual growth on these shores, a clear need had emerged for American teacher training. But none of the recognized teachers here who could have done so took the crucial step of establishing a training program—a fact, as we shall see, of far-ranging significance. Into this situation came two women—Judith Leibowitz and Deborah Caplan of New York—determined that the Alexander Technique would have an American institutional home. Neither was certified by STAT. Judith had worked extensively with Lulie Westfeldt and Alma Frank, and had established her own teaching practice during the 50's. Deborah, a registered physical therapist, had been trained in the technique by her mother, Alma Frank. Together with three students Judith had trained, they incorporated the American Center for the Alexander Technique in New York in 1964, and three years later commenced the first training class. ACAT has continuously trained teachers since that time, and Judith Leibowitz (d. 1990) lived to see a dream realized: in 1988, its Teacher Certification Program was accredited as a graduate-level program in higher education and also gained federal recognition for student financial aid and foreign student enrollment. Deborah Caplan still serves on the Senior Training Faculty there.

Change involves carrying out an activity against the habit of life.

Research Milestone!

In a memo dated November 4, 1991, John H. M. Austin, M.D., of New York, informed members of the Alexander community that his research on respiratory function and the Alexander Technique had been accepted for publication in a medical journal. Dr. Austin's study, co-authored by Alexander teacher Pearl Ausubel, is the very first to demonstrate, under conditions of accepted scientific rigor, improvement in physical functioning as a result of Alexander lessons. As such, it truly is a milestone.

It was a dozen long years ago that the results of Dr. Austin's first pilot study were reported in the premier issue of *The Alexandrian,* this country's first Alexander periodical, edited by me and published by the American Center for the Alexander Technique. Having known and worked closely with John these many years, I want to take this opportunity to introduce both him and his work to my readers.

But first, as they say, a brief historical note. Numerous respectable studies of various biomechanical, psychological, and behavioral aspects of the Technique began to be published around 1960, notably by Wilfred Barlow and Frank Pierce Jones. As early as 1938, however, a cogent monograph by Alma Frank, one of the first American teachers, had appeared in the journal of the Society for Research in Child Development. Beginning in the mid-70's, several academic theses and dissertations investigated the Technique, mostly in terms of music and music education. In a psychology dissertation, however, at Tufts University, to that point the most rigorous study in terms of design, Richard Brown demonstrated a significant relationship between Alexander experience and positive cognitive and emotional states.

A further word about this matter of rigor. It is the issue of control that is central to the evaluation of research. To infer that a result is valid, and thus generalizable, it is not sufficient to show that a particular treatment produces a change, regardless of magnitude. Rather, change in one group must be assessed relative to an equivalent group, called a control, which receives no treatment or an alternative treatment. The role of statistics in research is thus not to show if change has taken place—that is the role of measurement—but rather whether the degree of any measured change is statistically significant, i.e., truly the result of the application of an experimental procedure or merely due to chance. It is certainly true that there are other methods of conducting valid research, but this paradigm of the statistically-analyzed controlled experiment remains the accepted standard for *publishable* research in the sciences generally, including medicine and psychology.

John himself, now Professor of Clinical Radiology specializing in pulmonary function at the prestigious Columbia-Presbyterian Medical Center in New York, came to the Technique from his musical rather than his medical background. An excellent violinist and string bassist, he began Alexander study with Pearl Ausubel in the late 70's to deal with performance tensions. He became interested in experimental validation of the Technique, using his specialty of lung-function as a point of departure for research design. The reputation of the Technique in improving breathing inspired, so to speak, the major line of attack. Access to spirometry, a procedure that measures respiratory function, and other facilities of the laboratory at Columbia-Presbyterian, provided the necessary basis for quantifying experimental change.

In early 1980 John approached the American Center, where I was at the time in charge of such matters, for help in getting subjects for his study. Thanks to the Center's network of teachers, eight subjects were recruited and tested, both before and after a series of 20 lessons, yielding results of significant improvement in several aspects of respiratory function. Over the next couple of years John submitted an article reporting these findings to journals in the field, all of which declined to publish it, citing the small number of subjects and the lack of controls.

Somewhere along the line, excited by John's results in the pilot study, I got the idea of finishing my long-in-limbo doctoral degree by doing a similar study with wind-players. Encouraged by Dr. Harold Abeles, of the music department at Teachers College-Columbia University, I enlisted John for my dissertation committee, a "natural" given his professorship within the Columbia system and his willingness to lend full moral and technical support to the project. Over many a late dinner in our neighborhood Szechuan restaurant we worked hard on the study's design, which became the first to use a control group in investigating the Technique relative to improvement in physical functioning. To make a long story short, the project was duly carried out with seven experimental subjects and six controls. Unfortunately, there was no significant improvement in my experimental group, which did not prevent my getting the degree m 1987 but was certainly a considerable blow to my pride. In accounting for these results, John and I eventually speculated that wind players, being already strongly-habituated "respiratory athletes," probably would not show much change during a relatively small duration of Alexander study.

Genuinely attesting John's faith in the Technique's ultimate validation by experimental methods is the fact that, in the teeth of my disappointing results, and despite formidable logistical problems, he determined to repeat his study, this time with a target of 20 experimental subjects and an appropriate control group! In the smallest of nutshells, this quest that had become ever more frustrating and seemingly endless, eventually reached completion with the happy outcome announced at the beginning of this article. In John's own wads: "I am delighted to report that after a long haul of data analysis, a million rewrites, and difficulties with disbelieving medical editors, our research has finally been accepted for publication in the respected mainstream medical journal *Chest*." BRAVO, JOHN!

An Overview of Alexander Politics

Part III

We have seen to this point how the main avenues of Alexander teacher certification after F.M.'s death in 1955 became those deriving from STAT (Society of Teachers of the Alexander Technique, London) and ACAT (American Center for the Alexander Technique, New York). A third line, that of individual Alexander teachers whose training activities have been implied or explicit in varying degrees, remains to be discussed. These situations have been relatively few, both in England and abroad; we allude here to three of the most visible examples on the American scene.

Without doubt, the most influential teacher in this category has been Marjorie Barstow. A graduate of Alexander's first training class, Marjorie, now past 90, returned to the U.S. in the mid-30's and has remained in her family home in Lincoln, Nebraska, since about 1940. In the 60's she began offering extended summer and winter workshops in Lincoln. These workshops afforded virtually the only means for people not having a teacher in their area to get substantial work in the Technique. Marjorie, an acknowledged master, did not consider herself to be a trainer, but the fact is that over the years, quite a few people who worked with her eventually set themselves up as teachers, with more-or-less tacit approval. In the late 80's Marjorie recognized 26 of these by name, in a letter responding to the question of who could be eligible for membership in the newly forming national professional organization NASTAT (North American Society of Teachers of the Alexander Technique). Currently, the Performance School in Seattle, a joint effort of several individuals, and the Alexander School in Philadelphia, headed by Bruce Fertman, represent the main concentrations of Barstow-recognized teachers in this country.

Marjorie's contemporary, Catherine Wielopolska of Philadelphia, enrolled in the first training course but was not able to finish the last year and be certified. In the late 60's, Kitty (as she is known) returned to England and finished her training with Patrick Macdonald. She started her own training course in 1976, which, although basically a traditional three-year program, was not approved by STAT, for reasons unclear to the present writer. Kitty certified a relatively small number of teachers, probably less than 25, before her death at 88 in 1988.

A third teacher deserving mention in this group is Aileen Crow of New York. Originally certified by ACAT and a faculty member there during the 70's, Aileen left to establish her own training course in 1978. This program has been controversial in the eyes of mainstream Alexander because of its relatively short duration (approximately two years, based on monthly intensives plus more extended work at various times) compared to the traditional trainings. Aileen has probably certified about 20 teachers.

It took me years to reach a point that can be reached in a few weeks with the aid of any competent teacher.

An Overview of Alexander Politics

Part IV and Conclusion

Our longer-than-anticipated and now-thankfully-concluding series has brought us to the opening of the 1980's, at which point Alexander teachers of the U.S. were of three distinct camps: (1) ACAT (American Center for the Alexander Technique, New York & San Francisco; (2) STAT (Society of Teachers of the Alexander Technique, London); and (3) individual Alexander teachers, notably Marjorie Barstow, Catherine Wielopolska, and Aileen Crow. It remains to recount the formation of NASTAT (North American Society of Teachers of the Alexander Technique) and to offer an assessment of the current situation and future trends.

By the early 1980's, relations between ACAT and STAT—never officially established—had become unofficially yet definitely strained. ACAT graduates accounted for most of the practicing teachers in this country, yet were considered more or less "illegitimate" because of ACAT's founding by non-STAT-recognized teachers. Confounding the situation were rumors, not entirely without basis, of certain influences of non-traditional nature among some American teachers (mostly meditational or psychotherapeutic in origin). Yet certain STAT members continued to travel regularly to teach in the States, often using the facilities and membership of ACAT in New York and S.F. as their base of operation. It is understandable that in a few instances these visiting teachers came somewhat in the manner of apostles to the heathen, which of course did not help things either. In a fitting quirk of history, it was to be a Canadian who eventually brought about a conciliation.

David Gorman of Ontario had trained as an Alexander teacher in London, and, by dint of his gifts as illustrator and anatomist, was in demand in the U.S. in the early 80's for his lectures on "The Body Moveable." As he encountered American-trained teachers at firsthand, he found that they were in general as capable as their STAT-certified counterparts. He also found the U. S. Alexander scene crying for unification, having become, if not as chaotic as some abroad imagined, at least unhealthily fragmented, despite an almost 50-year history. To his great credit, it was largely Gorman's inspiration of a means to such unity and his labors as trusted broker on both sides of the Atlantic that moved STAT eventually to give its blessing to the project.

The plan as it evolved called for an American society of teachers incorporating training & certification standards acceptable to STAT, in effect a political alliance between STAT and ACAT. After much hard work (to put it mildly) by Gorman and a steering committee of American teachers, North American STAT (NASTAT) was finally incorporated in New York in 1987. This longed-for union of the mainstream English and American Alexander movements, almost matrimonial in its import, was truly a very great achievement, and as astounding to many of us on the inside as, say, recent events in the ex-Soviet Union, *mutatis mutandis*! Nor was this all. It had also been anticipated that the step of both organizations' making constitutional provision to allow reciprocal recognition of their respective societies would yield at a stroke a mechanism for an eventual network of allied societies worldwide, thus creating for the first time an international standard and forum for the profession.

This standard largely deals with the individual's training and qualifications to enter professional practice as a Teacher of the Alexander Technique. Although differing from society to society in details, the standard essentially requires completion of 1600 hours of training in no less than three years on an approved course. The intending director of a training course must be approved by the society, and the course itself must be at least 80% practical hands-on work, subject to monitoring and review, with a faculty-student ratio of no less than one to five. National societies now exist in Australia, Canada, Denmark, Israel, France, Switzerland, South Africa, The Netherlands and Germany, in addition to Great Britain and the U.S., with the steps toward full reciprocal recognition almost accomplished.

On the American scene, these overwhelmingly favorable developments came not without cost. At the outset, only STAT and ACAT-certified teachers were eligible for membership in the new national organization. It was felt by both American and English sponsors of NASTAT that, while ACAT had established a successful track record by maintaining organized training courses for twenty years, not enough was known of the qualifications of individuals trained or recognized by independent teachers to permit "grandfathering" them. Thus, even though due provision was made for such individuals eventually to become full teaching members of the society, through evaluation and/or additional training, the fact is that the establishment of NASTAT left unachieved the full unification of the American Alexander profession.

The reaction of non-NASTAT teachers to this scenario has been mixed. Several have successfully negotiated the waiver process and joined, or are in the process of doing so. Others have not, and perhaps will not. An organization called Alexander Technique International, numbering probably in the neighborhood of 50, has been formed to represent the interests of these and like-minded individuals. A special concern is the perpetuation of disunion through the continued operation of training programs by independent teachers. No one, in NASTAT or out, challenges a salutary degree of diversity, or the good intentions of all those serving the Alexander calling as teachers. But for such a tiny profession, in this era of increasing litigation and regulation, particularly in the health and alternative-health arenas, getting all Alexander teachers to pull together in terms of public perception and policy must be seen as a very high priority.

For its part, NASTAT has served the profession admirably during its first five years of existence. Its membership has grown from 134 charter members to 280 today, comprising a large majority of American teachers, with an additional 135 enrolled student members. It publishes a directory of certified teachers, approved training courses, and affiliated national societies, together with a reading list. It fulfills public requests for information from the national office in Champaign, Illinois. It conducts annual meetings that offer continuing education. It has adopted a Code of Ethics and guidelines for approval and review of training courses. It sponsors conferences of Directors of Training, itself an historic step within the Technique. It participated crucially in the establishment of an international standard of teacher education and qualification. Clearly representing the high road of professionalism, certification by NASTAT or one of its national affiliates is the basic professional credential that all Alexander teachers should have. For these reasons, for the public good as well as the private interest of all teachers of Alexander's great discoveries, it is to be hoped that the vision of NASTAT to unite the profession in this country can eventually be realized.

Habit is habit, and not to be flung out of the window by any man, but coaxed downstairs one step at a time.
Mark Twain

Sans Alexander

The thought of life's so bleak,

Imagine no Direction as day turned into week.

No Inhibition either to check us in our course,

Controlling our reactions at their very source.

Neck free head forward up our back

To lengthen widen there's a knack

Once got we never lose

As long as thought will only choose.

Oh, living with our discipline exacts its toll, no doubt;

For one I thank my lucky stars old F. M. found me out!

No. 10, Fall 1992

Poise and the Art of Lengthening

This article, excepting a few minor changes, originally appeared in the September 1991 issue of Thought Trends: New Dimensions for Living, *an Atlanta New Age and alternatives monthly. I am happy in reprinting it here to be able to include the source notes, which indeed form an integral part of the text.*

"Poise" is a curious word. A bit regal in tone and suggesting nowadays a certain personal command, it originated more prosaically in the language of weights and measures.[1] It can be traced back through the Middle English and Old French *pois*, "weight," to the Latin *pensum*, something weighed, and *pendere*, to weigh. Thus, poise has its basis not primarily in a mental state, but in definite physical action, a specific balancing of mass for mass, as in acrobatics, tight-rope walking, and similar skilled performances.

Perhaps few would consider standing up on two legs a particularly skilled performance, but it is in fact a most prodigious balancing act, as you can verify through recalling the infant's concentrated struggle to master it. Yet how many adults have a concern for, or even an intimation of, the distribution of their various body weights—head, arms, trunk, legs—over their base of support and around their center of gravity? For if these weights—the heaviest that most of us are ever required to lift—are not maintained in balance relative to each other within fairly narrow limits, the resulting strain on muscles, ligaments, and joints to keep the body upright leads inexorably toward the creaks, aches, and fatigue that all-too-familiarly herald and accompany the advancing years.

From this point of view, we should see poise as an active, whole-person process, an efficient managing of body weights, with an eye to what has been called *structural hygiene*.[2] The hygiene of poise is clearly what J. E. Goldthwait. M.D., a former president of the American Orthopedic Association, had in mind in saying:

> An individual is in the best health only when the body is so used that there is no strain on any of its parts. This means that, when standing, the body is held fully erect, with no strain on the joints, the bones, the ligaments, the muscles or any other structures. There should be adequate room for all the viscera, so that their function can be performed normally unless there be some congenital defect.[3]

One might thus be led to think that poise is simply a matter of standing up straight and being done with it. Reality will prove otherwise. Resolve for a day to "stand up straight" and generally attend to the use of your body. You will find embarrassingly few moments of awareness during the day's full round, and you will find that whatever change you can bring to bear in one position disappears as you move to another.

The attainment of poise is rather a matter of learning the art of lengthening. Lengthening means pre-eminently that in standing, sitting, walking, bending, or in any activity whatever, one must prevent both unnecessary muscular effort and the very common distortions of the natural curves of the spine. Encompassing a broad field of knowledge and practice, lengthening is an art rather than a precise technique because it involves skill and the application of principle on the basis of experience as contrasted with rigid adherence to arbitrary rules or so-called correct positions.[4,5] It should also be added that lengthening is a process practiced primarily by and not on the individual.

Obviously, the giving of precise, or even of general, instructions is beyond words alone, so here a hint must suffice. One first experiences lengthening, usually with the aid of a teacher, and then, like a gardener, one cultivates the conditions that tend to promote it. Much as a wind player keeps the breath going or a string player the bow, in lengthening one sustains the muscular tone that keeps the body up while inhibiting that which pulls it down. Indeed, the great secret is not to be pulling [or *falling*]* down on one's up, a principle that may be seen by some to extend farther than the present discussion.

It is crucial—though at the outset virtually impossible—to realize that one's lifelong habits, in both thought and action, form the sole standard of what feels right and correct within the self.[6] Against this omnipresent background, new responses are bound to seem unfamiliar, sometimes startlingly so. Students of lengthening can thus easily find themselves in the strange situation of being right and feeling wrong, quite the reverse of the usual order of things. It is in confronting this paradox in all its implications, and in the inevitable encounter of desire, habit, and the will that arises in all serious practice, that one has the possibility of gaining not only that which was initially sought but something more, an inner process of knowing at once dependent upon yet transcending the original goal.

———————————

*[In the sense of "collapsing" in contrast to Michael Protzel's "committing" of body weight. See citations in *Conceptual Foundations*, p. 69, fn. 1.]

124

[1] R. A. Dart, "The Attainment of Poise," *S. African Med. Jour.* (21, 1947), pp. 74-91.

[2] M.E. Todd, *The Thinking Body* (Hoeber, 1937), pp. 41-42.

[3] J. E. Goldthwait et al., *Essentials of Body Mechanics in Health and Disease*, 5th Ed. (Lippincott, 1952), p. 1.

[4] E. Langer, *Mindfulness* (Addison-Wesley, 1990), p. 6.

[5] F. M. Alexander, *Constructive Conscious Control of the Individual* (Methuen, 1924), p. 110.

[6] Alexander, *The Use of the Self* (Dutton, 1932), Chap. 1, "Evolution of a Technique."

In any attempt to apply my technique to changing and improving the use of the self, it is courting failure to continue to depend on the "feeling" which has been the familiar guide in the old habitual "doing" which "felt right," but which was obviously wrong since it led us into error.

A Psychological Perspective on the Alexander Technique

This article originally appeared in the Winter 1993 issue of Georgia Psychologist, *a publication for members of the Georgia Psychological Association. My thanks to Pat Gardner, CAE, Executive Director and Managing Editor, and Linda Campbell, Ph.D., Editor.*

I imagine that many psychologists, if they have heard of the Alexander Technique at all, have a more-or-less vague impression of it as a method for postural improvement or relaxation. I would like to convey a sharper view of this work, the original approach in Western culture to the modern fields of sensory awareness education and movement therapy.

It was actually just a hundred years ago, as Freud was launching his epochal investigations, that F. Matthias Alexander (1869-1955), a young Australian actor struggling alone and unaided to restore his own broken voice, discovered a relationship between unconscious muscular tension and many common problems, including learning difficulties, control of performance, and various other disorders. As with Freud, the self-analysis that Alexander underwent can be understood only in part intellectually. What can be said in brief is that as he observed his activities in a mirror over a period extending to years, Alexander learned to see certain patterns of posture and movement—or "use," in his term—that felt right and virtually instinctive to him, but that proved through experiment to be habits associated with his vocal malfunction. Once aware, he learned to modify his use in the direction of less tension. His efforts (or rather, his reduction of undue efforts) resulted not only in the recovery of vocal control, but also in the creation of a new behavioral paradigm and a practical technique, eventually articulated in four books, the first of which appeared in 1910.

Under this paradigm, cognition serves not only to specify goals of action (ends), but also to mediate, at a level heretofore unknown, the postural and movement processes (means) which alone make the pursuit of goals possible. Thus, where Alexander previously could recite his lines only by the habitual and, in his case, faulty, employment of the psycho-physical mechanisms loosely referred to as "his voice," he subsequently could "Let his neck be free, to let his head go forward and up, to let his back lengthen and widen," and so forth ultimately to speak, not with just his "voice," but, in a sense real enough to one who has had similar experience, with his whole self.

The practical technique that Alexander developed blended touch and idea in an ongoing transaction between teacher and student. Where Freud prescribed that his patients free-associate as they lay on the couch, Alexander instructed his pupils to "leave themselves alone"—neither to help nor hinder—as he guided them through common movements, such as sitting down in a chair or walking. It was the perceptual contrast between the guided and the habitual performance of the activity that revealed the unconscious habit.

In the psychological and educational worlds-at-large it is virtually unappreciated that both Freud and Alexander were dealing contemporaneously with different aspects of the same problem—unconscious obstacles to effective functioning—and that both introduced the same basic therapeutic strategy of bringing these obstacles to awareness where they could be dealt with consciously. As Alexander once remarked, with a perspicacity to satisfy any Freudian, "The things that don't exist are the most difficult to get rid of." And Freud, in almost pure Alexandrian tones, characterized the psychoanalytic therapy as "a re-education in overcoming internal resistances."

Not to push these similarities further at present—there are indeed great differences—my point is that whether by assent or reaction, the seminal idea of unconscious influences on functioning more than any other has shaped the vast modern therapeutic arena. And while within this frame of reference variations in theory and practice often appear more evolutionary than fundamental, some distinctions need to be maintained explicitly.

One is that there is a difference between naming a thing and understanding it. In my experience, for example, some people seem over-eager to get a conceptual grip on the Alexander Technique by labeling it, as in "Oh, it's behavior modification," or "It sounds like Reich," or some such. Freud's prefatory remark from his last book, *An Outline of Psycho-Analysis,* is worth quotation here:

> The teachings of psycho-analysis are based on an incalculable number of observations and experiences, and only someone who has repeated those observations on himself and on others is in a position to arrive at a judgment of his own upon it.

The same applies to all serious work, so far as I can see.

A more crucial distinction is that between intellectually accepting a belief and actually practicing it as a way of life. Under pressure from findings in advanced physics and to some extent from Eastern influences, our culture is gradually moving away from the rigid mind-body dualism, wedded to a notion of the priority of the abstract, that has dominated Western thought from Plato down to the present, Nautilus machines and Stair Masters not-withstanding. An example of this trend is the "organ-ism-as-a-whole" concept, one to which I imagine many psychologists would readily enough ascribe. But I invite you to reflect if, in reading this article, you have perhaps harbored the notion that the Alexander Technique is a form of "body-work." This would be an illustration of the dualistic bias to which I refer. Alexander tells us he came only by direct and hard-won experience to abandon his previously noncritical acceptance of "mental" and "physi-cal" as distinctly separate processes. As epitomized by the title of his third book, *The Use of the Self* (1932), Alexan-der's practice and theory of the whole person was revolu-tionary for his time and remains so to this day.

I must admit that when I began my investigation, I, in common with most people, conceived of "body" and "mind" as separate parts of the same organism, and consequently believed that human ills, difficulties, and shortcomings could be classified as either "mental" or "physical" and dealt with on specifically "mental" or specifically "physical" lines. My practical experiences, however, led me to aban-don this point of view and readers of my books will be aware that the technique described in them is based on the opposite conception, namely, that it is impossible to sepa-rate "mental" and "physical" processes in any form of human activity.

Reflections on the Alexander Method

This article first appeared in American Ensemble *magazine (Summer 1983). In her* From Stage-Fright to Seat-Height: An Annotated Bibliography on the Alexander Technique and Music, 1907-1992, *Julia Priest said of it: "Eloquent. Defines inhibition. Reframes students' frustration as 'creative tension.'" Thank you, Julia!*

Over the past ten years, musicians have been hearing more and more about the Alexander Technique as a resource far performance. In this article, I would like to share some of my experience with this technique, both as professional musician and Alexander teacher.

Briefly, the Alexander Technique is a method for acquiring skill in what F. M. Alexander (1869-1955) called "the use of the self." This concept encompasses our basic psycho-physical activities, such as standing, sitting, bending, walking, manipulating tools and instruments, speaking, and so on—all of our voluntary activity, in other words. Alexander, an Australian, developed his technique nearly a hundred years ago in response to a difficult personal problem: an actor by profession, his voice had begun to fail regularly during performances, and all available medical counsel and treatment had given no relief. Faced with the dilemma of giving up his career or finding out on his own what was causing the problem, Alexander chose the latter course and over the next several years carried out an amazing self-analysis, his only equipment a set of multiple mirrors in which he observed what he later called his "manner of doing." He came to learn that in all of his activities he was interfering with his inherent poise and flexibility by unconsciously overtensing virtually every muscle in his body. As he gradually learned to "undo" this faulty use of himself, the vocal problem improved and eventually ceased. Free to return to the stage, Alexander instead devoted the rest of his life to extending and teaching his discoveries in a career that eventually spanned half a century.

The most important aspect of this work concerns the significance of inhibition as a key factor in behavioral change. Inhibition in the Alexandrian sense is not the undesirable suppression of activity, but rather the delaying of an habitual response so that a different, directed response can take place instead. "Prevent the things you have been doing and you are halfway home," as Alexander put it, an observation that will be understood by any musician who has ever changed an embouchure or other major aspect of basic technique. The teaching of inhibition on a general basis has remained a hallmark of the Alexander Technique, and in fact is what mainly distinguishes it from other "body-works" that have developed in recent years.

My own involvement with the Technique began in 1972, while I was still clarinetist with The Saint Paul Chamber Orchestra. Those first lessons were a revelation to me, in experiencing the ease and lightness typical of the Alexander process. Five years later I began the Alexander teacher-training program in New York City, and received my certificate in 1979.

In practical terms as a clarinetist, I found the Alexander work most directly helpful in posture and breathing. Where previously I had done my best to follow advice such as, "relax," or "breathe from the diaphragm," I was now given direct experience of what those words really involved—namely, an awareness of what I was doing with myself, in order that I could release unnecessary tension, to allow a free response of my postural and breathing mechanisms to the on-going situation. The words in emphasis—awareness, release, and response—summarize neatly the Alexandrian dimension of potentially every learning process.

Another influence on my musical work has to do with my whole concept of practice, the musician's central activity. Practice I had always considered to be dealing with the clarinet, doing the scales, etudes, and other things that lead to musical proficiency. From my Alexander lessons I came to see that another kind of practice was possible, that of trying to use myself as well as possible in my other daily activities—walking down the street, waiting in line at the bank, rising from my chair to acknowledge applause, to name a few. I realized that I was indeed the instrument that played the instrument, and that working on myself amounted to working on the clarinet, in a different but highly significant way.

Learning the Alexander Technique requires definite efforts in definite directions, and there are always implications beyond our knowing what entering into such a process. In my own case, I certainly wasn't consciously looking for a new life when I took my first Alexander lesson, even though things worked out that way. Of course, most people who study Alexander are not moved to such major changes—they go on with their lives, using the Technique for practical help in their particular situations.

Also, the Alexander Technique is a serious study, like music, and as such involves frustration as well as reward. This frustration—the gap between our actual performance and our vision of it—I prefer to call "creative tension." An inherent factor in all serious efforts, creative tension requires not reduction or elimination, but rather under-standing, acceptance, and the energy to deal with it.

Energy seems mysterious enough to most of us, but one thing is clear. Energy bound up in inefficient neuro-muscular habits just isn't available for other purposes. Thus, whatever one's initial reason for studying Alexander, the real goal of the Technique is making more energy available for meeting "the stress of life," as Hans Selye so aptly put it.[*]

Musicians assuredly come in for their share of this stress: fortunately, they are well-equipped for dealing with it creatively because of their practical experience in developing skills. In this regard, it is encouraging to report that the Technique is being made increasingly available to music students as part of their formal programs of study. This is presently the case at The Juilliard School [and several others]. Unlike even ten [now twenty!] [now thirty!!] years ago, many Alexander teachers are now in private practice throughout the country. I wish to thank all of my own teachers in the Technique, each of whom has contributed uniquely to my present understanding of the art.

---

*Selye, an M.D., pioneered the concept and study of stress as a medical syndrome. His now-classic *The Stress of Life* (McGraw-Hill, 1956), is a synthesis and summary of his clinical and experimental work.

Teacher, Heal Thyself

Sometime last Fall, I noticed a pain in the "bunion joint" of my right big toe. It wasn't a steady ache or a swelling, but a sharp stab when I moved or put pressure on it in a certain way. At first I associated this pain with some vigorous exercise I had been doing on a rebounder (mini trampoline), so I stopped that, but to no avail. I admit the thought crossed my mind (though I admonish my students about such counterproductive notions), "Well, after all, you *are* getting older."

Then, shortly after New Year's, feeling myself too house and car-bound, but without conscious purpose relative to my pesky pain, I started some regular morning walks: no heavy aerobics, just a half-hour's easy pace for air, movement, bird-song, pleasant neighborhood scenery, and general Alexander awareness. One morning soon after, I looked down almost casually at my feet to see how they were "tracking" relative to forward direction and also to each other. To my surprise, I saw that the right foot was angled perhaps 10 degrees further out than the left, which was aiming almost directly forward, and also that the right arch was tending to collapse as it bore my weight during that phase of the gait cycle. In a flash of insight, in part from my long study of body mechanics, I understood that this pattern was making my right leg shorter than my left and skewing the weight-bearing axis of my right foot during the crucial activity, commonly called "walking," of taking my whole weight first on one side, and then the other, while moving forward.

On more focused kinesthetic observation I could sense the support of my left foot and leg as stronger and more solid than my right, giving experiential confirmation for the hypothesis I had already formed theoretically that it was the right limb needing to make the main change. Changing the limb's forward direction required a change of muscular coordination at the hip joint, so I experimented with rotating my right leg delicately inward to aim the knee forward as I maintained a primary awareness of head, neck, and back. Dealing with the collapse of the arch required actively tightening certain muscles of my calf in order to prevent undue stretching downward as my weight came over that side. If I looked away for a step or two, and then back, I could *see* that the right leg had reverted to habit, even though I couldn't feel it!

It's impossible to describe exactly the process I followed and the various muscular actions and awarenesses involved. Suffice it to say that after a couple weeks' practice I could tell "by feel" most of the time when the right leg and foot were doing what I wanted them to and when not. I should also add that I experienced very different muscular sensations from usual all along the right side of my torso. Remember, in walking the body's *whole* weight moves from one base of support (foot) to the other. If the two bases aren't equal, the system must compensate throughout in order to maintain balance. It's a shocker to realize that in walking one mile, the feet of a 150-pound person taking 30-inch steps endure a total stress of 158.4 tons! While properly-used feet take this and more easily in stride—so to speak—it's not difficult to see, given the indifference of most people to primary bodily support and movement, why there are both such a huge market for pricey athletic-type footgear and so many podiatrists in the Yellow Pages.

Getting back to my big toe, I had more-or-less instinctively developed, even before starting my walks, ways of avoiding the movements that caused the pain. (This natural process of compensation is the origin of much habitual misuse.) So, during the early period of walking, I wasn't aware of whether it (the pain) was still there or not. Then one day in March or April, I happened to make a movement that I realized as soon as I had done it was one that used to hurt. But this one hadn't! Rather gingerly, I tried it again. Still no pain! Over the next few days I gradually resumed the repertoire of erstwhile painful movements that I had been suppressing, and found that, yes, my pain was indeed gone! Not having myself come to the Technique through pain, and in spite of having heard many times from my students of pain relief through Alexander, I'm almost reluctant to say that I was really pretty surprised by all this. My pain was gone and all I had done was change my walk a little bit!

Well, maybe not so little. I cover about a mile on my walks. Supporting my weight of 135 pounds, my feet endure a total stress approaching 142.56 tons during that part of the day's activity alone. That's a lot of weight; I suspect that my first metatarsophalangeal joint on the right side came not to appreciate its unequal burden, and was letting me know by complaining. Lord knows what might have complained next! I'm not suggesting that through good use we can prevent all the "thousand natural shocks the flesh is heir to." But it's worth considering that if a ship in mid-ocean lose its bearing by a fraction of a degree, its landfall will be different from originally plotted to a greater or lesser extent as a function of the error projected over the distance. So it is with our bodies over time. Who knows what might be did we not continue so imperceptibly, so multifariously, and yet, for the most part, so inexorably off course?

[See No. 17 for the FMA quotation belonging to this issue.]

Inhibition, Direction, Primary Control

On the wall of my teaching studio hangs a whiteboard where is written "The essence of Alexander Technique: Inhibition, Direction, Primary Control." I define these concepts orally early on in lessons, and I often refer to them as the work progresses. Still, in the hurly-burly of practical teaching, it is easy enough to neglect their reinforcement through adequate repetition, which alone will render them as ready to the student's thought as "two and two are four" or "thirty days hath September": we tend to forget at what expense of time and effort Society insured to our consciousness the eternal presence of such useful engrams. Thus today's lesson. Repeat after me:

The essence of Alexander Technique:

Inhibition, Direction, Primary Control

Inhibition
Intercepting an Habitual Response

Direction
Planning a New Response

Primary Control
Maximal Organization for Activity

Inhibition. As Alexander himself said, "My technique is based on inhibition, the inhibition of undesirable, un-wanted responses to stimuli, and hence it is a technique primarily for the development of the control of human reaction" (*The Universal Constant in Living*, p. 114). Judy Leibowitz of New York, mentor to myself and a whole generation of Alexander teachers in this country, put it more pithily as, "You can't experience the new until you've stopped the old." How easy in words, how profound and subtle in actual practice! Whether we are inhibiting—intercepting and thus holding in check—an habitual response of pulling back the head, or of a less obvious behavior, such as (in my case) procrastinating, we are still exercising the control, however feeble and intermittent, without which deliberate change is impossible. To be confused neither with the Freudian sense of unconsciously suppressing a response, nor with the explicitly physiological process involving complex neurochemical reactions at the cellular level, inhibition in Alexander terms is simply, through awareness, catching oneself in the act ... and taking pause.

Direction. Alexander drew the important distinction between the correct conception of an action required and the muscular activity that actually produces it. Gaining a correct conception, both rationally and kinesthetically, is crucial to the process he termed "direction": how can you begin to approach doing the right thing without at least an idea of what that thing might be? Another aspect of direction is the sending of messages to the muscles from the brain via the nerves. Most people are familiar with this process in terms of learning skills like touch typing: you don't look at the keyboard, and you don't just take a wild stab: on the basis of remembered visual experience, you *think* the index finger of the left hand up and a little to the left of home position to get an "r," etc. In exactly the same way, but on the basis of remembered (though far less familiar) kinesthetic experience, you can *think* (or "direct") your neck to release, your head to aim up, and your spine to lengthen, before actually *doing* anything muscularly. Eventually, of course, muscles get involved, but the planning—direction—must come first.

Primary Control. More so than inhibition and direction, primary control can be approached intellectually but understood fully only in experience. At any given time, there is a maximal organization of the body in its own support and in its movement that derives, like that of all structures, from its disposition of constituent parts in a gravitational field. Maximal organization essentially demands that, in all activity, the body be at, or more accurately, *tend toward,* its greatest possible dimension. In other words, one must minimize the inappropriate muscular action that results in distortion of the natural curves of the spine: this we call simply "lengthening." Lengthening is primary because upon it depend not only the integrity of spinal support but also adequate internal space for normal functioning of the organs. And in order to lengthen, we must utilize, i.e. "control" in its sense as a verb, quite precisely our postural resources. We must neither brace stiffly up, nor sag depressively down. The control in primary control refers thus not to an elusive anatomical structure, position, or mechanism, but rather to an active, focused, continual, and—oh yes—*joyful* process of lengthening. Once again, students, all together:

Inhibition Means Pausing.

Direction Means Planning.

Primary Control Means Lengthening.

It's not getting in and out of chairs even under the best of conditions that is of any value; that is simply physical culture—it is what you have been doing in preparation that counts when it comes to making movements.

A Kinder and Gentler Nation

The graphic on this issue is from the title page of an
obscure book that I photocopied in the Teachers College
[Columbia University] library, after tracking it down from
an equally obscure source. The full title is *Body Mechanics: Education and Practice. Report of the Subcommittee on
Orthopedics and Body Mechanics. Robert B. Osgood, M. D.,
Chairman. White House Conference on Child Health and
Protection.* Published in 1932, during the waxing Great
Depression, and dedicated to "The Children of America,
Whose Faces Are Turned Toward the Light of a New Day
and Who Must Be Prepared to Meet a Great Adventure,"
this document faded quickly into the limbo inexorably
awaiting most of what is written (and certainly most
Government reports), but it speaks as clearly today, to
those with ears to hear (and certainly to the Alexander
Technique) as when it first came out over 60 years ago.

The gist of its 166-pages was that, on the basis of considerable empirical data, upwards of 75 per cent of the
country's youth exhibited subnormal and potentially
symptom-producing grades of body mechanics: is it likely
the figure would be less in our even more sedentary and
technologized society of today? The Subcommittee, consisting of four male physicians and a female physical
hygiene professor, called for widespread instruction in

body mechanics ("posture" to you, bub) at virtually every level of public and private education, from kindergartens to medical schools—truly health and not illness care! No isolated phenomenon, the report is a fair example of a body of medical literature from the first half of this century dealing with the relationship of body mechanics to health and disease, or of "use to function," in our Alexandrian lingo. The fact that organized medicine no longer takes such issues very seriously is not a reliable gauge of their importance, as fashions change in the medical arena as in others; developments in pharmacology and technology spurred by World War II, for example, have effectively obscured less spectacular but no less basic behavioral issues in the field of human well-being.

This past Fall, I had the privilege of editing a manuscript of a colleague from New York City, Michele Arsenault, who in the late 80's carried out a pilot project in teaching the Alexander Technique to elementary school children from the perspective of science, classical physics and mechanics, in particular. Through a grant from the Institute for Schools of the Future, Michele met weekly with kindergarten, fourth, and fifth graders at a public school on NYC's Lower East Side. As she later wrote, "They are easily engaged and challenged by a subject that has such personal relevance in their lives." Quoting her further: "five-year olds already exhibit mis-use and a significant decrease in flexibility in their hip and ankle joints ... nine-year olds complain of backaches and neck problems and move and collapse much like their adult counterparts; children have the same misconceptions about their bodies as their teachers; hands-on is a pleasure, response is immediate." The manuscript referred to above is a detailed teacher's manual, called *Moving to Learn* (not, as you might first think, the other way around), which, with its accompanying video, is eagerly awaited in published form by the Alexander community. Michele has done a tremendous job of conveying the subject matter, method, and *atmosphere* of her experience with these children!!

So often in my work with adults, who must patiently re-learn the proper use of themselves in order to relieve their aching bodies, I am told, "If only I could have learned this as a child in school!" Clearly, the full humanitarian potential of the Technique, in its moral as well as physical and intellectual aspects, will be realized only when its principles and associated skills are imparted to the young at the earliest stage of their education. Conventional curricula in physical education at any grade level do not remotely address this problem. It seems almost hopelessly utopian, in this era of AIDS, drugs, violence, and all the rest, to envision a system of early education where children learn along with the three R's that truly their back is basic! But envision we must, and Michele is taking us a distinct and necessary step in that direction by articulating the Technique at a level and in a form consonant with the mainstream of primary schooling in this country. Her work deserves all our support.

Its [the Technique's] *proper field of application is with the young, with the growing generation, in order that they may come to possess as early as possible in life a correct standard of sensory appreciation and self judgment.*
John Dewey

No. 16, Spring 1994

Strictly Personal

For the past year or so I have been fixing myself a bowl of
authentic Bircher muesli for breakfast. I have felt very
much better nourished in result, and in what to my
palate is truly a pleasing manner. So I've decided to share
this recipe with my readers, together with some of its
history and rationale, not by way of nutritional counsel-
ling (definitely outside the realm of my professional expertise) but simply as something you might enjoy.

Let me hasten to say that the original muesli is nothing
like any of the commercial products bearing the name,
which are mostly cereal with a little dried fruit and nuts.
The real thing must be made fresh on a daily basis, and
in fairly strict observance of what its originator, a medical
doctor, thought of more as a prescription than as a recipe. Not to scare you off, but just so you realize that Kel-
log's "Mueslix" it ain't.

Dr. M. O. Bircher-Benner was born in 1867, two years
before F. M. Alexander, and died in 1939. His clinic for
dietetic treatment and research was founded in 1897 near
Zürich, and has been carried on to the present by family
members. He had begun the practice of medicine in 1891
in an orthodox manner, until one day a few years later a
woman came to him unable to digest most of her food.
Nothing else having worked, Dr. Bircher took a friend's
advice and prescribed a diet of raw vegetables and fruit,
whereupon the woman, to everyone's surprise, recovered
completely. Bircher became convinced that nutrients as
near as possible to the living state provided a superior
quality of food energy, in contrast to the deterioration of
this energy that he now believed took place in cooking
and other processing. This was the basic premise upon

143

which, in spite of much early criticism, he founded his dietetic therapy. (For more on the Bircher-Benner approach to nutrition, which is by no means all raw food, see *Eating Your Way To Health*, Penguin Books, 1972).

The dish itself was originally called simply "fruit diet dish," and represented Bircher's adaptation of an old custom of the fruit-growing parts of Switzerland to eat a kind of fruit porridge, consisting of fruit, cereal, and milk, for lighter meals. At Bircher's time fresh fruit as a dietary staple had fallen into disrepute; such fruit as was consumed was taken usually as a dessert, preferably stewed and sweetened. The conventional wisdom held that people with delicate digestions should above all avoid fruit, so it was no small matter that Bircher undertook to make the consumption of fresh fruit once again a daily habit, resulting in his basic recipe and variations thereon.

Before getting down to it, there are some general points to be borne in mind: (1) muesli is primarily a fruit dish, thus no more oat flakes or cereal grains than called for should be used, "the spoon should not be able to stand upright in it"; (2) it must be freshly made just before eating, the fruit grated and mixed in at the very last moment; (3) it is to be eaten at the beginning of the meal and not as dessert; (4) the fruit as well as the grain may be varied according to taste and/or availability, the best apple being white-fleshed, juicy, and on the tart side. Also, I give here not the very original recipe, which calls for sweetened condensed milk, but two variations, one with yogurt and the other with almond purée.

Tools: corer, peeler, grater (¼" holes about right), nut chopper, mixing/eating bowl

Ingredients: 1 tbsp organic rolled oats soaked overnight in 3 tbsp water, 4 tbsp nonfat yogurt, 1 tsp lemon juice, 1 tbsp raw sugar or sugar alternative (aspartame), 1 apple (2½-3"), 1 tbsp chopped filberts or almonds

Procedure: Mix the oats, yogurt, lemon juice, and sweetener to a smooth consistency in bowl, chop the nuts, core and peel, then grate the apple directly into mixture, stirring as you go till all is blended, sprinkle nuts on top, enjoy! For the dairyless version, instead of yogurt, substitute 1 tbsp almond purée mixed with 3 tbsp water and 1 tbsp rather than 1 tsp of lemon juice.

Practical and Theoretical Observations: It will probably occur to you to try a blender or food processor rather than a hand grater. I did so myself during one brief period of muesli experimentation years ago, which I gave up partly because it was so much trouble to clean the machine. Also, hand grating gives one many opportunities to "let the neck be free," plus the satisfaction of using one's own hands and being less dependent on technology. Some few days I just don't feel like putting out the effort to make my muesli, and don't. But usually I do, with a little extra "direction," and find myself glad for it—tastes so good, you know!

Strictly Professional

Announcement in this issue of the imminent start-up of my Certification Program moves me to reflect upon the professional dimension of the Alexander Technique, both in terms of actual teaching and of preparation to teach.

The essence of teaching the Technique has been nowhere so clearly expressed, to my thinking, as by Alexander himself, in this anecdote related by my first teacher, the late Goddard Binkley, in his diary.* Binkley, a man of considerably robust build, found himself in difficulty at a certain period of his study with Alexander through just

145

trying too hard, prompting the Master, not 5-and-a-half feet tall and slight, to step back one day and remark, "You know, if one even expects to teach this work, one must above all, first and foremost, have acquired a fully adequate standard of conscious control in the use of himself. ... Why, Mr. Binkley, when I am teaching you, as I do now, I am able to convey to you what I want to convey, because as I touch you, and guide you with my hands in carrying out my instructions, I, myself, am going UP! UP! UP!"

Here Alexander was speaking in neither an exactly literal nor merely figurative sense, but rather in a kind of conceptual shorthand, in reference to certain conditions of psycho-physical competence that he had cultivated within himself and that had, over time, become reliable. He was trusting the communication of these conditions not to any particular "doing" on his part, but rather to staying with the "up" in his own process. As any Alexander teacher will tell you, maintaining within an expanded field of attention awareness of both one's student and oneself involves a peculiar discipline: this we call "nondoing," and its development to a consistent level remains the *sine qua non* of the teacher's education.

"Nondoing," like "going up," is neither literalism nor metaphor, but likewise a technical term whose meaning evolves from the individual's ongoing synthesis of experience, reflection, and practice. As a basis for action, nondoing certainly doesn't imply passivity, either mental or muscular, nor does it preclude knowledge in the conventional sense of concept-acquisition. What it does imply is a willingness to attend the fullness of time, a certain ripeness, whether that be in rising from a chair, in walking about, or in placing one's hands upon another person for the purpose of teaching. One may from time to time need or wish to move quickly, but one should really never hurry.

---

*Now published as *The Expanding Self: How the Alexander Technique Changed My Life* (London: STATBooks, 1993).

Trying is only emphasizing the thing we know already.

No. 17, Summer 1994

What's in a Name?

I have it from an eyewitness that one of the world's most senior and respected Alexander teachers [Walter Carrington, d. 2005], always a paragon of loyalty to the founder in his public statements, once privately remarked, in effect, "This work will never come into its own as long as it is known as the Alexander Technique." It is true enough that "never" is a long time, but it is also true that the Technique in its first century has not yet had the flowering that many bright and not-totally starry-eyed people feel it deserves—one wonders if somehow part of this might be in the name.

Just for openers, a current radio commercial here in Hotlanta regales us with the tale of a young man who dreamed of success in a certain type of business, prepared himself accordingly, made all the correct arrangements, opened up, only to fail within six months. Poor fellow called himself "Wilt's Flowers"! Regardless of whether you buy that or the rest of the spot's message, it does make you think. Freud, after all, author of the most influential and successful therapeutic method of this century in power and money terms, called it "psychoanalysis," and not the Freud Technique. Maybe there's a clue here.

Perhaps Freud, trained as a neurologist, realized (even at the conscious level!) that a work of fundamental import claiming a scientific basis should be identified by reference not to its originator, but rather to its *content: what is it,* and not *whodunnit.* So he came up with a nifty Greek-derived compound word that told a story all by itself. Obviously, the concept eventually must be understood beyond its self-contained reference, but that's

better, at least at the outset, than always having to explain "Who was Freud, anyway?" by launching into the
long story about this Viennese doctor who had weird
dreams.

I'm not suggesting here that Alexander should have, or
even could have, come up with some similar appellation
for his own work: he was coming from a totally different
perspective and his achievement stands, regardless of the
moniker. But for us latter-day Alexander types, engaged
in promoting a sophisticated and subtle service to a jaded
and ever more pop-culturized market, the fictional example of "Wilt" is at least suggestive if not downright instructive.

The foregoing is by way of introduction to my new brochure, *The Personal Body Mechanics Program.* I hasten to
say that I fully realize that "body mechanics" is a mere
intimation of the full scope of Alexander's work, and that
FMA himself had no truck with such labels.* That's OK.
My purpose is not to convert someone on the spot, but
just to get their attention with something of immediate
and understandable relevance in the very small interval of
time that the marketing analysts tell us is available,
which I have little reason to doubt judging from my own
attention span in appraising the barrage of printed material regularly confronting my eyes. And I also know that
what I teach is the Alexander Technique, regardless of
how characterized.

So, beyond adding that this new concept spins off the
currently popular "personal trainer" notion, as well as
that of "programmed instruction," I'll leave the piece to
speak for itself, as it must ultimately in the marketplace.
Much gratitude to Phyllis Mueller for her dedication to
visual as well as textual excellence. As always, I appreci-

ate your feedback, and hope to be able to report positive results.

———————————————

*7he Universal Constant in Living, p. xxxvi.

[From No. 13] *Unfortunately, we have been taught that all the ordinary, most necessary, and therefore the most oft-repeated acts of life should be automatic and unconscious; for this reason they have become indifferent.*

"So Long For Awhile …

… That's all the songs for awhile." Those of a certain age (as the French so delicately put it) may hear again in memory the theme song of old radio's "Your Hit Parade." Or maybe not. In any case, the sentiment was ready to mind as I began contemplating this piece and seems appropriate for the occasion of announcing my decision to move from regular to occasional publication of the *Atlanta Alexander News*.

A few factors have brought me to this. One is that I feel I've said, for the time being and in terms of newsletter format at least, most of what I needed to say. Appearances perhaps to the contrary, my writing energies are less than overflowing and what there are of them seem more and more drawn toward the broader themes of theory and practice in the Alexander Technique itself—my statement, as it were.

Another thing is that I've invested in a production-quality video camera is order to begin an exploration of this medium in both actually working with students and documenting aspects of my own teaching practice. I feel about this somewhat as I did in getting my first computer, just ten years ago, very excited about the prospects but daunted by the efforts involved, both technical and creative.

Some further factors are my new commitment in teacher-training (12 hours per week in clock time alone), the ongoing cultivation of my private clientele, and of course, my music. As the be-bopper said (on the sidewalks of New York) when asked how to get to Carnegie Hall, "Practice, man, practice"! All the aforementioned require me to make some space in my life, psychological as well as temporal.

So, having done *AAN* for four years and 18 issues now, it's feeling like time to move on. Many thanks to my contributors, both financial and literary, to those who sent or spoke words of encouragement and appreciation, and to my dear Zouzy, who helped fold, seal, and stamp many a copy. Bye for now.

Credo

Among the more prestigious students of the Alexander Technique over the years was the brilliant Raymond A. Dart, Professor of Anatomy in the University of Witwatersrand, Johannesburg. Dart was introduced to the Technique in South Africa around 1940, and subsequently became a staunch and articulate advocate of Alexander's work.

In 1981, in launching the first Alexander periodical in this country, (*The Alexandrian*, edited by myself and published by the American Center for the Alexander Technique), I quoted the last sentence of Dart's "An Anatomist's Tribute to F. Matthias Alexander" as follows:

> *It is a reasonable inference that each individual's part in the totality of human social behaviour is not confined in its effectiveness to the skill we succeed in attaining bodily and mentally in our use of ourselves but far beyond our daily acts and thoughts to our becoming as skilled as possible, as Alexander himself did, in communicating our knowledge about that better usage to others by the human practices of recording, of speaking and also of writing thereupon.*

This is the spirit that to this point has animated my communicational endeavors in the Technique, and that I trust will continue to do so.

What we need is an education for our bodies that shall be, on the bodily plane, liberal and not merely technical and narrowly specific. The awareness that our bodies need is the knowledge of some general principle of right integration and along with it, a knowledge of the proper way to apply that principle in every phase of practical activity. ... What is needed is a practical morality working at every level from the bodily to the intellectual. ... So far as I am aware the only system of physical education which fulfils all these conditions is the system developed by F. M. Alexander.

Aldous Huxley, *Ends and Means*

An Alexander Carol

(Tune: "Deck the Halls")

First, we let the neck be free-ee, Fa la la la la, la la, la, la!

Poise the head, just let it be-ee, Fa la etc.

Easy back, hips, knees, and ankles, Fa la etc.

Letting go all cares and rankles! Fa la etc.

Next we practice inhibition,

It's against all intuition,

'Tis the story need be told,

Seek the new by stopping old!

Now we're giving the directions,

Joining in our predilections,

Choosing ease for self and others,

Alexander sisters, brothers!

Fa la la la la, la la, la, la!

If you apply the principle to the carrying out of one evolution, you have learned the lot

.

Book III

Technical Topics & Research

1979 ~ 1999

Contents

Preface

This 3rd Series of my collected writings brings together the work of 20 years in the technical-theoretical and research dimensions of the Technique. With the exception of the paper on lumbar support and the original research of the functional reach study, the papers are all derivative, and yet they were done and are presently offered because they cover ground not usually encountered in our literature. "Breath As Postural Process" is a rather special case, being the written rendering, as it were, of a live presentation originally developed by me to convey a fuller understanding of the physiological mechanics of optimal respiration.

The papers on dysponesis and the work of N. Bernstein were done during my early ACAT-NY years, the former in 1979 as a kind of self-assigned final project of my training and the latter for a series of public programs at the Center called "Alexander Today" given in 1981. I was gratified to receive some positive feedback in correspondence with Dr. Whatmore, the originator of the dysponesis concept, and much later (1987) to learn, during my doctoral work at Teachers College Columbia, that Bernstein was one of the theoretical big guns of academic movement science. Also, "The Role of Reflexes in Normal Human Movement" was originally done in course work at TC.

Regarding the Coghill note, I wish to acknowledge a fruitful dialogue, initiated by Tim Kjeldsen in 2001, on the subject of the relationship of Coghill's "total pattern of behavior" to Primary Control. Through reading further into the sources than I had, he cited the view that "the total pattern and specific reflexes appear to develop in parallel, rather than the latter simply emerging in an orderly fashion from the former." Although this development doesn't materially alter the point of my note, which was to urge caution in citing Coghill's work on *Amblystoma punctatum* as decisively supportive of the Primary Control hypothesis, it does frame the matter in a broader perspective. Kjeldsen is a member of STAT and, to the best of my present knowledge, associated with the Cardiff (Wales) Consultancy for the Alexander Technique.

Regarding my doctoral dissertation, the abstract and some excerpts of which are given here, I confess that the day I learned of the non-significance, in statistical terms, of its results, was a dark one indeed. Obviously I had hoped in this study to show objective positive improvements in the respiratory function and performance of its wind-instrumentalist subjects, but such was not to be the case. Fortunately, the anecdotal reports were uniformly supportive, yielding much-needed consolation, and I did receive my degree in due course. Furthermore, the training involved in doing this project later enabled me to design, carry out, and publish the study on functional reach (reproduced in full beginning p. 39), which remains one of the very few in the literature reporting positive *findings* (as opposed to anecdotal reports) resulting from Alexander training.

It was the study of respiration that I did in preparing for the dissertation that led ultimately to the ideas and procedures, controversial among some Alexander teachers, advanced in my "Breath As Postural Process" work, the conceptual survey of which begins on p. 199. In this regard, it has been a matter of curious satisfaction to me that Jeroen Staring, a sometimes antagonist of mine as well as of the Technique, wrote on the flyleaf of my copy of his first published book, "Although pp. 279-281 speak about you as a 'fetishizing Alexander teacher' your BPP-method is only 1 millimeter short of real understanding." Wow, only one millimeter! But *pace* Staring, I thoroughly respect without totally accepting his voluminous and trenchant critique of our work.

"Breathe From Your Diaphragm and Other Myths" was written at the invitation of Jeremy Chance, after my presentation of Breath As Postural Process at the Engelberg Congress of 1990, for the "breathing" issue of *Direction*, and "The Question of Lumbar Support" was a response to Galen Cranz's virtual dismissal, in an AGM presentation, of any form of lumbar support. This latter article I consider especially important in that it reveals the hazards of taking a position based on incomplete analysis, in this case, that of treating the question of lumbar support in terms only of unsupported sitting, and not also of supported or reclined sitting, and even of lying supine, where lumbar support remains very much an issue though under materially different mechanical conditions.

Many thanks to Bob Britton for his bracing Introduction, and to the several others over the years who have in one way or another helped me along the way.

Ron Dennis
Atlanta, May 2007

Introduction

By Robert Britton

It is with great honor that I recommend these articles by Ron Dennis. Ron, as an experienced Alexander Technique teacher, is one of our most careful and insightful thinkers. The topics he has explored in these works are extremely helpful not only to an Alexander Technique teacher, but to anyone who is on the path of investigating the phenomena of being a living, standing, and moving human.

The introduction to the word "Dysponesis" alone is worth the price of admission. However for the same price we receive more understanding of Coghill's work (always helpful), insight and comparisons to the Alexander Technique in the work of the Russian physiologist Nicolai Bernstein on coordination, more confirmation of the help the Alexander Technique gives to wind musicians, a very helpful discussion of breath including insight into what the *recti abdomini* are really up to. In addition there is a wonderful discussion and evaluation of singing myths to help clear away some of the cobwebs of confusing singing teaching aphorisms, a valuable overview of human postural reflexes including a view into the work of one of the foremost experts on balance: T.D.M. Roberts, a discussion into the question of lumbar support, and a beautiful study of the improvement of arm reach after Alexander Technique lessons. All in all this little book (which is deceptively thin) (and delightfully readable) is a very rich and helpful collection of articles to help illuminate and question our understandings of what is happening when we are engaged in life.

I very much recommend this collection to you, and hope you gain as much from it as I have.

Dysponesis: Or, Misuse Revisited

Unpublished Manuscript, 1979

Two basic assumptions of the Alexander Technique are that the manner of use affects the general functioning of the organism, and that the organism is, for all practical purposes, an indissoluble psycho-physical unity. Thus, therapeutic results are seen as the natural concomitants of an improved use, by-products, as it were, of the educational process, rather than as "cures" brought about by specific remedies or procedures. This line of thinking has served the Technique well for three-quarters of a century, and has been essentially confirmed by discoveries and trends in modern physiology, psychology, and psychosomatic medicine. On the other hand, defining the Technique's aims and methods more rigorously seems desirable in a world attuned to scientific method and research, and a recent study in the medical literature is relevant in this regard. The purpose of the present paper is to summarize this study and advance some implications for the Alexander Technique.

Titled "Dysponesis: A Neurophysiologic Factor in Functional Disorders," the study is by George B. Whatmore and Daniel R. Kohli.[1] Dysponesis ("dys" meaning bad or faulty, "ponos" meaning effort or work) denotes a physio-pathologic state made up of errors of energy expenditure within the nervous system, and is seen as a hidden causative factor in various functional disorders. Dysponesis is neither a neurosis, in the sense that symptoms are a response to unconscious conflicts, nor a structural disease, where symptoms result from specific organic disorder. It is rather a maladaptive neurophysiologic response pattern, or more simply, a form of bad habit. "Effort" is defined as the production of nerve impulses or action-potentials in the nerve pathways of the voluntary motor system. The various sequences and combinations of effort that make up virtually all activity are classified in four categories:

1. Performing efforts—mainly learned motor skills, observable outwardly.

2. Bracing efforts—holding a body part rigid or "on guard," often contracting a muscle against its antagonist, ranging from obvious to virtually unobservable.

3. Representing efforts—thinking, remembering, imaging, and other forms of ideation, all involving specific sequences of effort. Daydreaming and worrying are forms of representing efforts, as are visual and auditory imagery.

4. Attention efforts—allowing some nerve impulses to have a greater influence on awareness than others, whether from within the self of from the external environment.

All these efforts constitute measurable energy expenditures that can act as an interference phenomenon in nervous system functioning. The explanation of how this takes place bears full quotation:

> The detrimental influence of these misdirected efforts results from the fact that action potentials (or nerve impulses) constituting effort follow not only the well-known pathways from motor and premotor cortex to anterior horn cells, and thus to muscle fibers, but they also feed signals (by way of side branches and feed-back mechanisms) into the reticular activating system, the hypothalamus, the limbic system, and the neocortex, thus producing widespread additional effects. These signals exert excitatory and inhibitory in-

fluences that are inappropriate to the immediate objectives of the organism. The result is an interference with many aspects of nervous system function, including the organism's emotional reactivity, its ideation, and the regulation of various organs of the body.[2]

Whether dysponesis is inherited or acquired, or both, has not been clearly established. It is probably acquired for the most part, resulting from stressful learning situations, trial-and-error methods, and imitation. Its effects on an individual depend on his heredity and environment, the current state of his nervous system, and the duration, magnitude, and distribution of the dysponetic influences. Symptoms can range from minor to severe, be intermittent or continuous, and present for an isolated period or throughout the lifetime.

Citing some ninety-eight studies in the literature, the authors detail and document the ways in which dysponesis can affect emotional reactivity, ideation, autonomic function, primary sensation, and reflex activity. Clinical syndromes showing evidence for the involvement of dysponesis include anxiety, depression, digestive and circulatory disturbance, impotence, frigidity, headache, backache, fatigue, exhaustion, insomnia, hyperventilation, eczema, neurodermatitis, obsessions, compulsions, hypochondriasis, schizophrenia, and myocardial infarction.[3]

Dysponesis is diagnosed on the basis of individual history, physical examination, and indicated laboratory and psychological tests. A main diagnostic procedure is the use of electromyometry, the electronic measurement of muscular activity. Since these measurements indicate bracing efforts primarily, the diagnosis of representing and attention efforts requires direct observation of the patient and clinical judgment, with stance, facial expression, gestures, breathing, speech, and general bearing as important clues.

The treatment of dysponesis is largely a teaching process in which the patient learns to recognize and control his misdirected efforts. This is a technical procedure of retraining specific circuits in the nervous system by biofeedback techniques. Essentially, the patient observes a given effort as indicated by the instrumentation and then learns by direct experience to bring the effort under conscious control. This skill is extended to other efforts, and gradually transferred to situations of daily life, a process which if successful, results in permanent elimination or reduction of symptoms. A caution in treatment is that the patient will understand the process intellectually, but will fail to develop his capacity for observation and control. As with any skill, regular training sessions, daily practice, and genuine interest in improvement are required for progress. Effort training potentially gives the patient something beyond relief from symptoms:

> He discovers a way of managing his energy expenditures, a way of living, that is extremely valuable to him in everything he does. He discovers a technique that enables him to reach goals and accomplish things that he could never do otherwise. He also discovers a way of meeting the hardships, disappointments, and misfortunes of life that is more effective than any method he has used. In addition he discovers that the joys, the satisfactions, and the pleasures of life can become richer experiences when he applies these same principles.

The study concludes with four illustrative case histories.

Although the dysponesis study is full of Alexander ideas and overtones, I still see two important insights for the Technique. The first is the significance of representing and attention efforts in the total effort pattern. These are the efforts involved in thinking, imaging, giving attention to, etc.—in other words, the efforts of Alexander directing, definite magnitudes of neural activity, and not different in kind from the efforts of performing or bracing. Thus, an individual who is directing is "doing" in a very real sense, in terms of producing action-potentials in nerve pathways. Although means of applying this insight to the Technique would no doubt vary, awareness of it, coupled with practical experimentation, does seem important.

The second insight is the elucidation of how the manner of use affects functioning in terms of the neurophysiologic mechanisms involved. The effects of misuse can now be discussed more rigorously in terms of the mutual interaction of brain and muscle nerve circuits, as well as in terms of an assumed mind-body unity. In general, I see Whatmore and Kohli's documentation of the effects of misdirected effort throughout the organism as a gain in credibility for the Technique vis-a-vis the research-oriented health sciences.

A concluding point. In citing Barlow, a physician and Alexander teacher, among others ,[4] Whatmore and Kohli characterize their techniques as "... an outgrowth of earlier, less sophisticated procedures which do not utilize so extensively the teaching advantages of modern instrumentation and do not direct the training so extensively to a monitoring of effort during daily activities." If the Alexander Technique is one of the "less sophisticated procedures" referred to, it is appropriate to recall Tinbergen, Nobel Laureate in Physiology/Medicine, who characterized the Technique as "... an extremely sophisticated form of rehabilitation, or rather of redeployment, of the entire muscular equipment, and through that of many other organs."[5] Thus, although there is value for the Alexander Technique in the dysponesis work, I suspect that ideas could flow beneficially in the other direction as well, considering the long experience of the Technique in dealing effectively with habit and change.

_____8

[1]*Behavioral Science*, Vol. 13 (March, 1968), pp. 102-124.

[2]The reticular activating system, hypothalamus, limbic system, and neocortex are neuronal networks of the brain stem, lower forebrain, forebrain, and brain surface, respectively.

[3]To which "clergyman's sore throat," Alexander's [putative] affliction, could probably be added.

[4]Wilfred Barlow, "Anxiety and Muscle Tension." In D. O'Neill (Ed.) *Modern Trends in Psychosomatic Medicine* (New York: Paul B. Hoeber, 1955), pp. 285-309.

[5]Nikolaas Tinbergen, "Ethology and Stress Diseases," *Science*, Vol. 185 (5 July 1974), p. 26.

A Note on Coghill[1]

The Alexandrian, Vol. I, No. 1, 1981

For many years now, the work of G. E. Coghill has been cited to support that of Alexander.[2] It now appears, however, that some of Coghill's generalizations were premature, and that their use in support of the Alexander Technique should he modified.

Briefly, in his studies on the small lizard *Amblystoma punctatum*, Coghill established that innervation developed in a cephalo-caudal (head-tail) direction, and that limb movements emerged from a more general pattern of trunk movement. He then theorized that behavior developed as the expansion of a "total pattern," rather than simply as the combination or coordination of reflexes, and suggested strongly that this might well be true for higher vertebrates, including man.[3]

Considering Alexander's emphasis on the importance of the head-neck relationship and of dealing with the whole organism, it is easy to see how he readily took up Coghill's ideas in support of his own. However, in *Aspects of Neural Ontogeny*, A. F. W. Hughes, Reader in Zoology, University of Bristol, summarizes several developments "... which have eroded the Coghillian dictum."[4] According to Hughes, studies on the embryos of chicks, sheep, and even another species of lizard, show that both total movements and local reflexes can be elicited by stimulation, and that there is no predictable stage of generalized reactivity in Coghill's sense. For example, from a study on chicks:

> Any part or combination of parts can he active, while other parts are temporarily quiescent, or all parts can

move simultaneously, but out of phase with each other. Such a picture defies all of Coghill's concepts.[5]

Or, from a study on a related lizard, *Amblystoma mexicanum*:

There is no evidence for the existence of a 'total pattern' in these forms.[6]

It should be emphasized here that Coghill's conclusions regarding *Amblystoma punctatum* are not at issue, but rather their wholesale extension to other species. It may be that a total pattern does characterize the development of behavior in some species, and possibly in man; however, we apparently may no longer assume this on the basis of Coghill's work with *Amblystoma punctatum*. In the present writer's opinion, these developments in research as summarized by Hughes suggest caution in citing Coghill's work in support of the Alexander Technique.

------

[1]Since this writing, I have learned that Dr. Wilfred Barlow has written on this topic and reached similar conclusions. See his "The Total Pattern of Behaviour," in *More Talk of Alexander*, Dr. Wilfred Barlow, ed. (London: Gollancz, 1978), pp. 240-245.

[2]Coghill's "Appreciation: The Educational Methods of F. Matthias Alexander" appeared in Alexander's *The Universal Constant in Living* (Dutton, 1941); a recent example is A. Rugg-Gunn, "Physiological Gradients" *(The Alexander Journal*, No.8, Autumn 1978), pp. 26-32.

[3]*Anatomy and the Problem of Behaviour* (London: Cambridge University Press, 1929).

[4]London: Logos Press, 1968, pp. 165-170.

[5]Ibid.

[6]Ibid.

A Modern Theory of Coordination and Its Implications for the Alexander Technique

The Alexandrian, Vol. II, No. 2, Winter 1983

This paper has its origins in my first Alexander lessons, where some questions came up that I pondered for several years before reaching some satisfactory answers. The gist of these questions was: "Why are the sensations of incredible lightness and ease in movement that I experience in Alexander lessons so different from those I experience when making the same movements by myself?" I recall asking my teacher about this, and being led to think there really wasn't any reason why I couldn't, in time, experience the same sensations by myself that I experienced in the lesson. But as time went on, although my commitment to the Technique grew, accompanied by perceived positive changes in myself, I continued to puzzle about this disparity in feeling between the guided and unguided movements.[1]

I think it was sometime early in the teacher-training (1977 or 78) that the essential answer struck me—that being guided in a movement was an objectively different phenomenon from doing more or less the same movement "unaccompanied." There was, in fact, someone else there in the situation, touching and guiding me, so that the experience necessarily had to be different from that of acting by myself. So, from a logical viewpoint at least, my questions seemed answered, but it was some time later before I encountered the ideas that extended my understanding.

These ideas are contained in the writings of Nicolai Bernstein, a Russian physiologist and philosopher who applied scientific and mathematical methods to the study of movements from roughly 1910 until his death in 1966.

The results of his work are summarized in English in *The Co-ordination and Regulation of Movements*, a densely technical but curiously exciting book that has, I believe, many implications for the Alexander Technique.[2] I first came across Bernstein in an article called "On voluntary action and its hierarchical structure" by the cognitive psychologist Jerome S. Bruner,[3] and pursued my inquiry with some other sources which included a text on contemporary learning theory[4] and an article from *Scientific American* called "Brain Mechanisms of Movement."[5] I also found useful material in Norbert Wiener's *The Human Use of Human Beings*.[6]

I would state Bernstein's major thesis as follows: Coordination consists not only of programmed responses of the central nervous system (CNS) to external stimuli (the classical stimulus-response model), but consists also, and perhaps more so, of continuously monitored and modulated series of responses of the CNS to information arriving from throughout the system, and particularly from the proprioceptive mechanisms, the structures such as muscle spindles and tendon organs that inform the kinesthetic sense. In other words, in terms of controlling ongoing activity, events at the muscle and joint level (the "periphery," in Bernstein's terminology) are just as significant as events at the brain level. Furthermore, because of the extreme intra-connectedness of the nervous system, any change in proprioceptive input, however small, can radically affect motor output, so that apparently identical movements can have markedly different patterns of innervation, with consequently different muscular actions, depending on the state of the system at the precise time of the variations. In Bernstein's words, "Movements react to changes in one single detail with changes in a whole series of others which are sometimes very far removed from the former both in space and in time, and leave untouched such elements as are closely adjacent to the first detail, almost merged with it."[7] In Alexander terms, this suggests that guided movement is innervationally different from unguided movement, because the CNS responds differently to stimuli originating in the brain centers, as in movement initiated by intention, imagery, memory, etc., than it does to stimuli originating in the proprioceptive mechanisms mentioned above. It is this qualitatively different response of the organism to stimuli originating in different places in the system that I currently believe accounts in part for the difference in sensation between guided and unguided movements.[8] It feels different because it is different in some significant degree, however subtle. This seems very obvious to me now, but for a long time it wasn't!

The evidential basis for the foregoing is beyond the scope of this paper, but I would like to develop further a model of the behavioral system suggested by these concepts. This model represents the characteristics of *self-regulating systems,* sometimes called closed-loop systems. The theoretical treatment of these systems is cybernetics (from the Greek, "helmsman"), developed largely during and since World War II, and first applied mainly to weapons-control systems. A more familiar application is that of the furnace controlled by a thermo-stat-when the temperature in the house falls below a pre-set level, the furnace is turned on, and vice-versa. Living organisms are extremely complex self-regulating systems with both electrochemical and mechanical aspects, speaking from the purely physical point of view. In terms of our line of interest, the purpose of the model is to represent both the structures and functional relationships of a system capable of coordinating its own purposeful movements.

The main operational characteristic of self-regulating systems is that they can both detect and correct their

own errors.[9] Complex activities require ongoing evaluation as to whether the actual muscular actions are in fact
implementing the necessary movements which are in turn
producing the desired results. This kind of evaluation
implies a feedback mechanism, which can inform the
system of the neuro-muscular activity in progress, and a
reference mechanism, which can compare the required
value for the intended movement against the factual value
of the feedback. Then this difference in required and
factual values must be calculated and delivered as a
modified output value, and then converted to the appropriate nerve impulses and resulting muscular action,
which is then submitted again to the feedback process
until the action is in some sense completed. Hence the
name, closed-loop system, or in Bernstein's term, *re-
flex-ring system.*

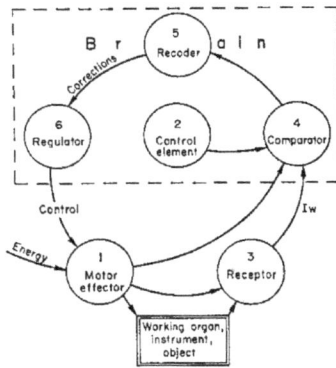

B r a i n
Corrections
5 Recoder
6 Regulator
2 Control element
4 Comparator
Control
Iw
Energy
1 Motor effector
3 Receptor
Working organ, instrument, object

Reprinted by permission of Pergamon Press, Ltd.

The diagram shows schematically the elements and
relationships of this kind of system, particularly illustrating the role of sensory information in controlling activity.
Looking at the diagram in terms of the furnace example
mentioned above, the house is the "working instrument,"
with a sensory receptor for heat, a thermostat, which
typically consists of a bi-metallic strip that arches one

way or the other depending on the amount of heat present and the differential rates of expansion and contraction of the two metals forming the strip. The "controlling element" is a mechanism for adjusting the distance of an electrical contact from the strip, which determines how far the strip must bend before closing a circuit, and therefore how much heat is required to bend the strip that distance. The furnace itself, controlled electrically, is the motor element, its output providing heat for the house that is also information for the thermo-receptor. *Note that a change in the system's behavior can originate at any point along the circular path of activity.* This is the key concept in understanding how the lightest guiding touch can significantly affect the sensation and quality of a movement.

In terms of human neuro-muscular activity, relatively more is known about the motor and sensory systems, as compared to the little known of the controlling, comparing, re-coding, and regulating systems. Even the existence of these latter has not been established by direct observation, but has been largely inferred from the design theory and practice of man-made self-regulating devices.

I believe that Bernstein's conclusions have both theoretical and practical implications for the Alexander Technique, and will discuss them in that order. To introduce the theoretical implications, here is a rather long quote from Bernstein, which is in effect a digest of his theory of coordination:

> The mastery of co-ordination must consist in the ability *to give the necessary impulse at the necessary moment,* seizing the fleeting phases of higher conductivity of force and avoiding those phases during which this conductivity falls to low values .... The role of coordination at this level must therefore consist in

173

the preparatory organization of the motor periphery in order to guarantee optimal selection of conductivity. ... Co-ordination at the level described lies basically not in the character and accuracy of a tetanic [contractile] effector impulse but in the accuracy of some sort of preparatory (not tetanic) effector impulses *which organize and prepare the periphery* for the reception of the right impulse at the right moment. The co-ordinational process does not enter into the composition of the tetanic impulse, or follow immediately after it; it goes before, clearing and organizing the path for it, and therefore must operate through quite different paths and employ quite different innervational processes ... . We find it very tempting to draw upon the concepts of *tonus*, a very generalized state of the motor periphery of preparation (in particular of the neck and body) for the accomplishment of positions or movements, to explain the phenomenon described here . ... It is clear that these systemic reflexes of high degrees of plasticity, as studied by the school of Magnus, are decisive co-ordinational prerequisites to movements or positions and that their physiologic purpose is not limited to the communication of a necessary and simultaneous rigidity to the trunk of the body but incorporates the entire preparatory reaction of the periphery to the conditions of the external (static and dynamic) field of forces [italics added].[10]

We seem to have here a striking support for Alexander's hypothesis of a *primary control of use,* but on a much broader neuro-physiologic basis than has yet been advanced. Alexander seems to have discovered empirically the phenomenon that Bernstein predicted theoretically. Paradoxically, in this case the discovery came before the prediction! Also, Alexander's processes of *inhibition* and *conscious direction* suggest themselves as possible psycho-physical counterparts of Bernstein's "non-tetanic preparatory impulses" that organize and prepare the organism for optimal coordination. Finally, every Alexander teacher experiences as a daily fact "giving the necessary impulse at the necessary moment, seizing the fleeting phases of conductivity," or as he or she may call it, "staying in the moment." In the foregoing considerations we see not only Alexandrian practice enlightened by Bernsteinian theory, but also the reverse, a significant correlation [better to say, to avoid confusion with statistics," an interesting and perhaps meaningful relationship"] from a theoretical viewpoint.

In terms of practical Alexander teaching, I currently think it's important to let a student know from the outset that what he experiences with hands on will necessarily be different from what he experiences on his own. I often ask a student to follow a guided movement with a similar movement by himself, so that he experiences the difference in the lesson situation, and can get clarification if necessary. The whole notion of the preparatory impulse I find valuable, possibly the more so from my experience as a musician, who always conceives the down-beat as a function of a preparatory up-beat. Not that these ideas are totally new—Alexander himself expressed their essence—but their reinforcement from Bernstein's perspective has been significant for me.

I will close on a philosophical note with three quotations that re-identify and emphasize the larger significance of the Alexander work. First, from Alexander, who said, "... throughout his long career man has been content to make progress in acquiring control of nature in the outside world, without making like progress in acquiring its essential accompaniment, the knowledge of how to control nature within himself."[11] And then from Norbert Wiener, the father of cybernetics: "We have modified our

environment so radically that we must now modify ourselves in order to exist in this new environment."[12] And
finally from Bernstein: "The progressive growth in the
complexity and power of technical devices has demonstrated very clearly that problems of control and regulation form an independent area of study—a study which is
in no way less complex, important or comprehensive than
that of the energies which are subordinated to these
controls. The problem of the rider has begun to overshad-
ow the problem of the horse."[13]

---

[1]In my own teaching experience, pupils have expressed or implied
similar questions.

[2]New York: Pergamon Press, *1967.*

[3]*Beyond Reductionism* (New York: Macmillan, 1970).

[4]Jack A. Adams, *Learning and Memory: An Introduction* (Homewood,
Illinois: Dorsey Press, 1976).

[5]Edward V. Evarts (September, 1979).

[6]New York: Doubleday, 1954.

[7]Bernstein, p. 69.

[8]Another factor is the small but real magnitude of supporting force
in the teacher's touch.

[9]In fact, a main difficulty with the older models was that they didn't
adequately account for the inherent plasticity of ongoing activity. A
stimulus just came in, and was transformed by the system into a
response that went out—a too-simple account of even such an act as
getting a hot spoonful of soup from bowl to mouth, to say nothing of
playing a concerto or giving an Alexander lesson!

[10]Bernstein, pp. 110-112.

[11]Edward Maisel, ed., *The Resurrection of the Body* (New York: Delta
Books,1974), p. 87.

[12]Wiener, p. 46.

[13]Bernstein, p. 145.

Musical Performance and Respiratory Function in Wind Instrumentalists: Effects of the Alexander Technique of Musculoskeletal Education[1]

The Congress Papers, Brighton, England, 1988

Abstract

Introduction

The Alexander Technique, an approach to reducing unnecessary muscular tension and improving general bodily co-ordination, has attracted considerable attention in recent years as a resource for musical training and performance. This study tested the hypothesis that twenty Alexander lessons would result in functional improvements in young adult wind instrumentalists.

Related Literature

The study derives from prior research, notably Armstrong (1975) – "Alexander Technique and Videotaping of Piano Performance," Huttlin (1982) – "Spirometric Measurement of Vital Capacity in Young Adult Wind Instrumentalists," and Austin and Pullin (1984) – "Alexander Technique and Spirometric Measurement of Respiratory Function in Normal Adults."

Method

The study employed thirteen volunteer subjects assigned randomly to experimental (7) and control (6) groups. Pre-tests and post-tests were administered to musical performance, via videotaping, and respiratory function, via standard spirometry and maximal static mouth pressures. The independent variable was a series of twenty lessons in the Alexander Technique.

Operationally-defined dependent variables for musical performance were:

1. posture and movement during non-playing;

2. posture and movement during playing;

3. breath control; and

4. overall performance.

Dependent variables for respiratory function were:

1. forced vital capacity (FVC);

2. forced expiratory volume at one second;

3. peak expiratory flow;

4. expiratory flow rates at 25%, 50% and 75% of FVC;

5. maximum voluntary ventilation; and

6. maximal static mouth pressures.

Video tapes were judged by six expert observers with pre-observational training; ratings were analyzed with t-tests. Experimental subjects provided brief anecdotal reports.

Results

There was a significant association among judges' ratings of musical performance (inter-judge reliability). The control group performed significantly better than the experimental group in maximal voluntary ventilation. There were no other significant differences between groups.

Anecdotal reports suggest a positive effect associated with the Alexander lessons.

Discussion

Results suggest "Critique of Method" and "Recommendations." Future studies with group designs should employ finely-tuned variables and measures. Single-subject designs and ethological methods may offer viable research alternatives.

Appendix

Rating form, respiratory data, verbatim anecdotal reports.

Excerpts of Dissertation[2]

Discussion

The hypothesis of this experiment was that a course of twenty lessons in the Alexander Technique would result in observable improvements in the musical performance and respiratory function of young adult wind instrumentalists. The objective findings of the study did not support this hypothesis. One finding, that for maximum voluntary ventilation (MVV), showed significant improvement for the control (non-Alexander) group. In the test for MVV, subjects are instructed to breathe in and out as rapidly and deeply as possible for a period of 15 seconds. In the experimenter's (RJD) view, the finding for this single variable is probably not of major relevance to respiratory function as involved wind performance, and can possibly be accounted for in terms of subject bias (see below, 'Subjects').

The experimental subjects' anecdotal reports indicated that positive effects were associated with the Alexander

lessons—this seeming disparity with the objective findings of the study suggests that the subjectively sensed
improvements were not objectively observable under the
conditions of the experiment. This interpretation warrants
both:

1. a critique of method; and

2. recommendations for further research.

Critique of Method

Subjects

Two methodological limitations concerning the subjects
are that:

1. they were volunteers; and

2. it was not possible to prevent them from knowing
which were experimental, and which were control subjects.

Both these factors relate to the experimental issues of
sampling and bias. In the present study, both musical
performance and respiratory function tests were possibly
influenced by these sources of error due to the assumption, on the subjects' part, that one group was supposed
to improve and the other not. This type of assumption is
explicitly stated in Anecdotal Report 3:

*However, I must say that my undemanding of the pur-
pose of this experiment war to find out whether the Alexander Technique lessons would alter the respiratory
functions in mind players.*

Particularly in the highly effort-dependent tests of respiratory function, this foreknowledge may have motivated control subjects to try harder on the post test, a conjecture not inconsistent with the data, which show that three controls actually improved in this regard. In the musical performance tests, the performance of the experimental (Alexander) subjects may have suffered because of anxiety about demonstrating improvement, although this consideration is conjectural. In any case it seems clear that some degree of subject bias was present in the study and probably contributed to the non-significance of results. In the experimenter's view, this bias was unavoidable in the context of the research problem.

Procedures

Note: Several issues regarding the assessment, via before and after videotapes of the musical performance phase of the study, are omitted here.

A major issue of the respiratory function phase of the study was how the subjects' baseline (pre-test) forced vital capacity (FVC) compared to the predicted, or normal, values. Austin and Pullin reported evidence suggesting that eight normal adults improved in the FVC after twenty Alexander lessons, but that study did not investigate wind instrumentalists, already "respiratory athletes"—a term of Dr Austin's—by virtue of their instrumental training and practice. If the subjects' baseline FVC were already higher than normal, as suggested by previous studies, then the possible effects of Alexander lessons on this variable seem an open question. In the present study, the mean (average) predicted FVC of all subjects, as a function of height and as provided by the laboratory report, was 4.4 liters. Their actual mean measured baseline FVC was 4.6 liters. The difference between these independent means was not significant ($t=7$, $p<20$, $df=24$), but suggests caution in interpreting the study's results and in using FVC as a dependent variable for such subjects.

A second issue of this phase of the study concerns the appropriateness of FVC as an indicator for wind instrument performance. Nolin had already raised this question in his review of Huttlin's dissertation, remarking, "Of greater potential interest to our field might be what the musician does with the lung capacity, once inhaled." The experimenter, tending to agree in this regard, suggests that expiratory flow rates (not reported by Huttlin, but reported by the present study) might be variables of interest for further investigation. It might be speculated, for example, that the present data, which show virtually no difference between groups in FVC, do show a trend of difference between groups in forced expiratory flow (FEF) at 25% and 75% of FVC. This trend is evidence by the higher *t*-scores for these variables (.74 and .82 respectively [statistical significance would have required a t-score exceeding 1.711], indicating a greater degree of difference between the groups than that indicated by the score of .02 found for FVC. The reported means show that the experimental group tended to perform slightly better than the control group on these intra-breath variables— particularly on FEF/75—an improvement in late expiratory flow rate [which] would seem to imply the ability to sustain a faster air stream longer into the breath, with greater potential control of tonal quality and dynamics.

Another important consideration in both areas, musical performance and respiratory function, is the influence of previously-acquired behaviors on new ones—in this regard, an observation by Fitts and Posner bears full quotation:

> *The effect of old habits upon new is remarkably persistent and continues into the final phase of skill learning*

even after overt errors an eliminated. This is shown by the high correlation which usually exists between early progress and later performance. The initially, more difficult task remains more difficult, even after both tasks are well practised. In addition, the effect of interference from previous habits may appear as actual errors when one is confronted with new demands [emphasis added]. Even though you have "learned" to turn on the correct faucet and have made no errors for a long time, you may under stress, revert to the older habit ...

Given the relatively short period of Alexander lessons, and the strength of musical performance habits acquired through years of practice, it would seem plausible to attribute in some degree the non-significance of results in the present study to the effects of old habits vs new under testing conditions involving some stress.

Recommendations

1. Studies such as the present one, employing a classical group design and performance-oriented testing procedures, will need to be planned with the subtlety of behavioral change associated with the independent variable—the Alexander Technique—clearly in view ... finely-tuned variables and measures, combined with a relatively brief experimental treatment of twenty to thirty lessons [probably] represent the most viable approach to Alexander research with classical group designs.

2. An alternative mode of empirical research, single-subject design would appear to offer great promise to future researchers in the Alexander Technique. [The crux of single-subject research is continuous measurement across time, and establishment of evidence of treatment effectiveness through replication.]

3. Another potentially valuable method of Alexander research would seem to be offered by the discipline and methods of ethology. [The ethological approach emphasizes extensive and detailed observation of behavior as contrasted with testing and measurement. The identification of suitably precise variables for Alexander research would presumably be a function of an ethological method.]

Indeed, because the present research base is still quite small, such detailed observational studies are probably a prerequisite to meaningful empirical investigations of the Alexander Technique in any field of application. In this regard it would seem, in retrospect, that the present experiment was in some respects an exploratory study, its contribution as much in revealing dimensions of the research problem, as in actual results. However that may be, it is the experimenter's opinion that empirical validation of the Alexander Technique is a worthy goal, and one that can absorb the best efforts of interested workers for some time to come.

---

[1]Ed.D. Dissertation, Teachers College, Columbia University, 1987

[2]Since the main results of this by-no-means decisive study nevertheless cannot be viewed as favorable to the Alexander Technique, excerpts from the "Discussion" chapter were included to help the reader understand, not only the results themselves, but also the broader issues of scientific method. The full paper is available from: University Microfilms Inc., 300 N. Zeeb Road, Ann Arbor, MI 48106, Order No. 8721097

[3]Bracketed passages [thus] are the author's emendations to original text of the document.

The Role of Reflexes in Normal Human Movement

The Alexander Review, Vol. 4, 1989

A version of this paper was originally written in partial fulfillment of the course requirements of TR4060, Motor Learning, Prof. Antoinette M. Gentile, Dept. of Movement Science & Education, Teachers College-Columbia University.

Although the basic nature of reflexes has been known since the studies of Pavlov and Sherrington early in this century, their exact role in normal human movement remains unclear. Easton (1972), for example, said:

> "They [reflexes] may very probably underlie all or most volitional movements in man and the lower animals, and their involvement is certainly great enough to justify the fruitful hypothesis that the muscles engaged in associated movements arc functionally connected by reflexes" (p. 591).

On the other hand, Roberts (1982) came to the following conclusion:

> "The role of the reflexes [in motor control] may be seen as that of prompts in the early *learning* [emphasis added] of how best to deal with adverse changes in the environment. As the nervous system matures, the superior timing of the newly acquired `anticipatory pre-emptive actions' (Roberts, 1973) has the consequence that the conditions for eliciting pure reflex responses are seldom allowed to arise" (p. 151).

The purpose of this paper is to assess these apparently conflicting positions via a review of the underlying theory and data.

Overview of Human Reflex Activity

A reflex may be defined as an involuntary response to a stimulus (Snell, 1980, p. 330). In humans, reflexes are known to be associated with basic defense responses (Chusid, 1976, p. 206), as well as with the maintenance and regulation of muscle tonus, the basis of body posture (Snell, 1982, p. 330). Reflex behavior varies in complexity, ranging from simple, one-joint movements (for example, the knee-jerk or patellar reflex) to complex postural adjustments, as in the pattern of jaw-side extension and skull-side flexion of the limbs shown in the tonic neck reflex. Reflexes may be classified both as to (a) location of manifest occurrence, or (b) level of CNS (central nervous system) representation. The former include superficial (skin, mucous membrane) reflexes, deep (myotatic, or tendon) reflexes, visceral (organ) reflexes, and pathologic reflexes. The latter include spinal, bulbar, midbrain, and cerebellar reflexes (Chusid, 1976, p. 206). Reflexes have long been important in clinical neurologic diagnosis, and were the point-of-entry for this century's efforts to understand motor coordination and adaptive movement. From both physiologic and psychological aspects, the central problem in this line of inquiry has been to establish a link between the patent necessity of reflex behavior and the apparent freedom of human activity as actually experienced. In terms of this paper, the reflexes of primary interest are those which have been conjectured to be involved with normal voluntary movements, namely, the postural and righting reflexes resulting from afferent and efferent activity at many different levels of the brain and spinal cord.

Mechanism & Typology of
Postural & Righting Reflexes

The basic mechanism of the reflex is known as the *reflex arc,* an image conveying the notion of an open-ended input-output circuit, i.e., without the joining of the ends of the arc that would imply circular processing of information via feedback. The components of the simplest reflex circuit consist of (1) a receptor (various sensory cells of vision, touch, pain, etc.), (2) a nerve to the CNS [Central Nervous System] (sensory nerve), (3) a nerve from the CNS (motor nerve), (4) an effector (muscle, gland). The only reflex presumed to be of this dineuronal-monosynaptic type is the *myotatic* or tendon reflex resulting from sudden stretching of the muscle spindles, although Chan (1983, p. 468) cites data suggesting that even these elementary reflexes are mediated via a long-loop pathway. The postural and righting reflexes almost certainly involve complex polysynaptic connections and suprasegmental control.

According to Easton (1972), the reflexes likely to be directly involved in voluntary movement include (1) long spinal reflexes, (2) tonic neck reflexes, (3) tonic labyrinthine reflexes, (4) labyrinthine positional reflexes, (5) labyrinthine, (6) body-on-head, (7) neck, and (8) body-on-body righting reflexes, all of which serve to integrate larger units of response than the elementary spinal reflexes. Roberts (1976) refers to the more collective role of "vestibular and neck *receptors* [emphasis added] in locomotion." Chan (1983) discusses "segmental and suprasegmental *contributions* [emphasis added] to long-latency stretch responses." The trend in terminology seems clearly to broaden the conceptual base of the question of reflex participation in voluntary movement to include the notion of the higher levels of control assumed to be involved in complex behavior.

Easton's Position: Theory & Data

Easton's (1972) is essentially a theoretical paper in which the hypothesis that reflexes underlie volitional movement is supported by relevant data. His line of argument is in three broad phases:

1. Identification and discussion of known reflexes, particularly those that coordinate on a reflex level much larger groups of muscles than do the spinal reflexes and bear a much closer resemblance to volitional movements (p. 592).

2. Citation of findings supporting the notion that reflexes may be activated by the higher levels of the CNS as well as by peripheral stimulation (p. 593).

3. Construction of a model of six quadrupedal gaits consistent with the hypothesis of a "reflexization" of the flexion-extension coordination of the required interlimb movements (p. 593 ff.).

Concerning Point 1, the main data cited are those collected from decerebrate preparations (e.g., Severin, Shik, & Orlovski, 1967; Shik, Orlovski, & Severin, 1966; Woods, 1964). These preparations demonstrate that the more CNS tissue left intact below the level of the section and connected to the musculature, the more complex, accurate, and appropriate the motor repertoire elicitable from an animal (p. 592). Lower animals (rats) are more capable than higher (cats, dogs) after decortication; man thus apparently depends more on cortical activation than the lower forms.

Substantiation of Point 2 is first approached via evidence that certain complex reflexes (tonic neck, tonic labyrinthine, righting, and positional) appear in normal human

188

movement. Fukuda (1961), which offers convincing if not conclusive evidence of reflex involvement in certain postures of sport, dance, and visual art, is the main prop of this phase of Easton's argument. Also cited are the studies of Hellebrandt, Houtz, & Partridge (1956), Hellebrandt, Schade, & Carns (1962), and Hellebrandt & Waterland (1962), which showed that voluntary head-neck movements in the pattern of the tonic neck reflex increased work output. The importance of the tonic reflexes in normal movement is supported by Cohen (1961), which showed severe disturbance of movement in monkeys and baboons that were cervically deafferented by anesthetization. Finally, Easton cites evidence supporting the idea that flexion reflex interneurones may be directly affected by various brainstem sources and cortical areas (p. 593), representative studies being Eccles & Lundberg (1959), Holmqvist & Lundberg (1961), and Lundberg & Voorhoeve (1962).

Regarding Point 3, Easton's model is based on a logical inference deriving from Points 1 and 2: "the basic units [reflexes] are known to exist [Point 1] and they seem to be used" [Point 2]. He first sets up a schema hypothesized to account for flexion and extension of limbs via spinal and higher-level reflexes, deducing therefrom the footfall sequences of six different gaits (transverse crawl, slow transverse walk, normal walk, walking pace, fast walk, trot) in terms of the required interlimb phase shifts. From the model, Easton concludes "Thus may one aspect of locomotion, the footfall sequence of a gait, be approximated by a simple array of reflexes activated in the proper order" (p. 597).

Remarks on Easton's Position

Easton does not claim sufficiency, but rather consistency, for his model in accounting for the general problem of how movement is orchestrated by the neuromuscular system; he wishes to advance the notion that reflexes form the basic language of the motor program (p. 598). Suggesting the term "coordinative structures," he proposes "to add to the word 'reflex' the hypothetical quality of underlying all volitionally composed movements (p. 591). It is curious that Easton does not refer explicitly to servomechanisms and central pattern generators (though he does cite Graham Brown and refers to synergies), but seems rather, in a somewhat Procrustean way, to relegate all such structures to status as reflexes. Perhaps the more specific terminology was not yet current when Easton was writing, but in any case it would seem preferable to reserve for the term "reflex" the meaning of a specific central response, however simple or complex, to a given peripheral stimulus, whether proprio- or exteroceptive.

Roberts' Position: Theory & Data

In contrast to Easton, Roberts (1982) might be termed a critical-theoretical paper. Roberts aims to examine the assumptions underlying certain current ideas that he believes to be incorrect, namely (a) that upright posture is maintained by reflexes whose combined action is to detect and correct for deviations from the gravitational vertical; (b) that there exists a "gravity sensor" in the labyrinth; and (c) that the alternation of limb movements in locomotion depends on the cyclic activity of rhythm generators located in the spinal cord (Roberts, 1982, p. 142; subsequent refs. to the same unless noted). His argument proceeds in three basic phases:

1. Criticism of commonsense notions about the action of gravity,

2. Analysis of kinetic and kinematic requirements of balance and locomotion,

3. Criticism of unimodal models (such as the servomechanism idea) of motor control.

Regarding Point 1, the crux of Roberts' notions about the action of gravity is that stress forces differ from gravitational forces in their effects on distributed masses (p. 143). Stress forces arise from intermolecular relationships in deformable structures (such as the human body) as the structure is accelerated toward the center of the earth by gravity. Gravity acts equally on every particle of the structure; however, stress gradients are established at the regions of contact of the structure with earth, in the case of upright human posture, the feet. These "contact forces," rather than gravity per se, represent the actual information available to the system about its relationship to the supporting surface. Likewise, the labyrinths are deformable structures with associated accelerations of the ocotonia. Roberts concludes that the labyrinth thus signals the effect of contact forces on the skull and not direct gravitational information (p. 144). He suggests that a system of reflexes linked by servomechanisms to the otolith signal would not be sufficient to stabilize the skull with respect to the direction of thrust because animals move their heads about freely. The general direction of Roberts' argument through this portion of the paper, supported by his own work on reflex balance in decerebrate cats (Roberts, 1970, 1973), is to indicate the range of decision processes bearing upon the organism's interpretation of the "behavioural vertical" (p. 146), encompassing not only neck and labyrinth signals but also visual cues and the whole interplay of brainstem and cerebellar influences.

Regarding Point 2, Roberts is concerned to classify the command strategies required for motor activities of all types. Roberts (1976, pp. 542-43) characterizes these as (1) *set*, (2) *hold*, (3) *drive*, (4) *punch*, (5) *catch*, and (6) *throw*, all involving different modes of motor control and command strategies. With respect to limb control in balancing and locomoting reactions, Roberts (1982, p. 148) adds *aim, thrust*, and *furl*, each involving a separate set of muscles operating in one or more of the modes of set, hold, and drive. The net effect of this analysis, too involved to detail here, is to emphasize the complexities of neuromuscular control under the actual kinetic and kinematic requirements of various actions.

Under Point 3, Roberts criticizes aspects of both the notion of central oscillators in locomotion and also unimodal schemata of motor control such as the servo-mechanism idea. Regarding the question of central oscillators, he points out that, in natural locomotion, each leg must in turn be discontinued in its thrust, furled, and then aimed again in a new direction. Decerebrate preparations suspended over a treadmill do not show all these phases, and cannot be taken as adequate examples of locomotor activity. Oscillatory action implies that later parts of a cycle may be predicted from earlier parts. No such predictions, and hence no inference of oscillatory drive, can be made from natural locomotor activity, which must vary according to the requirements of the environment. Regarding unimodal schemata, Roberts argues that "the nature and variety of the motor tasks in the repertoire systematically catalogued above (set, hold, etc.] make it clear that no single system can provide enough flexibility to encompass all the requirements" (p. 149). He also suggests that in the alleged servo-regulation of balance, that since the organism cannot respond directly to the gravitational vertical, there is thus no reference signal from which to derive an error signal, and hence no servo operation.

In terms of an alternative to the hypothesis of reflex involvement in normal voluntary movement, Roberts suggests that learned "anticipatory pre-emptive actions" (p. 151) begun very early in life gradually supplant purely reflexive activity. This suggestion is based on research in hopping (Roberts, 1976). Subjects standing on one leg were gradually overbalanced by the application of external horizontal forces, and thus caused to hop. The induced hops were of two distinct varieties. In one, the leg is flexed slightly just before take-off; in the other, there is no preliminary flex. In the former, subjects reported that they hopped deliberately; the latter was not accompanied by the feeling of deliberateness. Roberts termed the first a "voluntary," the second a "reflex" hop. It is not certain what is the adequate stimulus for the reflex hop. Roberts speculates that it may be the inclination of the support vector at the foot, which is always less for voluntary than for reflex hops. Roberts' articulation of the concept of anticipatory pre-emptive action bears full quotation:

"The implication is that the nervous system is able to recognize when conditions are changing in a direction which might ultimately lead to the development of a reflex response, and that the nervous system then interposes a voluntary corrective action which takes effect before the stimulus has actually reached the threshold for initiating the reflex. Motor control is pre-empted by voluntary processes and does not pass to the reflex mechanisms" (1976, p. 557).

Remarks on Roberts' Position

Roberts is concerned in this paper (1982) to ensure that what is actually performed in voluntary actions is set forth with adequate rigor and that experiments to test the predictive value of explanatory descriptions are devised accordingly (p. 151). In the writer's opinion, Roberts has successfully delineated the complexities of voluntary action through his analysis and classification of the command strategies involved in motor control. However, in his statement "the nervous system then interposes a voluntary corrective action" (quoted above), it is not really clear how such an interposition can in fact be a voluntary action. It seems as though in this instance we are looking at CNS activity somewhere between intention and reflex. But this is precisely the area of contention, and Roberts' argument may be circular in this regard.

Conclusions

The exposition and assessment of Easton's and Roberts' views on the role of reflexes in normal movement have resulted in reservations about each position. Easton seems to have promoted an inadequately precise conception of reflex activity, while Roberts has failed to demonstrate that anticipatory pre-emptive action is something other than a reflex with another name. On the positive side, Easton has supported his hypothesis fully with data, and Roberts has rigorously analyzed the full dimension of the problem. A succinct summary of the state of knowledge about the role of reflexes in motor patterns is offered by Keele (1982, p. 180):

> "A motor program is a hierarchical representation of action that proceeds from general goals to specific selection of muscles. Much of the learning is concentrated at higher levels in the hierarchy that specify the general sequence of action. Lower levels are free for alternative specification such as speed or [left or right] arm. Final details may partly be taken care of by innate reflex patterns."

In the writer's view, Roberts' notion of anticipatory pre-emptive action may be the more viable in terms of empirical investigation, because of its potential for operational specificity, in contrast with Easton's more general hypothesis that muscles engaged in associated movements are functionally interrelated by reflexes.

Afterword

Among Roberts' concluding remarks in the 1982 paper are the following (p. 151):

> "In many habitual and much-practiced activities, such as those involved in balance and locomotion, sequences of 'elementary motor acts' come to be assembled by the inclusion ... of sensory messages ... occurring during the consummatory phase of other 'elementary motor acts' performed earlier in the sequence. For this reason it is often very difficult, as Alexander has pointed out [*The Use of the Self*], to modify an habitual pattern of motor activity. ... The task of the therapist ... is to lead the patient, or pupil, into a situation in which voluntary intervention *can* [emphasis added] be effective. *If this crucial stage is omitted, the most assiduous practice serves merely to reinforce the undesired habit*" [emphasis added].

References

Chan, C. W. (1983). Segmental versus suprasegmental contributions to long-latency stretch responses in man. In J. E. Desmedt (Ed.), *Motor control mechanisms in health and disease* (pp. 467-487). New York: Raven Press.

Chusid, J. G. (1976). *Correlative neuroanatomy & functional neurology.* 16th ed. Los Altos: LANGE Medical Publications.

Cohen, L. A. (1961). Role of eye and neck proprioceptive mechanisms in body orientation and motor coordination. *J. Neurophysiol., 24,* 1-11.

Easton, T. A. (1972). On the normal use of reflexes. *Amer. Scientist, 60,* 591-599.

Eccles, R. M. and Lundberg, A. (1959). Supraspinal control of interneurones mediating spinal reflexes. J. *Physiol. London, 128,* 565-584.

Fukuda, T. (1961). Studies on human dynamic postures from the viewpoint of postural reflexes. *Acta Oto-Laryngologicn,* Suppl. 161.

Hellebrandt, F. A. et al. (1956). Tonic neck reflexes in exercises of stress in man. *Am. J. Phys. Med., 35,* 144-159.

Hellebrandt, F. A., and Waterland, J. C. (1962). Expansion of motor patterning under exercise stress. *Am. J. Phys. Med., 41,* 56-66.

Hellebrandt, F. A., Schade, M., and Carns, M. L. (1962). Methods of evoking the tonic neck reflexes in normal human subjects. *Am. J. Phys. Med., 41,* 90-139.

Holmqvist, B. and Lundberg, A. (1961). Differential supraspinal control of synaptic actions evoked by volleys in the flexion reflex afferents in alpha motoneurones. *Acta Physiol. Scand., 54,* suppl. 186.

Keele, S. W. (1982). Learning and control of coordinated motor patterns: the programming perspective. In J. A. Scott Kelso (Ed.), *Human motor behavior: an introduction* (pp. 161-186). Hillsdale: Lawrence Erlbaum Assoc.

Lundberg, A. and Voorhoeve, P. (1962). Effects from the pyramidal tract on spinal reflex arcs. *Acta Physiol. Scand., 56,* 201-219.

Roberts, T. D. M. (1970). Changes in stretch reflexes in limb extensor muscles during positional reflexes from the labyrinth. *J. Physiol., 211,* 5P-6P.

Roberts, T. D. M. (1973). Reflex balance. *Nature (London), 244,* 156-158.

Roberts, T. D. M. (1976). The role of vestibular and neck receptors in locomotion. In R. M. Herman, G. Grillner, P. S. C. Stein, & D. G. Stu art (Eds.), *Neural control of locomotion.* New York: Plenum Press. (pp. 539-560).

Roberts, T. D. M. (1982). Problems in the understanding of balance and locomotion in man. In D. Garlick (Ed.), *Proprioception, posture and emotion* (pp. 142-153). University of New South Wales: Committee in Postgraduate Medical Education.

Severin, F. V., Shik, M. L., and Orlovskii, G. N. (1967). Work of the muscles and single motor neurones during controlled locomotion. *Biofizica, 12,* 762-772.

Shik, M. L., Orlovskii, G. N., and Severin, F. V. (1966). Organization of locomotor synergism. *Biofizica, ll,* 1011-1019.

Snell, R. S. (1980). *Clinical neuroanatomy for medical students.* Boston: Little, Brown and Co.

Woods, J. N. (1964) Behavior of chronic decerebrate rats. J. *Neurophysiol., 27,* 635-644.

Breath As Postural Process

THE CONGRESS PAPERS, Engelberg, Switzerland, 1991

An authority on respiration, W. O. Fenn, has said, "The mechanics of breathing is a problem requiring on the one hand the detailed knowledge of a classical anatomist and on the other hand the analytic understanding of an engineer."[1] The purpose of the Breath As Postural Process (BPP) presentation is to bring together this level of anatomical and biomechanical information in a practical synthesis of working knowledge for the Alexander teacher. The emphasis is on understanding the structures and forces, as a co-ordinated whole, that produce the movements resulting in what I now call the "lengthening breath."

My work in this area derives from my background as a professional clarinetist and also from my doctoral dissertation, which dealt with respiratory function in wind instrumentalists as influenced by the Alexander Technique.[2] The changes I have been able to make in my own breathing since 1984 have resulted not from being shown or taught by someone else, but from an original conceptual understanding as applied to and combined with practical experimentation and skill development. I have learned, and through BPP try to help others learn, as Alexander recommended, "to command the maximum functioning of the psycho-physical mechanisms concerned with the satisfactory expansion and contraction of the walls of the thoracic (chest) cavity."[3]

From a biomechanical standpoint, the crux of the BPP work may be briefly described as follows: The lower segments of the *recti abdominis*, properly energized, provide tonic (continuous) support to the viscera and to the lumbar spine, while the upper segments release to accommodate downward movement of the diaphragm in inspiration. "Single segments of the muscle [*rectus abdominis*] can contract separately."[4] The muscles below the *umbilicus* therefore can be contracted independently of those above it." The upward support of the viscera in opposition to the downward movement of the diaphragm is a mechanically crucial factor in the lifting and expansion of the rib cage without the narrowing of the back, as made clear in Kapandji and De Troyer.[7] The foregoing comments and references are totally consistent with what Alexander wrote as early as 1907:

> *The respiratory mechanism should be re-educated, for this would mean a re-education or strengthening of the supports Nature has supplied . ... The improvement in the abdominal conditions (the improved position of the abdominal viscera and the development of the abdominal muscles) is proportionate to that of the respiratory movements . ... The intra-abdominal pressure is more or less raised, and there is a gradual tendency to the permanent establishment of normal conditions.*[8]

I would like to emphasize at this point that these and other observations of Alexander, which in my previous readings had had virtually no meaning for me, became perfectly clear once I actually experienced in myself the specific co-ordination and movements of BPP.

The BPP presentation itself is a group experience via a series of illustrations with commentary, demonstration, and dialogue in what I call "contemplation of structure." Coming to a level of understanding beyond where a little knowledge can be a dangerous thing requires at least three hours. I tell participants that, despite some resemblance to a lecture, their main task is not verbal but visual: to transform a series of two-dimensional images into a single four-dimensional inner "seeing" of a total process in time. This inner vision corresponds to Alexander's first specification—"the conception of the movement required"—in his four-part approach to the performance of any muscular action by conscious guidance and control.[9]

In closing I will mention that for me actually to be able to present BPP in public required something beyond my understanding of and practical ability to perform it. Pondering the question of practical demonstration, I knew that the movements of my entire torso at the skin level would need to be visible. For a time I could think of no way, short of disrobing, for dealing with this. Then I discovered the unitard—a unisex kind of leotard—a garment that provided the desired exposure combined with the necessary modesty. At my first presentations I had the unitard on under my street clothes, and dramatically undressed to reveal it at the proper moment. Coming to feel in this a little too exhibitionistic—though I am a performer, after all—I have taken just to holding it up at the outset and announcing that I will be demonstrating in it. Not being the usual sort of thing that goes on in Alexander circles, this serves to pique the group's curiosity and generally get us off to a good start.

[1]Quoted by E. J. M. Campbell in the first edition of *The Respiratory Muscles* (1957), p. 2.

[2]*Musical performance and respiratory function in wind instrumentalists:effects of the Alexander Technique of musculoskeletal education,* Dissertation Abstracts International 1988; (7, Jan.).

[3]*Constructive Conscious Control of the Individual*; Centerline Press, p. 201.

[4]Spalteholz, *Hand Atlas of Human Anatomy*, 7th 1-Vol. ed., p. 295.

[5]Goldthwait et al., *Essentials of Body Mechanics in Health and Disease*, 5th ed., p. 271.

[6]Kapandji, *Physiology of the Joints, Vol. III*, 2nd ed., pp. 136-151.

[7]De Troyer, "Mechanical Action of the Abdominal Muscles," *Bull. Europ. Physiopathol. Respir.*, 1983, 19, pp. 575-581.

[8]*Man's Supreme Inheritance*, Dutton, 1918, p. 337.

[9]*MSI*, p. 200.

Afterthoughts on Breath as Postural Process

NASTAT NEWS No. 16, Summer 1992

Having given "Breath As Postural Process" some half-dozen times now, I know that when it's over I'll feel an essential frustration in realizing that, no matter what or how much I say or do, it is only the experience—which in this case cannot be given directly, but must be patiently sought by each individual —that ultimately tells the tale. I am grateful this time around, though, through *NASTAT NEWS*, to have the opportunity to share some post-BPP reflections.

One point that I perhaps did not emphasize sufficiently was that in our Alexander discipline, global awareness—primary control, as it were—must always precede, accompany, and modulate more focal awarenesses, such as of feet, legs, upper and lower abdomen, etc., as FMA makes abundantly clear in "Evolution of a Technique." Certainly the upper back, shoulders and neck release to comply with the upward, forward, and outward movements of the thorax, which is what I imagine Barbara Conable was concerned to point out, and with which I agree 100%.

I can empathize with those who feel the breath is an area of functioning that shouldn't be meddled with: I don't meddle with my own digestion, for example, beyond being somewhat aware of what I eat and under what conditions. Some yogis, on the other hand, are reported voluntarily to influence a very wide range of normally automatic functions, a practice that I (with FMA) don't advocate but can't in honesty condemn either, not having had the relevant experience. At a certain point, however, we all must stand with FMA in applying "the test of principle in new ways for old" (*UCL* ,Chap. IX), since we never will be able to acquire the requisite experience empirically to evaluate all potential behaviors of interest.

"Postural process" is a very broad concept. It includes everything we're doing, not doing, and how, and when. At times FMA seems to tell us that if only interference is eliminated, the rest will take care of itself. As he said, "Prevent the things you are doing and you are half way home." But he didn't say you are *all* the way home, which as much as anything has led to my concern with what *to do* as the necessary complement of what *not* to do: this is the essential nature of skill. It is possible that FMA may have meant that Nature will take one the rest of the way, but then why, in addition to Inhibition, do we need Directions, Guiding as well as Preventive (*CCCI*, Chap. III)? I personally cannot read Chapter V "Respiratory Mechanisms" of *CCCI* without concluding that FMA is very much involved with facilitating the acquisition of skill, through the inhibition of habitual responses and the direction of new ones in the respiratory act.

It seems to me that some confusion has arisen in our understanding and use of the primary control concept. As a word, "control" functions both as noun and verb. "Control" as a noun refers to some sort of thing, such as a thermostat, which mechanically and predictably influences the behavior of a system."Control" as a verb, however, refers to a *process,* such as driving a car, in which inputs are ongoingly integrated with outputs in a plastic and contingent manner that, certainly in situations where a human being is the controller, necessarily includes the factor of judgment. So whether our understanding of "control" is oriented toward "thing" or "process" will to some considerable extent affect our teaching behaviors, as I see it. Those oriented toward "thing" will tend to be involved with getting "it" working, so that it can fulfill its overarching controlling function. Those oriented toward "process" will tend to be involved with recognizing and coordinating the various input, output, and judgment factors in such a way as to bring about improved patterns—skills—of response and behavior.

These, in brief, are the core ideas that I want to explore in depth in a future paper, and that ongoingly allow me to pursue, in clear Alexandrian conscience, the cultivation of skill in the postural processes that result, to quote FMA, in "due increase in the movements of expansion and contraction of the thorax until such movements are adequate and perfectly controlled" (*MSI*, Dutton 1918, p. 336). For myself, the breath work has been a tremendous source of insight into FMA's earlier writings, as well as associated with perceived psycho-physical benefits, not the least of which has been a marked freedom from colds and flu (none) over the past six years.

Breathe From Your Diaphragm and Other Myths

DIRECTION, Voice Issue (Vol. 2, No. 3, 1994)

My all-time favorite book title, partly due, no doubt, to my own half-Swedish heritage, is John Louis Anderson's *Scandinavian Humour and Other Myths*,[1] hence my now obvious starting point for these present reflections. Certainly when dealing with *voice*, one must at some level deal with *breath*, and there is certainly no dearth of opinion among the world's performers and teachers of singing, acting, and speech, as to how the latter properly should relate to the former. Depending on its particular source, such opinion ranges from what might on the one hand reasonably be termed "informed" to what on the other can only, in the light of physiological fact, be viewed essentially as myth.

Praise be to Science and Higher Education, there exists actual evidence for this assertion. A peer of mine in the doctoral program at Teachers College-Columbia University, Kathleen Wilson Spillane, produced a dissertation called *Breath Support Directives Used by Singing Teachers: A Delphi Study*,[2] in which she collected and mounted, so to speak, specimens of the various verbal/conceptual means through which the pedagogues of her experimental sample—395 randomly selected members of the National Association of Teachers of Singing—attempt to initiate their charges into the respiratory mysteries. Readers of *DIRECTION* will be pleased to note that, at one end of the scale, the second-highest-ranked directive was "Good posture via Alexander Technique; breathe calmly, expanding lowest ribs and filling back without shoulder tension." By contrast, the directive with the second-lowest rank was "Muscular action is the same as defecatory movement." (The lowest was "Beginning students should not think about breathing.") Without dwelling here on whether defecating is really all that much like singing, or on further discussion of Spillane's findings or aspects of method—the Delphi technique of developing a consensus of opinion, for example—I certainly recommend her ingenious, thorough, and enlightening work to anyone involved in the teaching of voice, wind instruments, glass blowing, and other breath-dependent activities.

Among her conclusions Spillane notes, with due scholarly restraint, "Despite the advanced Degrees of many of the subjects [singing teachers], a certain lack of understanding of the physiological process seems to be indicated by the results of this study." Herein lies the source of the general confusion pervading instruction in this area, most properly termed "breath management." I myself, even though at the time a clarinetist of some thirty years experience and an Alexander student and teacher of twelve, only arrived at an adequate understanding of these matters after 1984, through the study of respiratory function in preparation for my own dissertation.[3] The problem is, that without an accurate conception of the internal forces and movements that actually produce airflow, one can only attempt to convey one's personal technique by the method of "show and tell," which, though perhaps more-or-less effective in immediate objective, lends itself in the student's interpretation to distortions both gross and subtle—as Alexander experienced at the hands of an early acting teacher, as recounted in *The Use of the Self*.[4]

It is beyond the scope of this article, and probably of any piece of writing, reliably to convey an understanding of what, as one authority has put it, "is a problem requiring on the one hand the detailed knowledge of a classical anatomist, and on the other hand, the analytic understanding of an engineer."[5] There are some journeys that are—or should be—undertaken only in the company of an experienced guide, an apt metaphor for the three-hour presentation I give called "Breath As Postural Process,"[6] where dialogue with the questioning audience is as much a part of the proceedings as exposition and illustration of the subject matter itself. My limited goal here will be to give a glimpse of this landscape by exposing what, in my experience, are three of the commonest "breath teaching" myths:

1. Breathe from your diaphragm
2. Keep your shoulders down
3. Breathe like a baby

Who among us hasn't been admonished, at one time or another, to "Breathe from your diaphragm"? But the physiological fact is, it is impossible *not* to breathe from it, or more correctly, not without its contribution, together with that of the abdominal and thoracic muscles and abdominal viscera, to the internal resolution of forces causing the movements that increase the volume of the thorax, resulting in a region of lowered pressure, into which air from a region of higher pressure—outside the body—flows. This mythical directive is often implemented in practice by pushing out the entire abdomen, from rib cage to pubis, on inspiration, an action requiring a pronounced voluntary contraction of the diaphragm in conjunction with a general relaxation of the abdominal musculature. The problem with this action, when employed as the major or sole breath-management strategy, is that in pushing the abdomen out, at the expense of letting the ribs go up, expansion of the thorax is limited, resulting in a reduction of breath capacity—remember, the lungs live in the rib cage, not the belly.

What truth there is in "breathe from your diaphragm" stems in part from an oft-observed tendency under stress to hold the abdominal muscles stiffly, thus reducing their necessary motive contribution to controlled expiration and inhibiting the necessary downward excursion of the diaphragm on inspiration, as well as abetting the misdirected attempt to expand the thorax by lifting the shoulders and/or over-extending—arching—the spine.

This last-mentioned tendency is, no doubt, what has given rise—so to speak—to the myth of "Keep your shoulders down." Breath, whether managed or not, takes place through complex muscular synergies—groupings of co-ordinations—that may be termed "primary" and "accessory." The primary synergy, accounting for most of the muscular action in normal, unforced breathing, is that involving the diaphragm, abdominals and intercostals. (Animal intercostals, you know, are the ones some like to eat barbecued.) The accessory synergy is that involving muscles connecting the ribs to higher points in the skeleton. The accessory synergy is recruited, becomes active, as respiratory demand increases—watch your neck and upper torso muscles work if you exercise to the point where you're really heaving! But, if one is overusing the accessory synergy relative to the primary in activities of relatively low respiratory demand—speaking, singing, wind instrument playing—the action is inefficient with respect to both capacity and control of the breath. Thus, the intuitive teacher's natural response to observing this kind of misuse is "Keep your shoulders down:"

I hope it might be obvious by this point that, however well-intentioned, this directive very often has the effect of inducing the student to tighten the accessory musculature in order to prevent the shoulders from rising, an action that, unfortunately, prevents the upper rib cage from expanding. In contrast, by skillfully allowing the correct recruitment of muscular activity from primary to accessory, the entire thorax moves easily from bottom to top. This doesn't mean, however, that the lungs fill from bottom to top, another oft-perpetuated myth. The inspired air inflates the lung equally in all directions, as in blowing up a balloon. One could improve the mythical directive by rephrasing it, "Allow the shoulders to stay down," but even better would be "Let the shoulders rise on the tide of the breath," a verbalization that, though by no means a sure thing, at least contains nothing in its imagery to encourage unnecessary constriction.

Which brings us to "Breathe like a baby." As a clarinetist, I remember being told by my teacher in college—who was very fine, by the way—that if I wanted to understand breathing, to watch a baby lying on its back and imitate it. Not having a baby handy, I can't recall actually follow-ing this advice, but I did accept it intellectually—as well as lying down myself, observing my breathing, trying to play, etc., all rather inconclusively—and I distinctly re-member repeating the same thing to my students over the many years that I taught the clarinet. This is how much "knowledge" is transmitted. Somewhere along the line, after I had begun Alexander and was sens-ing/moving/thinking critically through many issues, breathing among them, I had the insight that the objec-tive conditions—orientation to gravity, absolute size, sensory-motor development, etc.—of a baby's lying down are very different from those of an adult, who not only stands up, but indulges in extremely complex voluntary activities. From that point forward, I have been extremely cautious about the use of analogy in teaching—the point of course being that, at some point, every analogy breaks down under the reality of comparative objective condi-tions.

Having completed our basic agenda, I wish to make two further points in closing. The first is to respond to an assumed query on the part of the reader as to whether there's anything "practical" in what I've written here.

Probably not, at least in the sense of one's being quickly able to do something competently and reliably. Modifying one's breath management habits on the basis of a rational understanding of structure and process is something that takes time, practice, and, above all, *interest*. To the individual who feels the stirrings of attraction toward these matters, I can do no better than to recommend the relevant pages in Kapandji's *Physiology of the Joints*, "… an anatomy text which is notable for its expressively aesthetic illustrations of movement on the one hand, and the clear engineering interpretations of human joint structure and muscular vectors on the other."[8] The initial work is perhaps best approached as a *contemplation* of these diagrams and texts with the intention of understanding them one at a time, though not necessarily in page-by-page order. "Understanding," in this sense, means an inner "seeing" of the movements in both space and time. Some are easy, and others—the crucial ones— difficult. But if you look enough, and with genuine interest, something will probably emerge (try starting with the diagram below).

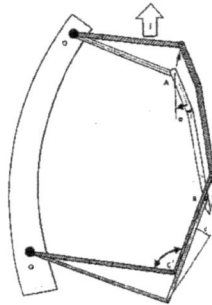

Shape Changes of the Thorax in Inspiration: No one understanding this diagram would ever give a breath directive such as "Keep the upper chest down" (after Kapandji).[7]

My second and concluding point is that artistic values are not to be confused with hygienic or ethical values. The purpose of *art* is self-expression, and not health or efficiency. Relative to voice, for example, from the artistic standpoint one uses oneself in a particular way to make a particular sound. But if the truly desired sound can be produced only by means that ultimately compromise the voice or the organism in general, then that represents one of the prices that the individual pays in being an artist. The issue, of course, is one of choice. But one can only choose if there is awareness of alternatives, and a willingness to take a risk. In our use of voice, and in manifold other ways also, too many persist in habitual and counter-productive patterns though ignorance and/or fear of failure.

---

1. Anderson, John Louis, *Scandinavian Humour and Other Myths,* Nordbook, Minneapolis (1986).

2. Spillane, Kathleen Wilson, *Breath Support Directives Used by Singing Teachers: A Delphi Study,* University Microfilms International, 300 N. Zeeb Road, Ann Arbor, MI 48106. Order No: 8721175. Price information at 800-521-3042.

3. *Musical Performance and Respiratory Function in Wind Instrumentalists: Effects of the Alexander Technique of Musculoskeletal Education.* Available as in Footnote 2, Order No: 8721097. Abstract in *The Congress Papers: 2nd International Alexander Congress, Brighton, England,* Direction, Sydney *(1994) pp.84-88.*

4. Alexander, F. Matthias, *The Use of the Self* (Dutton, New York, 1932), pp.17, 18.

5. W. O. Fenn, quoted by E.J.M. Campbell in the first edition of *The Respiratory Muscles* (1957).

6. *The Congress Papers: 3rd International Alexander Congress, Engelberg, Switzerland,* Direction, Sydney (1993) pp. 68-69.

7. I. A. Kapandji, *The Physiology of Joints, Vol. 111,* 2nd ed., ISBN 0 443 012091, pp.136-151:

8. Mathews, Troup, "Parliamentary Procedure & The Breath—Ron Dennis at the AGM," *NASTAT News,* No. 16 (Summer 1992) p.13.

Group Teaching

NASTAT NEWS 23, Winter 1994

The first group teaching I did was a few years after being certified in 1979. To my knowledge I offered the first public Alexander group class in New York City at the Hebrew Arts School (now the Elaine Kaufman Cultural Center, and the home of ACAT), beginning in 1983 and continuing until 1990, when I moved to Atlanta. During the same period, I also taught groups at The Juilliard School, the Swedish Institute (massage, not cultural), Teachers College, and in the Music School of the Chautauqua Institution. So I have seen my share of people coming to grips (so to speak) with the Technique in the context of group study. And I know from their feedback that many got quite a lot out of it.

Nonetheless, I no longer offer such classes to the general public. This is partly a matter of economics. During my training, groups were thought to be a way to get private students. I, sad to relate, have never had one student from all of my group classes come for regular private lessons. Why? In offering a group, you implicitly represent that it is an appropriate mode of study for the Technique and you also provide a considerable financial incentive: who would come for private lessons under these circumstances? On this subject I like to quote that great iconoclast Ezra Pound saying, "The economic problem of the teacher (of violin or of language or of anything else) is how to string it out so as to be paid for more lessons" (*ABC of Reading,* New Directions Paperbook, p. 85). These days, earning my total keep as an Alexander teacher, I find that I have a better chance at "stringing it out"—sufficiently challenging as that is anyway— with a student who has had the motivation to come for private lessons in the first place.

Beyond the financial there are educational and personal factors as well. I like being alone with people at the beginning of their Alexander experience. I think they appreciate a space where, for a while at least, they don't have to perform, and can focus exclusively on their own process. Table work is important in my approach, and I want plenty of time and psychological space available for it. Paradoxically, in my first year or so of teaching, I strongly resisted giving table work. It seemed too passive, too indulgent of students' desires to "relax." And yet I also felt at a certain level that I *should* be giving it; I had had lots myself, other teachers did it, why not I? Conflict, in a word. One day without particular motive I was just sitting and thinking and my thoughts drifted back to my own first lessons with Goddard Binkley. I remembered how good his table work felt, and how much—even at the time, and certainly in retrospect—I felt I learned from it. It then occurred to me that in not giving that experience to others, I was actually hoarding the wealth, perhaps unconsciously afraid that if I shared it I wouldn't have enough for myself. Praise Freud, from that moment on I was freed to give table and it has become a mainstay of my work.

By no means, though, do I undervalue the uses of group work in the overall Alexander picture. There is, in the first place, the objectification of the Technique that comes through observing others. Seeing is believing: one learns through unselfconsciously watching others that these oh-so subtle and delicate changes are nonetheless real, and often produce striking improvements in action and appearance. In the second place, there is the social aspect of it all; people often enjoy doing things together, and that is a strong reinforcement to the learning process. Feldenkrais, not without reason if perhaps a bit self-servingly, wrote, "The whole problem is a social one and reeducation has much better prospects of success if conducted in groups and not in the seclusion and pretended secrecy of the consulting room ... The number of silent sufferers who dread the consulting room and cannot afford it, is far greater than is generally realized. The group ... solves the two problems; the whole procedure is that of adult re-education and not treatment" *(Body and Mature Behavior,* last paragraph). Be that as it may, it is certainly true enough, in my experience, that group work can serve as a useful and enjoyable kind of halfway house between the intimate transaction of the private lesson and the hurly-burly of actual daily life.

Considerations such as these have gradually evolved into my current policy, featuring two broad restrictions, for the offering of group study: (1) to the public, only in clearly pro bono type situations, i.e., within academic or arts institutions, or to senior citizens and others with genuine financial constraints; and (2) to those of my own students who first complete ten private lessons. As I wrote in my newsletter in announcing the latter:

> Over the years I have felt concern for those students who study enough to get a minimal feel for the Technique and then stop, perhaps for financial reasons or perhaps because of uncertainty about "where they're going" with it. Emphatically, Alexander isn't about lessons forever. But the deeper learning that I would hope for students—a liberation of energy, subtle or otherwise, seeking its proper channels— is most probable as a function of guided practice over time. It seems to me that these issues are addressed by the opportunity to work regularly in a group after initial study in private lessons.

Here in Atlanta, I've found this approach personally and philosophically satisfying, as well as increasingly rewarding, strangely enough, on the financial level.

The Longer and Shorter of It:
Data Collection at the AGM

NASTAT NEWS 29, Winter 1995

At my presentation for the Research Panel during the AGM [1995, Oakland CA], I had to exercise considerable inhibition not to spill the beans about the data I wanted to collect. Naturally, I wanted everybody there to know all the details of this brilliant research project I had come up with, but on the other hand couldn't tell them because of the issue of subject bias. So this article is to clear up the mystery and hopefully to elicit some further participation.

This past year, I finally came into possession of an article I had first learned about 15 or so years ago in Mabel Ellsworth Todd's *The Thinking Body*. This was "A Resumé, with Comments, of the Available Literature Relating to Posture" by Louis Schwartz, Surgeon, US Public Health Service (*Public Health Reports*, Vol. 42, No. 1, May 26, 1927, pp. 1219–49), in which the author reviewed and summarized 154 documents as well as giving complete bibliographic information for each. (I will make a copy available to NASTAT for distribution if there is a demand.)

Under a section called "Definitions of Correct Posture" I especially noticed this one that I take the liberty to quote in full, for its tone (so to speak) as well as substance:

> Floyd A. Rowe defines good posture as a winning fight of the human organism, muscle, and will power, against the pull of gravity, and he grades posture by measuring the length of the body when horizontal and when it is vertical and by dividing the vertical length by the horizontal length. This gives what he says is an exact percentage of posture.

I was intrigued by the possibility of researching this variable because:

216

1. It is eminently Alexandrian—"lengthening the stature" is one of our basic tenets.
2. It is quantified—measurements, not judgments, yield the data.
3. The variable in question requires no performance by the subjects.
4. The instrumentation and research protocol are simplicity itself.
5. A large sample would be potentially available at the AGM.
6. The results would constitute a verifiable statement about one aspect of Alexander teachers' use—their "Functional Length Index" (FLI), as 1 chose to call it, rather than Rowe's "percentage of posture."
7. The FLI of Alexander teachers could eventually be compared with that of samples of other populations—"normals," most notably—the hypothesis here being that in standing we Alexandrians "lengthen," i.e., functionally use a greater percentage of our structural length, more than they do.
8. This comparison, if favorable, might begin to quantify the actual benefits of the Technique, and in any case would represent "harder" knowledge than has as yet been usual in our work—of course, the results might not confirm the hypothesis, the HHH (Hazard to Hopeful Hypothesis) of all empirical research.

So without further ado, here are the numbers you've all been waiting for. In a sample of 42 Alexander teachers, mean age 45 and mean years of teaching 9.5, the mean length differential between standing and lying-down was -1.06 inches, resulting in a mean FLI of .98. Preliminary statistical modeling suggests that a mean difference of -1.625 inches in another population sample would represent a difference at less than the .05 level of significance between that sample and that of Alexander teachers. In other words, if it turns out that we Alexandrians use at least 5/8" more of our structural length in functional upright posture than other folks do, other things being comparable (like *variability,* for example), that's pretty big news!

The next step is to obtain some preliminary data on "normals" to get some idea of whether such a difference actually exists; this is where the community could really get involved. If we all would begin to take measurements on our new students, we would soon have an FLI data pool that would answer the question of whether this variable bears further investigation. I will provide a copy of the data form and research protocol to NASTAT for any teachers wishing to participate. ('The protocol calls for subjects to be measured before 10 a.m. without shoes, in case you want to jump right in.)

As a closing note, I want to point out the presence in our current Alexander sample of 11 females 50 years of age or over. The mean FLI of this group is .98, exactly the same as that of the entire sample (all right!). It would be especially instructive to compare this FLI with that of a "normal" population sample of the same sex and age group, relative to concerns about osteoporosis. Without much knowledge of the subject, it nevertheless is my impression that little is said in medical circles about a possible postural component in osteoporosis, and comparative FLI's might begin to shed some light on that.

[Subsequent data from a group of "normals" here in Atlanta were not encouraging, but the research hypothesis and design are still$_{2014}$ viable. For example, data collected from beginning Alexander students, as suggested above, might yield significant results.]

The Question of Lumbar Support

NASTAT News, Issue 34, Autumn 1996

At the NASTAT AGM of 1995 in Oakland, Galen Cranz, Ph.D., presented her work on seating and the chair, in which she made a statement about the undesirability of lumbar support that I consider to be an over-generalization. This statement has been uncritically cited in a review of Dr. Cranz's presentation (Laura Klein, *NASTAT News*, Summer 1995, p. 18), thus accruing credibility and further motivating the present response.

At issue is Cranz's virtual dismissal of the common type of ergonomic seating that provides direct support to the lumbar concavity, justifying this only by the assertion that pressing in on an arch weakens it. Though this be true for some arches some of the time, it is not true for the lumbar spine all of the time, as will be shown. Cranz's unstated but more substantial argument derives considerably from A. C. Mandal's paper "Investigation of the lumbar flexion of the seated man" (*Intl. J Industrial Economics*, 8:75-87, 1991), which she kindly supplied to me in post-meeting correspondence. Mandal does convincingly debunk the notion of lumbar support as a "magic formula" for workplace seating, showing that such support is not biomechanically appropriate for "Most forms of work, [which] take place in the forward bent position with the gravity point in front of the sitting bone" (p. 86).

What Mandal and Cranz fail to point out is that a good deal of work in fact takes place in the *reclined* position; I refer specifically to that of driving motor vehicles, and to reclined sitting in general as in theaters, etc. In these situations, given the type of seating available, the alternatives for maintaining an appropriate degree of lumbar concavity are (1) muscular effort or (2) mechanical support. Qualitative task analysis of Alternative 1 suggests that its consequences include (a) tension-induced restriction of circulation, (b) narrowing of the interdiscal spaces by the same mechanism, and (c) excessive energy expenditure. Alternative 2, however, substantially ameliorates these consequences, as has been shown by B. J. G. Andersson, *et al.* ("Lumbar disc pressure and myoelectric back muscle activity during sitting," *Scan J Rehab Med*, 6:104-114, 1974): "By using a proper backrest, it is possible to reduce the myoelectric activity of the posterior muscles of the back . ... When sitting supported [reclined], a decrease in pressure is obtained both by an increase in backrest inclination and by an increase in lumbar support" (p. 113). Mandal, citing this finding, also admits the effectiveness of lumbar support in the reclined position, "with the gravity point behind the sitting bones" (p. 86). My point, thus, is that lumbar support ain't necessarily all bad: it depends on what you're doing.

The question of whether the sitting posture is (a) erect or forward-bent on the one hand, or (b) reclined, on the other, leads to consideration of the PosturEvolution™ appliance recently marketed to the Alexander community and beyond, whose design also reflects an ideological opposition to lumbar support. The brochure states: "What's needed is a way of supporting your back while permanently training your back muscles to properly support you." Since the appliance is designed for use in reclined sitting, this argument does not convince by the same reasons given for Alternative 1 above. Granted, that PosturEvolution™ is an advance over seating that allows the lumbar spine to flex while still supporting weight, as do many car seats and easy-type chairs. Granted also that many back muscles do need training. But both evidence and task analysis suggest that, for the purpose of muscular training, positions other than the reclined are more appropriate. To be sure, if PosturEvolution™

were supplied with an adjustable lumbar support, it would be a superior biomechanical aid [it now is so equipped].

A more general issue deriving from both foregoing discussions is whether a given biomechanical means is appropriate for the specific task at hand. Take for example Alexander lying-down work; certainly lumbar support is not usually provided here, and would be considered by many [teachers to be] an "interference." Yet, Andersson *et al.* cite evidence that such support in the supine position actually decreases intradiscal (inside the disc) pressure, and presumably spinal stress, for the reason that the support maintains the shape of the disc closer to that of the "normal" posterior wedge shape (p. 111). Thus in table and floor work I regularly employ the "Spinatrac," a small plastic appliance that supports the lumbar concavity, with positive reports from most students [contact me for more information]. Likewise, I often support the cervical spine with a rolled-up towel, rather than routinely propping the head up on books, which in many people tends to over-straighten the neck. I emphasize that these are not arbitrary decisions, but rather procedures virtually dictated by relevant empirical evidence, as well as confirmed in experience.

It is this issue of arbitrariness that I would like to address in these closing remarks. At an international congress I once heard a Most Senior Teacher say, relative to putting hands on the chair, "That's the way F. M. did it, and that's good enough for me." No blame attaches to doing things in the usual ways, providing that a reasoned decision to do so has been worked out, relative to alternatives. As Alexander himself observed, speaking of the "extraordinary variability of the cases presented," "On broad lines it is evident that the misuses must be diagnosed by the instructor who may be called upon to use considerable *ingenuity and patience* [my emphasis] in correcting the faults, and substituting the correct mental orders for the one general order which starts the old train of habitual vicious movements" (*MSI*, 1918 ed., p. 212-13.). More poetically perhaps, Jung once remarked, "Learn your theories as well as you can, but put them aside when you touch the miracle of the living soul (*Psychological Reflections*, Bollingen Paperback, 1973, p. 84).

Functional Reach Improvement
in Normal Older Women
after Alexander Technique Instruction

Journal of Gerontology: MEDICAL SCIENCES
1999, Vol. 54A, No. 1, M8-M11
Reprinted by Permission

Background. Functional Reach (FR) is a clinical measure of balance. The Alexander Technique (AT) is a non-exercise approach to the improvement of body mechanics. This study investigated a possible relationship between FR performance and AT instruction.

Methods. Three groups, comprised of women over 65 with the exception of one male control, were studied: (i) a pilot group; and (ii) and (iii) experimental and control groups. Groups 1 and 2 were given eight 1-hour, bi-weekly sessions of AT instruction with pre- and post tests in FR, while Group 3 was given only pre and post tests in FR.

Results. Groups 1 and 2 both showed significant improvement in FR performance. Group 2 was retested 1 month after posttest and showed a slight decrease in FR performance. For Groups 1 and 2, a questionnaire allowing qualitative responses on a four-item scale showed an overall positive response to the AT instruction.

Conclusions. AT instruction may be effective in improving balance and thereby reducing the incidence of falls in normal older women.

Functional Reach (FR) is a clinical measure of balance, representing the maximal distance one can reach forward beyond arm's length while maintaining a fixed base of support in the standing position (1). The Alexander Technique (AT) is a method of postural control employing a non-exercise, or co-ordinational repatterning, approach to the improvement of body mechanics (2, 3). Since falls are a major source of morbidity in older adults (4), and since body mechanics are assumed to be associated with balance, the present study was undertaken to investigate a possible relationship between FR performance and AT instruction.

In the present study, "body mechanics" refers to the mechanical correlation, or static and dynamic alignment, of body segments in posture and movement (5, 6). Although the exact relationship between body mechanics and balance is unknown, that such a relationship exists may be inferred from observation of the normal infant's process of learning to stand and walk, where increasing control among body segments eventually leads to successful performance. That body mechanics do not necessarily remain invariant after the acquisition of upright stance and locomotion may be inferred from the observation of the posture and movement of elderly persons relative to that of infants. Most authors on the improvement of body mechanics, e.g. Goldthwait, Brown, Swaim, and Kuhns (7), prescribe a regimen of exercises, after qualitative analysis of existing mechanics has suggested the muscle groups to be appropriately stretched and/or strengthened. Alexander, however, devised a method for improving body mechanics in the context of ordinary daily movement tasks, such as standing, sitting, bending, and walking (8). This method involves direct guidance of the student by the instructor, toward the goal of more efficient movement, using both tactual and verbal cues. In AT instruction, exercise per se plays no role.

Three groups were studied in this investigation: (i) a pilot group; and (ii) and (iii) experimental and control groups. Groups 1 and 2 were given AT instruction with pre- and post tests in FR, while Group 3 was given only pre- and post tests in FR. At posttest, Groups 1 and 2 both showed significant improvement in FR performance. Group 2 was retested 1 month after posttest and showed a slight decrease in FR performance. For Groups 1 and 2, a questionnaire allowing qualitative responses on a four-item scale showed an overall positive response to the AT instruction. These results indicate that AT instruction may be effective in improving balance and thereby reducing the incidence of falls in normal older women.

METHODS

Subjects

All subjects were normally ambulatory volunteers, aged at least 65 and giving informed consent. Group 1 (six females, age range 71–88, median 85.5) was recruited in Fall 1994 from the population of a senior residence; Group 2 (seven females, age range 66–83, median 72) was recruited in Spring 1995 from the membership of a senior educational facility, as was Group 3 (five females, one male, age range 65–78, median 71). Subjects in Groups 1 and 2 received free AT instruction; Group 3 subjects were paid $15 each for service as controls.

Apparatus

FR testing required (i) one piece of plywood 3/4" thick by 14" wide by 24" long; (ii) one sheet of 14" by 17" newsprint drawing paper for each *S*; (iii) a red marking pen; (iv) a wooden yardstick; (v) a Stanley #42-287 line level ; (vi) a wooden ruler 12" long; (vii) "sticky" putty; (viii) data recording forms. AT instruction required a straight chair with no arms for each *S* and a room in which *S*'s could sit in a circle with about an arm's length of space on each side.

Procedures—Quantitative

For FR testing, the yardstick was prepared by affixing the line level, bubble forward, with dots of sticky putty at the center on the calibrated surface, and by placing dots of sticky putty near each end on the other surface. Near one end of a wall clear of obstruction for about six feet, the plywood was placed with narrow side against the baseboard. A piece of the drawing paper, secured with dots of sticky putty, was placed on the plywood equidistant from each end. For each S, an assistant levelled the yardstick and affixed it with sticky putty at a position shoulder height and about 12" forward of the shoulder. With S standing approximately centered on the drawing paper, the side of the body next to but not touching the wall, the red marker was used to make an outline of the feet, ensuring a similar stance for all tests. The assistant then instructed S to raise the right arm forward of the body and parallel to the yardstick, without reaching forward, thumb up and hand loosely closed. The assistant established the base line for reach by using the 12" ruler to establish a perpendicular between S's bent index finger proximal interphalangeal joint and the yardstick, announcing the measurement to the nearest eighth-inch, which the researcher recorded on the data form. The assistant then instructed S to "lean forward as far as you can, keeping your arm level with the yardstick, without losing your balance and without touching the wall." No further instruction or coaching was given as to S's method of reaching. The extent of reach was observed and recorded as above, with FR being the difference between the first and second measurements. The interval between pre- and post tests was 1 month for all groups. In order to assess retention of learning, Group 2 was retested 1 month after posttest. The same assistant performed all observations and instruction for all tests.

226

Procedures—AT Instruction

The researcher, an Alexander Technique Teacher (9), gave all AT instruction. Groups 1 and 2 met 1 hour twice each week for four weeks. The median number of sessions attended was 6.5 for Group 1 and 8 for Group 2. Instruction consisted of conceptual (verbal) and hands-on guidance in the body mechanics of unsupported sitting (erect, no back support), supported sitting (back of chair), rising to standing from a chair, sitting down in a chair, standing, walking, and lowering the body in space (commonly called "bending" but more properly "folding" the body). For example, in the mechanics of sitting down in a chair, the verbal part of the guidance typically was, "Let the knees fold forward and the hips fold back," while with the hands the experimenter suggested the desired direction of segmental movement in space. Where *S* was able, instruction was also given in moving down to the floor to recline in a "constructive rest" position—supine with legs folded, feet on floor, knees pointing up, head and neck supported with books and/or a cervical roll (folded towel) so as to maintain spinal alignment—and in returning to standing. The regular (daily) practice of constructive rest has been found clinically useful in temporarily redistributing postural muscle tone, especially of the torso, leading to gradual modification of body image in upright stance and commensurate improvement in body mechanics. None of the instruction dealt with leaning movements per se.

Procedures—Qualitative

At the end of AT instruction, *S*'s in Groups 1 and 2 responded anonymously either "none," "a little," "a fair amount," or "a lot" to a questionnaire on their perceived improvement in (a) balance, (b) leg strength, (c) posture, (d) overall ease of movement, (e) general body awareness, (f) self-confidence in movement, (g) enjoyment of classes,

(h) extent of learning in classes. At the FR retest, S's in Group 2 responded on the same scale to questions regarding (a) retention of instruction during the month, (b) desirability of additional instruction, and (c) helpfulness of instruction in daily life.

Statistical Methods

Data for Group 1 were analyzed by the t-test for correlated means. Since Groups 2 and 3 were recruited separately, allowance was made for the non-equivalent control group (10) by using Welch's t' (t-prime) statistic, sometimes referred to as the separate-variance t-test, which is characterized by the use of separate sample variances and modified degrees of freedom (11). As improvement after instruction was anticipated, t-tests were 1-tailed.

RESULTS

Quantitative Results

Table 1, "Summary FR test data in inches ($\bar{x}$, SD, SEM)," gives sample means, standard deviations, and standard errors of the mean for all FR tests. Analysis showed that Group 1 improved FR performance by 1.71" ($p < .025$), and Group 2 improved by 1.50" relative to Group 3, whose mean FR decreased by .74" ($p < .005$, $df = 8$). In Figure 1, "Graphical display of functional reach pre- and posttest scores," each point is an S whose posttest performance is readily visible relative to the dashed line representing the case where all pre- and post scores be equal. At retest 1month after posttest, FR performance of Group 2 decreased by .32".

Table 1. Summary FR Test Data in Inches (Mean, *SD, SEM*)

Group	Pretest	Posttest	Retest
1, $N = 6$	7.42, 3.80, 1.70	9.13, 2.68, 1.20	n/a
2, $N = 7$	6.96, 2.86, 1.17	8.46, 2.24, 0.92	8.14, 2.86, 1.17
3, $N = 6$	11.57, 2.27, 1.02	10.83, 2.17, 0.97	n/a

FR, functional reach; n/a, not available.

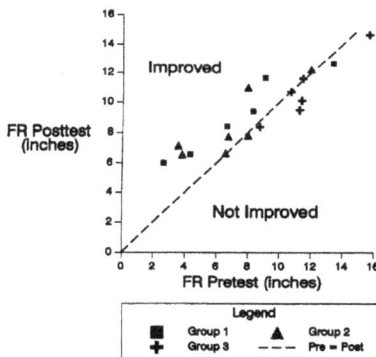

Figure 1. Graphical display of functional reach pre- and posttest scores.

An alternative analysis for the data in terms of percentage of change for each subject was carried out; this transformation from the raw scores compensates for bias introduced by differing lengths of body segments, e.g., arms, legs, and torso, for the different subjects. These data are given in Table 2, statistical analyis of which shows that Group 1 improved by 40.8% ($p < .05$), and that Group 2 improved by 32.2% ($p < .025$, $df=6$). Group 2's retest performance relative to posttest decreased by 5.2%.

Table 2. Percent FR Change by Subject (S)
Between Pre- and Posttests

	S_1	S_2	S_3	S_4	S_5	S_6	S_7	Mean
Group 1	52.0	125.6	28.5	26.2	−0.8	13.1	n/a	40.8
Group 2	1.2	14.8	71.8	100.0	−2.1	37.5	2.1	32.2
Group 3	−11.4	1.0	−4.2	−15.9	−0.7	−6.7	n/a	−6.3

FR, functional reach; n/a, not available.

Qualitative Results

Table 3, "Post-instruction questionnaire responses, Groups 1 & 2," shows response frequencies for each question (12 responses are shown in each row because one questionnaire from Group 1 was not returned). Table 4, "Retest questionnaire responses, Group 2" shows response frequencies of Group 2 for three questions: (a) How much Alexander awareness [a technical term known to S's as a function of AT instruction; to the reader, body awareness relative to AT instruction] would you say you have retained during the month? (b) How helpful do you think additional or ongoing study would be? (c) How helpful do you think the Alexander Technique has been to you in your daily life? (one S did not respond to questionnaire).

Table 3. Postinstruction Questionnaire Responses—Groups 1 and 2

	None	A little	A fair amount	A lot
Improvement in				
Balance	1	3	5	3
Leg strength	3	3	3	3
Posture	0	2	5	5
Ease of movement	0	3	5	4
Body awareness	0	0	3	9
Self-confidence	0	2	6	4
Enjoyment of class	0	1	2	9
Extent of learning	0	0	2	10

Table 4. Retest Questionnaire Responses—Groups 2

Question	None	A little	A fair amount	A lot
a	—	—	4	2
b	—	1	2	3
c	—	—	1	5

Questions: (a) How much Alexander awareness would you say you have retained during the month? (b) How helpful do you think additional or ongoing study would be? (c) How helpful do you think the Alexander Technique has been to you in your daily life?

DISCUSSION

Remarks are in order on five specific aspects of the quantitative procedures and data:

1. At the senior educational facility, not enough volunteers responded to the initial solicitation in order to assign randomized experimental and control groups. A second solicitation 1 month later offering compensation yielded the necessary controls.

2. Note that the control group's mean FR at pretest was 11.57", 4.61" greater than that of the experimentals at 6.96". The published mean for 14 females in this age

231

group is 10.47", $s = 3.53$ (1). Thus, both experimentals and controls fall within one standard deviation of the published mean, though the experimentals are borderline on the low side. It is possible that factors associated with the self-selection of volunteers are responsible for this difference, e.g., the experimentals being more motivated to volunteer because of felt need.

3. That the control group's FR performance decreased by .74" at posttest raises the issue of test-retest reliability, which is claimed for the FR measure by its authors (1). However, since descriptive statistics on the variable show no particular abnormality, such as influence by extreme scores, the lower posttest score is attributed to inter-test variability of unknown origin.

4. That the experimental group's FR performance at retest decreased by .32" raises the issue of retention of learning. This issue might be addressed by further testing at monthly, bi-monthly, or longer intervals. Such recurrent testing would raise the issue of practice effects on the test itself, although it is clear that optimal maintenance levels of instruction should be investigated. Within the context of the present study, the observed decrease seems reasonable, given the short period of AT instruction relative to lifelong habits of body mechanics.

5. A question could be raised as to the quantity (eight sessions) and quality (group vs. individual) of AT instruction employed in this study. On this point, Austin and Ausubel give the orthodox AT view that 20 private sessions constitutes an entry level with up to 100 sessions over two years for permanent improvement (13). It is the researcher's experience that such a course of study, however valid as an ideal, is seldom realized even in the non-geriatric population, and is, for most practical purposes, unnecessary in the geriatric context. Based on the

experience of the present study, the researcher ventures to suggest that the group session for seniors is educationally viable, more financially feasible, and probably socially preferable. Of course, it would indeed be desirable to study geriatric AT instruction on a more extensive basis than eight sessions, say 16, which would hopefully be an outcome of the present study evidencing the validity of the method.

Regarding the study's qualitative results, the usual cautions concerning subject bias preclude a too-enthusiastic interpretation of the overall positive trend that is especially strong in the areas of body awareness, enjoyment of classes, and extent of learning. Nonetheless, Langer's important work has demonstrated the beneficial effects of mindfulness as defined in various operational contexts (12). Clearly, awareness, enjoyment, and knowledge of one's own body in practical daily use form such a context. Based on the evidence of the present study, it appears that some older adults profit mentally as well as physically from re-examining fundamental movement skills they originally acquired as infants. Illustrating the point are two among several comments that were returned on the post-instruction questionnaire:

1. My legs are stronger and I am less fearful of falling.

2. I have been walking one hour daily for eighteen years. I was afraid I would have to quit because I felt like I was trying to carry a heavy load. I learned from the Alexander technique how to stand tall and get rid of that burden. *I feel in control* [emphasis added].

Although the AT has been taught since early this century, it is still little known as an alternative therapy. At the 1997 national meeting of the American Association on Aging, the researcher served as a panelist on "Complementary Therapies and Aging," where the new watch-words seemed to be aerobics, massage, and *t'ai chi*. The present study shows that AT instruction can also be an effective intervention in some geriatric contexts, and that a viable research protocol is available. Further cooperation is called for between the geriatric and AT professional communities (16) in replicating and extending these results. Certainly our graying population stands to benefit from fuller access to this self-empowering resource.

ACKNOWLEDGMENTS

Sincere appreciation is extended to King's Bridge and Life Enrichment Services, Inc., both of Atlanta, for cooperation in securing subjects and providing teaching facilities; to my AT colleague Judith Stern, MA, PT, for originally bringing the FR measure to my attention; and to my student Patricia Zobel, MA, for competently and faithfully assisting me in administering the FR testing.

REFERENCES

1. Duncan PW, Weiner DK, Chandler J, Studenski S. Functional reach: a new clinical measure of balance. *J Gerontol Med Sci*. 1990;45:M192–M197.

2. Barlow W. *The Alexander Technique*. New York: Alfred A. Knopf, 1973.

3. Austin JHM, Ausubel P. Enhanced respiratory muscular function in normal adults after lessons in proprioceptive musculoskeletal education without exercises. *Chest*. 1992;192:486–490.

4. Tinetti ME, Doucette J, Claus E, Marottoli R. Risk factors for serious injury during falls by older persons. *J Am Geriat Soc*. 1995;43:1214–1221.

5. Osgood RB. *Body mechanics: education and practice. Report of the subcommittee on orthopedics and body mechanics.* New York: The Century Co.; 1932:5.

6. Howland IS. *Body alignment in fundamental motor skills.* New York: Exposition Press; 1953:103.

7. Goldthwait JE, Brown LT, Swaim LT, Kuhns JG. *Essentials of body mechanics in health and disease.* Philadelphia: J. B. Lippincott; 1952:262–281.

8. Alexander FM. *Man's supreme inheritance.* 2nd ed. New York: E. P. Dutton and Co., Inc.; 1918:273–311.

9. U.S. Dept of Labor. Occupational Title "Teacher, Alexander Technique." Occupational Code 099.227–581.

10. Campbell DT, Stanley JC. *Experimental and quasi-experimental designs for research.* Chicago: Rand McNally & Co.; 1966:47–50.

11. Ott L, Mendenhall W. *Understanding statistics.* Boston: PWS-Kent Publishing Co.; 1990:316–318.

12. Langer EJ. Mindfulness. Reading, MA: Addison Wesley; 1989.

Book IV

Later Writings ~ 2003–2014

Contents

Preface₂₀₁₄

The major theme of these later pieces—sometimes more and sometimes less explicitly—is the question of the historical and ongoing and marked underperformance of the Alexander Technique in the human potential and wellness marketplaces. My concern with this question is by no means academic: I, along with most Alexander teachers, experience the struggle for students that is a stark reality of our intending professional life.

In pondering this question over the years, three possible reasons—perhaps not mutually exclusive—have come to me: 1) the Technique's "time" has not yet come (or *has* come and already passed); 2) by its very nature the Technique is elitist and esoteric, and thereby unsuited for attracting a wider following; or 3) as its advocates, we teachers have failed to communicate the Technique in a manner that the broader public we seek can more readily understand and accept.

While not finally ruling out 1) or 2)—who can say, after all?—for the sake of my own *raison d'être* I can only deal with 3) as a basis for personal "response-ability" and action.

Thus I've written persistently, consistently, and insistently about what I consider to be basic *mis*-understandings of the Technique within our own Alexandrian community. This in order that, through clearer self-knowledge, we may more effectively communicate a message that will progressively bring the Technique to its surely rightful place in the world, in the words I wrote for the AmSAT Mission Statement, "a *basic and recognized* [italics added] resource for health, productivity, and well-being."

A Commentary

For a time *AmSAT News* ran a feature in which three training course directors were each invited to comment on sayings of F. M. Alexander as originally noted down by his assistant, Ethel Webb, and variously published. The saying for this issue (No. 61, Fall 2003) was "We can throw away the habit of a lifetime in a few minutes if we use our brains."

Who knowing me would be surprised that I caution against too sanguine a reading of this pronouncement? For it at least implies that by rational comprehension and inhibition (using our brains) we can be quickly and permanently rid of deeply stereotyped behaviors and attitudes (habits of a lifetime). This is less than the case in my experience, though my intention in so saying is not to cast wholesale doubt, but to suggest that intelligent use of any isolated assertion (proverb, saying, aphorism) as a "principle of life" (FMA, "Notes of Instruction" in *The Resurrection of the Body,* Edward Maisel, Ed.) means understanding when it applies and when not.

We need to recognize, I think, that there are habits and habits. Some, such as sitting down in a chair, carry relatively little emotional charge *(cathexis,* in psychoanalytic terms). Others, such as public performance of various kinds, are often utterly loaded in that regard. The former are eminently more amenable than the latter to the specifically Alexandrian mode of behavior modification through conscious inhibition and direction. There is also the notion, well-developed in psychology, that a habit is never really extinguished, but rather is gradually replaced by the acquisition of new habits. Reversion to habit under stress is a common experience of us all.

I suppose FMA could be generously interpreted as meaning that we can renounce (which is not the same thing as remove) an undesirable habit immediately and decisively upon becoming aware of it. As he was also quoted by Miss

Webb, "The things that don't exist are the most difficult to get rid of." All things considered, however, I much prefer Mark Twain's wary observation that "Habit is habit, and not to be flung out of the window by any man, but coaxed downstairs a step at a time."

Call for Colloquia

AmSAT News No. 68, Fall 2005

We are warned by John Nicholls in his impressive 2005 Memorial Address about taking out of context F. M. Alexander's statement "There really isn't a primary control as such. It becomes a something in the sphere of relativity" (from a ca. 1943 letter to Frank Pierce Jones). This is reasonable; we should always be on our guard when dealing with quoted material. However, as the person mainly responsible for the use of this quote in support of certain of my own beliefs, I would point out that, even though first mentioned in my 1999 article "Primary Control and the Crisis in Alexander Technique Theory," no direct qualification to it has yet been brought forth. Some statements in their simple clarity seem to stand on their own, virtually independent of context. Personally, about the only qualification to this statement of Alexander's that I can imagine would be if he had followed it to the effect of, "Naturally I jest." Naturally I jest. From all indications Alexander was anything but given to levity in regard to his work, and the words as writ clearly reveal his evolving understanding of Primary Control not as a reflex or mechanism but rather as a co-ordinational process.

Much more important than the issue of this particular quotation is that in the face of new facts, old facts differently viewed, and ongoing experience, serious challenges have arisen around the Technique concerning its historical development, its conceptual foundations, and, to some extent, its methods. I refer mainly though not solely to the extensive and detailed work of Bouchard, Protzel, Staring, and myself, published in these pages and elsewhere. These challenges cannot, or at least should not—in a community ostensibly motivated by values of critical inquiry as well as of self-validation—be dismissed by fiat, generalization, or appeal to authority.

The Alexander professional community in general, and in particular AmSAT, the Society that in 1994 officially disavowed certain of Alexander's statements about blacks, needs and deserves a more thorough-going and leisurely exposure to the challenges mentioned above. To this end, I call for colloquia to be held in plenary session at our Annual General Meetings, beginning at AGM 2006. A possible format could be that of a panel presentation, with panelists giving timed opening statements and then being questioned by other panelists and members of the audience in a predetermined structure (similar to the Presidential debates). Given the backlog of issues—at least several years' worth but in truth more like 50—a 3-hour session (with break) would probably provide suffi-cient temporal and psychological space for such an enter-prise, at least at the outset. Whatever the format, we need to be together, we need to speak and listen together, and we need to think together if we are to gain a more con-scious, if not an immediately more unified, perspective on the grounds of our work.

[Such a colloquium in quite limited form—as an option for an otherwise free Friday evening—was indeed included in the program for the Annual General Meeting of 2006, and the talk that I delivered for it follows below.]

Colloquium Talk

In the blurb I wrote for this Colloquium [in the Annual Meeting brochure], I used "heresies" to characterize certain views represented here tonight. I've since encountered a definition of "heresy" that indicates just how appropriate, at least in my case, that word is. "Heresy is the dislocation of some complete and self-supporting scheme by the introduction of a novel denial of some essential part therein." Those familiar with my thought will know that my particular heresy is with regard to Primary Control: as initially announced by Alexander and carried on by many of his successors, I do not consider it to be a credible conceptual foundation for our work, a position I first advanced in "Primary Control and the Crisis in Alexander Technique Theory," published in the Summer 1999 issue of *AmSAT News*.

This view of mine that has been maturing over 25 or so years wasn't at first the result of an intellectual skepticism, but rather of my own experience, or, more accurately, *non*-experience. That is, in practicing the Technique in my own daily life, I didn't actually *experience* Primary Control as my lessons and my reading of Alexander had led me to expect. I simply couldn't perceive that my head-neck relationship was in some manner acting as a general control of the use of myself. What I *did* feel was I myself controlling my own behavior so as to maintain, as far as possible, this manner of use, but that is quite a different thing from its controlling me. To anticipate a bit, that is why I say that the "control" in Primary Control is a verb— a doing—and not a noun naming a specific mechanism.

In case you aren't aware of it, Alexander didn't begin to use the term Primary Control until sometime in the 1920's. It doesn't appear at all in the writings up to and including *Constructive Conscious Control* in 1923. The only reference I've found to it before its full-blown appearance in *The Use of the Self* in 1932 was in a 1925 lecture note titled "An Unrecognized Principle in Human Behavior." Significantly, I think, in 1924 Magnus had published *Körperstellung*, his study of body posture in which he posited a *zentralcontrolapparat*—"central control apparatus"—to account for the complex of reactions—the so-called tonic neck reflexes—associated with certain passive movements of the head and neck. This work had likely become known to Alexander through his medical connections, and it's probable that he seized the opportunity to explain his own technique wholesale in terms of Magnus's quite limited results—a huge conceptual leap. Neuroscience has of course made great strides since then, and, while the general explanatory schema remains one of hierarchical organization, suggesting *some* kind of primariness in control, the action pathways, both motor and sensory, are seen to be manifoldly and widely distributed throughout the nervous system. This I wrote about at some length in "A Modern Theory of Coordination and Its Implications for the Alexander Technique" (see p. 169).

It is to Alexander's credit that he eventually outgrew the simplistic notions of Primary Control as first put forth. As I have quoted several times—and for which have been obviously though anonymously criticized in two out of five of our recent Memorial Addresses—some sort of record, perhaps—by 1943 or so Alexander was saying in a letter to Frank Pierce Jones, "There really isn't a Primary Control as such. It becomes a something in the sphere of relativity." Vis-à-vis my critics, it *is* true that I haven't seen the entire letter, in spite of several attempts to obtain it. [I since *have* seen it, with no prejudice to my citation of this sentence.] However, apart from the unequivocalness of the statement itself, and the absence of any credible refutation, there is further evidence in the words of the Master himself that his view of Primary Control underwent substantial change. In the 1932 first edition of *US*, he put it thus: "As is shewn by what follows, this [putting the head forward and up] proved to be *the* [italics added] primary control of my use in all my activities." By contrast, the third edition of 1945 has, in exactly the same place in the text, "The experiences which *followed my awareness* [italics mine] of this [putting the head forward and up] were *forerunners of a recognition of that relativity in the use of the head, neck and other parts* [italics mine] which proved to be *a* [italics mine] primary control of the general use of the self." Quite a different and much less categorical statement.

By contrast, many of Alexander's followers seem not at all to have followed their mentor's lead. Among laypersons, there was Aldous Huxley, who declared that "When the head is in a certain relation to the neck, and the neck in a certain relation to the trunk, then (it is a matter of brute empirical fact) the entire psychophysical organism is functioning to the best of its natural capacity." On the professional side, the very influential teacher Patrick Macdonald called Primary Control "a master reflex of the body, so that by organizing it one can modify all the postural relationships throughout the body," and so the line has generally run down the years.

Of course, the issue is less *what* is said than the *basis* of what is said. Perhaps Huxley, Macdonald, and everybody else, including yourself, have indeed perceived the action of a master reflex—or something like it—when heads, necks, and backs somehow enter into that special relationship. Perhaps, after all, I'm just an oddball with an Oedipal ax to grind, who has recklessly mouthed heresy based only on personal experience. Be that as it may, these are the questions I would pose for us here tonight, and ongoingly: Does Primary Control indeed have its reality only in a subjectively-shared, inner experience—an article of faith, as it were? If not, then in what *does* its reality consist? If so, then is the Technique something other—a religion, say?—than the scientifically-based discipline that it has always purported or at least aspired to be?

Jeroen Staring's *Frederick Matthias Alexander, 1869–1955:*
The Origins and History of the Alexander Technique

AmSAT News, No. 70, Spring 2006

What to make of my fitness to speak about this book? On the one hand, I've had neither the desire nor the will to read it through, even the text portion of 294 pages as distinguished from the references, 671 pages altogether in 8-point (very small) type. On the other hand, I *do* have more than a passing familiarity with the author's work, his previous book for example—*The First 43 Years of the Life of F. Matthias Alexander*—two volumes of 1,000+ pages that I read and *heard* word-for-word with my then-trainee Blake Ferger as we pursued, through reading aloud, the book's content as well as practical work in the use of the self. What then to make of Jeroen (juh-roon') Staring, the Dutch anthropologist-medical diplomate-Alexander researcher, who, on the one hand, has become the world's foremost authority on the history and literature of the Alexander Technique, but, on the other hand, Alexander's and (inevitably by association) the Technique's harshest critic?

Having raised these perplexities relative to this notice (hesitating to term it a "review" proper), the very first thing to be said—and emphatically—is that every teacher and every intending teacher of the Alexander Technique should own this book, and should regularly read in it, refer to it, and reflect on it. For the voluminous factual content and abundant illustrations alone in its handsome and high-quality cloth binding it is well-worth the price, hefty to be sure but no more so than many college textbooks. The point is that nowhere else can one find in a single source (or even in multiple sources) such a wealth of information about not only Alexander himself but also the context and world-view in which he lived, moved, and had his being. To be knowledgeable of its content is to be an educated and not only a trained Alexander professional.

Staring's motivation in all of this arose, according to his own admission, as it did or does for most of us, in an Alexander *experience*. In 1979, at the ashram of Bhagwan Shree Rajneesh in India, he was given by a Rajneesh follower what was described to him as an "Alexander massage." The resulting and unexpected feeling of lightness sparked the interest that became his passion, as he set out to learn all he could of Alexander and the technique he had developed. Like most of us, Staring has pursued the Technique over several years for its practical and personal benefits, working with a Dutch teacher from 1986–1993. But *unlike* many of us, his quest has been additionally and powerfully drawn toward the historical and conceptual bases of it. By amassing and analyzing— in what may only be termed a herculean labor—the extant historical, sociological, philosophical, and medical literature, he has arrived at an estimate of Alexander far different from what is got through the usual texts, i.e., Alexander's own writings plus those of various followers.

In brief, it is Staring's conclusion that, whatever else Alexander was as teacher, writer, and personality, he was also a plagiarist, a eugenicist, and a racist. On the evidence there seems little doubt that he was the latter two, at least to some degree: *Man's Supreme Inheritance* (1918 ed.) is explicit in positive references to "race culture"— eugenics by definition—and also contains the negative reference to "Negroes in the Southern States of America"—racism by implication if not by definition—that was officially disavowed by AmSAT in 1994. However, it is the *context* and not the fact of Alexander's eugenicism and racism that remains more open to discussion and interpretation than Staring would have it. Of the charge of plagiarism (in the broader and not solely literary sense of taking another's work without attribution), Staring's case is conceivable but not compelling. Cause-and-effect is something easier to demonstrate in the laboratory than in the hurly-burly of life as it's lived, and particularly so in the swirling currents of contemporary ideas. Bearing in mind the logical fallacy "post hoc ergo propter hoc" (after this therefore because of this), it is nevertheless instructive to learn how some of Alexander's key concepts and practices (e.g. inhibition and faulty sensory appreciation as well as aspects of the manual technique) were expressly anticipated in the late-19th century medical and therapeutic literature.

Speaking three sentences ago of "Staring's case" for Alexander's alleged plagiarism has suggested a hopefully useful analogy for dealing with this entire book, that of the adversarial nature of proceedings at law. Well-known are the roles of prosecution and defense attorneys, each to present their respective side of the case to the exclusion of the other's, their only obligation not to falsify the facts. In our situation, up to and continuing in the present, Alexander's story has been presented almost exclusively by himself and by obviously friendly witnesses. Now comes Staring, an obviously hostile witness, with a different and by no means trivial version. As in court, there can be no question of an outside authority to determine the conclusion. Hearing the different testimonies and arguments, a decision must come from ourselves as individuals in the unenviable but necessary capacity of judges or jurors and upon our weighing of the evidence. Unlike a trial, however, where there must be a clear-cut verdict (or a hung jury), in our case there need be no such black or white but rather, in at least a provisional and *personal* truth, varying shades of gray.

F. M. Alexander, Theorist First

AmSAT News No. 72, Winter 2006

"Alexander started by discovering something that works and then later coined a term to describe it."[1] Thus is the belief succinctly and confidently asserted that, in the Alexander Technique, theory follows practice. Judging from my own experience of 34 years in the Technique (most recently at the 2006 AmSAT AGM), there is little doubt that this belief is shared, explicitly or implicitly, by most Alexander teachers and students. But I believe it to be incorrect, or at least misleading, and, to that extent, harmful. Furthermore, there appears to remain in the Technique a not-so-subtle derogation of theory, an inheritance from FMA's contrarian manner of referring to "the practice and theory of my work." Of course, the issue turns on FMA's—and our own—understanding of these terms, and beyond that, how they relate to real things and events, questions this article aims to clarify.

Certainly there is *no* question that 'theory'[2] in common usage encompasses several meanings, six of which (there may be more) I've previously identified:[3]

Theory$_1$, formal predictive theory, as in the germ theory of disease.[1] [See next page for this footnote.]

---

[1] David Langstroth, "Reply to Ron Dennis' 'Primary Control and the Crisis in Alexander Technique Theory.'" See p. 33, also at http://alexandertechnique.com/ats/pcdavid.

[2] In this article, enclosure within single quotes (aside from the conventional usage for quote-within-quote) is equivalent to inserting the phrase "the word or concept *as such* of" directly before the material so enclosed. In functional Alexandrian terms, inhibition of the habitual understanding is suggested.

[3] "Reply to A Reply," See p. 42.

Theory$_2$, formal descriptive theory, as in music theory.

Theory$_3$, informal predictive theory, as in hunches, intuitions (my theory about the race tomorrow ...).

Theory$_4$, informal descriptive theory, as in explanations (his theory on the Technique ...)

Theory$_5$, formal speculative theory, as in Plato's theory of virtue.

Theory$_6$, informal speculative theory, as in opinions (her theory regarding the case ...).

'Practice' (as a noun) also has different meanings according to usage. Particularly as distinguished from theory, according to Webster, it is "the actual performance or application of knowledge."[2]

It is clear from the foregoing that theory is necessarily[3] a function of brain activity, in the form of symbols (words and images), while practice is necessarily that of muscle activity, in the form of contractions (our only means of affecting the environment). But it is equally clear that in a human being there can be no arbitrary separation of brain activity (mind) and muscle activity (body): at least under the organism-as-a-whole assumption, they do not co-exist as separate entities but are rather separate *aspects* of a total and unified functioning. Perhaps in

---

[1] The numeric subscripts are a device of Korzybski's General Semantics; see Susan Presby Kodish and Bruce Kodish, *Drive Yourself Sane: Using the Uncommon Sense of General Semantics*, Rev. 2nd Ed. (Pasadena: Extensional Publishing, 2001).

[2] *Webster's New International Dictionary of the English Language* (Second Edition Unabridged, 1940).

[3] Though obviously not solely.

some rarified sense the newborn is a virtually practical being and the dreamer a virtually theoretical one, but, for a language-imbued, conscious, and otherwise normal adult, the real-life hazards to clarity are those of (1) premature cognitive commitment[1]—taking a position in advance of sufficient information, and (2) reification—regarding or treating an abstraction or idea as if it had concrete or material existence.[2]

FMA himself came to understand this latter hazard with regard to mind and body, as he relates in *The Use of the Self*,[3] but apparently not to theory and practice. For him, the fact of his having gradually worked out the Technique as a response to a real and present problem, in contrast to having thought it through first, and then applied it, constituted practice. Explaining *how* it worked—theory—in contrast to *that* it worked—practice—came, or would come, afterward. But this "afterward" is precisely the realm of *formal descriptive theory* (Theory$_2$, above), and not that of *informal predictive theory* (Theory$_3$) that is decisive in all creative work. Everyone has experienced the process of trial-and-error (more properly, "hunch-and-trial"[4]) in working out problems great and small. Indeed, FMA launched the investigations that led ultimately to his Technique based on the hunch (hypothesis, if you like) voiced to his doctor as reported in *US*, " 'Is it not fair, then,' I asked him [his doctor], 'to conclude that it was

---

[1] Ellen J. Langer, *Mindfulness* ((Reading, MA: Addison-Wesley, 1989).

[2] *The American Heritage Dictionary of the English Language* (1969).

[3] Chap. 1, "Evolution of a Technique."

[4] Although quite sure of not having made it up, I can no longer find my source for this phrase. However, the pivotal role of insight—hunch, intuition, lucky guess, etc.—in problem solving is illuminated by Hubert L. Dreyfus in *What Computers Can't Do: The Limits of Artificial Intelligence*, Rev. Ed. (New York: Harper & Row, 1979), pp. 112-120.

something I was doing that evening in using my voice that was the cause of the trouble?'" [FMA's italics].[1]

Thus, by his own testimony, FMA was mistaken in referring to "the practice and theory of my work," not only in point of historical precedence but also in point of emphasis. Indeed, how could the Technique have come to pass at all without that particular hunch, intuition, hypothesis, or Theory3, call it what you will?![2] Nor was it a trivial error, for this facile transposition of terms has influenced the mindset and thought of Alexandrian generations down to the present. It is truly unfortunate that FMA, as consciously the leader of a new and important movement, spoke with such effect, to the detriment of truth, about this aspect of his work.

I hope it might be clear by now why I speak of FMA as theorist first. Not that he "discovered something first and then described it," but that he had an idea first and then worked on it. Working on it led to new ideas—theories—and so on and so on. Theory is not a separate and concrete thing, but rather the name given to the psycho-physical process that enables us to reflect upon and so contingently to modify the beliefs and opinions that decisively affect our ongoing use-of-self. Likewise, practice refers to the relatively stable physico-psychical means by which ideas are realized. Theory and practice should be joined so—theory-practice—as, in a late letter, FMA ad-

---

[1] *US* (Centerline Press Ed., 1984), p. 8.

[2] Even Theory1 —*formal predictive theory*—has become viable in the Technique, as shown by Michael Protzel's work in "weight commitment" ("Why Do We Tense Our Necks," *AmSAT News*, No. 62, pp. 17-19). His theory, developed through practice and at least personally testable, essentially predicts that *when body weight is correctly committed, certain favorable postural reactions occur.* Thanks to Michael and also to Bruce Kodish for their valuable assistance in preparing this article.

vised Frank Pierce Jones to do with 'mental' and 'physical.'[1] To commit prematurely, to understand practice as somehow self-contained, without the contributions of generative, corrective, and explanatory thought, is fundamentally to *mis*understand the very nature of human voluntary action. Thus, if we do wish to use these terms at all, we should *not* do so in ignorance of their full dimensionality and in a manner that influences for the worse the quality of the very thinking-doing we seek to enhance.

---

[1] Letter dated December, 1945, copy courtesy of John Nicholls. "Join the words mental and physical with a -- so (mental-physical)."

Our Next Mission Statement

AmSAT News No. 77, Summer 2008

Actually, I was ready to broach this material in its entirety at our recent AGM but refrained out of consideration for the Mission Statement Committee, whose efforts and results I had taken part in, for the Meeting itself, which I thought should be spared undue even if procedurally correct deliberations, and also for my own wish to air these present views in a more reflective, less reactive venue. For those who weren't at AGM, last February after the Committee had submitted its report for publication, I conducted an informal survey among my recent students to get a feel for which candidate-statement had the most "audience appeal." To my surprise and discomfiture, out of 36 people surveyed with 16 responses, eight chose the statement that I had set out two years ago to replace: "To define, maintain, and promote the Alexander Technique at its highest standard of professional practice and conduct." Not conclusive, to be sure, but impressive, this result certainly challenged my own, and, I daresay, the Committee's prior assumptions about that particular mission statement (Statement #1 received no votes, #2 and #3 each received four votes.)

It wasn't the numbers, however, that decisively moved my thinking, but this unsolicited comment of one of my respondents: "As my husband says, members of the public who looks [sic] to the mission statement to see whether Alexander Technique is a sexual practice or an investment strategy will find no guidance in *any* [italics added] of these choices. They are all rather vague and some sound a bit more like spiritual principles than help for those of us with sore backs." This pithy observation jump-started and expanded a line of thought I'd taken up many years before, in "What's In A Name," from my own

Atlanta Alexander News (No. 17, Summer 1994)). In this article I quoted Walter Carrington's comment, as reported to me by Michael Frederick, who had heard it in person, "This work will never come into its own as long as it is known as the Alexander Technique." To me, this unexpected remark shows the genuine concern of a supremely dedicated and revered Alexander teacher over the exact issue posed offhandedly by my student's husband, namely, *the Alexander Technique of what?* This lack of specificity in our name and aim surely is a liability in our effort to gain broader acceptance, and is what makes the *right* mission statement, one that truly serves us rather than being mainly an exercise in idealism, especially important for us.

Of course, the right mission statement needs the right words, and we're all aware of the difficulty in pinning down the Technique conceptually or definitionally. For every proposal along these lines someone will quickly point out in what manner or degree the attempt is lacking. And this is no doubt due in large part to the overarching nature of the Technique itself, as FMA himself and others — John Dewey, notably — were at pains to point out. But it is also because we have had a hard time saying anything really incisive about the Technique without trying to say everything about it, an obviously futile effort. It is this attitude, at least in part, that contributes to our tendency to think and speak about it in the language of "spiritual principles," as perceived by my student's husband, and our reluctance to seek out and articulate its essence in worldly and "sore-back" terms. In this sense I can wholeheartedly agree with the charge "to define" the Alexander Technique, provided that we now take it seriously and act upon it.

Not, as has been pointed out, that the mission statement need (or can) provide a genuinely descriptive definition of the Technique (see my "Defining Primary Control," *AmSAT News* No. 64), but rather that it can and should sufficiently *characterize* it in *plainly recognizable terms*. A couple of points, however, before going into that dangerous zone. The first is that the problem really isn't one, or at least can no longer be considered one, of *branding*, as implied by Carrington. "Alexander Technique," for better and worse, has without doubt become deeply and permanently rooted as our public identity. (As an aside, one might ponder how psychoanalysis would have fared as "The Freud Technique"; many's the story would've been told about this Viennese doctor who had weird dreams!) No, not branding, the issue rather is one of *positioning* — "determining exactly what niche your offering is intended to fill"— in the realm of educating people about products and services, otherwise known as *marketing* (Jay Conrad Levinson, *Guerrilla Marketing*, 1984, p. 23).

Getting back to the mission statement, as I said in Committee deliberations, " ... in the broader world, where our mission statement presumably will appear prominently on web site, stationery, [brochures and other informational materials,] etc., we certainly must conceive it as epitomizing AmSAT [and the Technique] to whomever encounters it for whatever reason." *It is this always-together association coming as the first impression of us that makes the mission statement such a crucial element of our public image.* It behooves us therefore to devote whatever further effort may be necessary, including professional assistance, to get it right — not only a mission statement that we agree on but one that *works* for us. Thus, as I have come to see it, our mission statement should be less for our own guidance, as has been proposed, than for the public's, who, surveying a broad field ranging, as it were, from aerobics to Zen, needs therein to place the Technique *quickly, accurately, and positively.* Thus we come to it, my candidate for our next mission statement: *To establish the Alexander Technique of therapeutic postural education as a basic and recognized resource for health, productivity, and well-being.*

Whatever your immediate reaction to these words, and trusting in your inhibitory powers, I ask you to bear with me just a bit further. Regarding "therapeutic," beyond the benign meaning of the word itself — "Having healing or curative powers; *gradually or methodically ameliorative*" [italics added] — aren't any regulatory concerns about it considerably less pressing now than previously in view of favorable precedents and growth in the alternative health arena? Isn't the "postural" dimension of our work already widely understood and accepted as its focus among people who seek us out? Isn't it precisely *this* "education"— to be sure, through inhibition, direction, primary control, and all the rest — that most Alexander teachers in fact have been and are doing with most of their students most of the time? If you can't answer yes to these questions as readily as I, then I can only encourage you to think through and communicate your own answers and reasons.

Two points in closing. First, I re-surveyed the 16 respondents of my original group (nine males, seven females, age range 21-62, median 48), asking them to indicate which statement they thought stronger between the first-round winner ("To define, maintain, and promote etc.") and my "next mission statement." This time, of 16 responses, 11 chose the latter and four the former, with one undecided; collating both surveys showed that six chose the latter even from the eight choosing the former the first time around. Surely, as we move ahead, proposed mission statements or components thereof should be subjected to similar "real-world" testing. Second, I did a literal (in quotes) search on the web of "therapeutic postural education" and found exactly zero instances, suggesting that this phrase might serve quite handily "to delineate exactly the niche our offering is intended to fill."

On "Postural Education"

AmSAT News No. 80, Summer 2009

With the creation of the Ad Hoc Committee at AGM 2009 comes to the fore the question of whether an explanatory phrase should be included in our mission statement and, if so, what such a phrase should be. After three years of active thought and research, my opinion is that the mission statement gains strength by such inclusion, and that the phrase should be "postural education."[1] Yet I realize, judging from the incredulous reactions I got when running it by some colleagues at AGM, that this language will be initially resisted because it is perceived as too limiting and misleading for the Technique's true scope. At first blush this objection seems valid enough, but there also can be little doubt that "postural education" in its various aspects—musculoskeletal, respiratory, vocal—is the principal reason that people come for lessons, and further, that this phrase communicates broadly to delineate our professional expertise across several audiences— general, medical, academic, artistic. Thus, in this article I will argue that rather than rejecting it as too narrow, we instead expand our own view of "postural education," so as not to squander this powerful communicative concept.

---

[1] All assertions in this article, and indeed any assertions on the subject, may and should be tested by appropriate survey or interview techniques. For example, in my "Food for Thought" handout at AGM 2009, which detailed responses of six members of a nonprofit small-business consulting organization, as to their preference of my mission statement versus the Board's, three of the six—two explicitly— favored an explanatory phrase, while one suggested that the Board's statement left open the possibility that "the undefined product could change at the whim of the teachers"!

I begin with the easier word "education," which seems already generally accepted in our community. Alexander, however, consistently spoke of "re-education," and there are those who think this usage should be respected and retained. But, in terms of actual meaning, "re-education" seems faulty. For if "education" (as opposed to "learning") implies the intentional and systematic inculcation of broadly adaptive understandings and behaviors, and if virtually no one has been so educated in their habits of use "BA" (Before Alexander), then it follows that pursuing the Technique later in life is distinctly an educational and not re-educational process.

Regarding "postural," my argument relies on two sources, the first an obscure article (though one discussed at length by Raymond Dart in "The Attainment of Poise") by Beckett Howorth, M.D. of New York, from the *Journal of the American Medical Association* in 1946, and the second from the massive *Neurophysiology of Postural Mechanisms* of Tristan D. M. Roberts, a world-class physiologist of Glasgow, already somewhat known in Alexandrian circles mainly via Walter Carrington and associates.

The title of Howorth's article, "Dynamic Posture," is revealing, the first paragraph meriting full quotation as to his central theme:

Posture has long been thought of in terms of standing and sitting, and correct posture as the erect position assumed when one is under inspection, but posture should really be considered as *the sum total of the positions and movements of the body throughout the day and throughout life* [my italics]. It should include not only the fundamental static positions in lying, sitting and standing, and the variation of these positions but also the dynamic postures of the body in motion or in action, for *it is here that posture becomes most important and most effective* [my italics]. Posture has a direct relation to the comfort, mechanical efficiency and physiologic functioning of the individual.[1]

Here and throughout is a conception very close to that of Alexandrian Use, though Howorth's analysis of dynamic posture, conveyed partially through simple line drawings illustrative of poor and good posture in both static and dynamic modes, seems primitive in comparison with that of Alexander, who understood and exploited the unifying principle of Length. But my purpose here really isn't to compare the two but to point out that in "dynamic posture" is a conception allowing us vitally to broaden our own view in this area.

Although Roberts' work is gigantic in comparison with Howorth's, they are alike in providing the information requisite to our present need in their first paragraph. Here then is Roberts:

A movement may be thought of as a change in posture. Alternatively, one might be tempted to regard the voluntary movements of the hands in man as something different from the posture of the rest of the body, so that 'posture' and 'movement' could be dealt with separately. However, even such small movements of the fingers as occur in writing, commonly involve adjustments in the activity of the muscles of the arm, and often there are accompanying head movements also as the eyes follow the task in hand. These adjustments of the head and arms alter the disposition of the weight of the body in relation to the supports, so that muscles in many different parts of the body become involved, as, for example, in the other arm, or in the legs and trunk. All this background activity needs to be accurately co-ordinated for the successful performance of the desired movement of the fingers. *There is no difficulty in regarding the background activity as 'postural'* [my italics]. Accordingly, because this background activity is essential to the successful performance of the

------

[1] *JAMA*, August 26, 1946, pp. 1398-1404.

voluntary movement itself and has to be co-ordinated with it, there are advantages in *treating the whole process as a unity* [my italics].[1]

What a magnificent statement of Alexander's conception of Use! And to be sure, in our mission statement, we would prefer to proclaim "the Alexander Technique of Use Education"! Alas, because the concept of Use in our sense is unknown to those with whom we want and need to communicate, it just isn't possible. But fortunately it does become possible, in light of the foregoing and in the security of our own heightened understanding, for us confidently to speak, to those who would hear, of "postural education." Surely, when they come, our students can and will be led to the fuller meaning—the unique heritage of our work—in this phrase.

I close rhetorically with a question I would have asked actually at AGM had the opportunity arisen: How many of us are aware of Posture-Based Chiropractic? I wasn't at all until recently, when, doing some Web research into postural analysis software, I found that several such programs were being used by chiropractors for purposes of patient screening and recruitment. Now, I do hope that we as Alexander teachers *know* that posture, however we define or refine the concept, is *our* field of expertise, and that we also know, or should, that the chiropractic profession has never been shy about promoting itself. Thus, lest we slumber too long before clearly staking out our professional claim, I ask you to hear anew that historic cry, now directed squarely at us, "The Chiropractors are coming, the Chiropractors are coming"!

---

[1] *Neurophysiology of Postural Mechanisms*, Second Ed., Butterworth & Co., 1978, p. 9.

Posture, Postural Education, and the Alexander Technique

AmSAT News No. 81, Winter 2009

This article is both for general readers—notably but not exclusively those of scientific-critical outlook—and also for specialists in the Alexander Technique and like-oriented disciplines. For both groups, my purpose is illumination of the three title-designated subjects in rigorous but accessible form and language. As will be shown, "posture" can be more fully and usefully understood in terms of its overall nature and significance in bodily functioning, in contrast with its more usual relegation in popular thought to bodily appearance as in, for example, military drill, balletic display, or "standing up straight." The section symbol § has been employed to suggest that the present material—really an outline—could indeed be expanded by way of documentation, explanation, and/or illustration.

---

§1. **Definition:** Posture comprises the flow through space and time of all activity of bodily support and movement in the course of living.

§2. The effect of posture as response to gravitational stress on bodily functioning is constant (*stress* as in Mechanics—"an applied force or system of forces that tends to strain or deform a body").

§3. Support and movement do not exist apart from each other in the living person; all support involves movement, all movement involves support.

§4. Neither do body and mind exist apart from each other in the living person; rather, these terms refer to different aspects of one unified process. Posture must be viewed inclusively as support-movement, body-mind, or, as characteristically in the Alexander Technique, *psycho-physical* activity.

§5. A comprehensively valid approach to posture must recognize and take into account in its theory and practice this constant, unified, psycho-physical process.

§6. Posture is not fixed from biological inheritance but evolves as a learning process from its genetic and developmental base; posture is a function both of innate factors (reflexes, broadly speaking) and of habit (acquired stereotypical behavior).

§7. Because the innate and acquired aspects of postural development proceed continuously and simultaneously from birth onwards, only in very general terms can a distinction be made in the living person between the given and the acquired.

§8. Generally, the acquired or habitual aspect of posture develops contingently (by learning) rather than systematically (by training), as a function of the individual's conscious and unconscious responses to the physical, emotional, and cognitive demands of the life as actually lived.

§9. To the extent that postural habit is learned, it can through conscious effort be re-learned or modified.

§10. All the foregoing, particularly the *contingency* of postural habit as acquired (§8), imply an issue of *quality* in the individual's posture, i.e., to what extent this particular posture that has developed is a factor for better or worse in terms of overall functioning.

§11. Where quality is an issue, assessment is relevant; postural quality can be assessed.

§12. Postural quality varies from moment to moment; the assessment of postural quality, whether by an outside observer or by the individual in question, is always conditional relative to the present moment. Assertions about stable postural quality ("I *have* good/bad posture") are thus undue generalizations, subject to further observation and assessment. "Right now" is the only available time for such assessment.

§13. The assessment of postural quality by an outside observer implies comprehensive knowledge of posture as here delineated combined with experience in applying this knowledge to individual variability. Such knowledge and experience comprise the professional qualifications and practice of a Teacher of the Alexander Technique.

§14. Ultimately, the assessment of postural quality may be accomplished only by the self-aware individual, through comparing manifest action in real time with *a sufficiently valid subjective criterion of postural quality.*

§15. Psycho-physically, this criterion is termed "accurate proprioceptive perception."*

§16. Accurate proprioceptive perception gives a *sense* of manifest posture corresponding to the actuality of that posture: disparity between perception and reality can occur because *postural habit conditions postural percep-*

---

* Proprioception is the normal ongoing awareness, mediated by the action of proprioceptors, of the position, balance, and movement of one's own body, or any of its parts; a proprioceptor is a receptor [nerve cell sensitive to stretch, pressure, displacement] located in muscle, tendon, joint, or vestibular apparatus, whose reflex function is locomotor or postural (*Blakiston's Pocket Medical Dictionary*). Kinesthesis (movement sense), often used synonymously, is actually a subset of proprioception.

tion. For example, the individual with a clearly observable head tilt does not necessarily perceive it as such because visual mechanisms compensate to maintain an upright or "straight" visual field, leading to an unconscious and often-inaccurate postural self-assessment. Many examples of this association between postural habit and proprioceptive perception could be cited; experience over its long history qualifies the Alexander Technique to claim that inaccurate proprioceptive perception is not only common but also detrimental to normal functioning in varying degrees among so-called normal as well as symptomatic individuals.

§17. The development through an educational process of accurate proprioceptive perception is thus the main purpose of work in the Alexander Technique.

§18. This educational process provides direct experiences in real time of correct or normal posture: *correct experiences condition the individual toward correct and accurate perception.*

§19. Posture is *normal* when the individual's bodily movement and support are carried out with the skeleton in general and the spine in particular at optimal structural dimension. Minimizing structural stress and preventing strain require that the jointed bodily structure is mechanically well-organized over the base of support. Statically, this organization is usually termed "alignment;" dynamically, there appears to be no descriptive term other than the generic "movement." The Alexander Technique incorporates both static and dynamic aspects of bodily organization in the practical process called "lengthening."

§20. Conceptually, "lengthening" means that in standing, sitting, walking, bending, or in any activity whatever, one must prevent both unnecessary muscular effort and undue distortions of the natural curves of the spine; full appropriation of "lengthening," however, comes only through experience.

§21. Posture is sub-normal when, through incomplete response to the gravitational challenge and/or unduly contracted musculature, the individual is not lengthening.

§22. "Lengthening" by whatever name is the required principle that unifies the theory of posture as both support and movement. In practice, this principle enables the Alexander Technique teacher to assess postural quality reliably and, through the employment of manual and verbal cues and without arbitrary physical exercises, to provide experiences of normal posture leading to accurate proprioceptive perception.

Letter to the Editor

AmSAT News No. 84, Winter 2010

Michael Protzel alleges "significant error" in aspects of my "Posture, Postural Education, and the Alexander Technique" (*AmSAT News,* Winter 2009, Issue #81). He says that human beings do not "respond" to gravity, but rather "partner" with it, apparently because responses (in the narrow sense) can only occur as a function of prior stimuli, as in classical Stimulus-Response theory. If I understand Protzel's point correctly, he would evidently argue that, because gravity is a constant, there can be no question of a response, but only of an ongoing relationship, "partnering," as it were.

However, there is a broader conception of "response" as "some more or less complex collection of movements which can be selected from a repertoire of such movements and described with sufficient exactitude so that common agreement among observers can be attained" (B. R. Bugelski, *An Introduction to Psychology,* 2nd Edition, New York: Bobbs-Merrill, 1973, p. 41). Surely there would be common agreement among observers that humans do adjust to different gravitational requirements of the terrestrial environment (as in walking up and down hill, for example) by such more or less complex collections of movements.

Protzel states that "Gravity is not the problem," implying that I think it is. But I do not think so, neither did I say so: gravity simply *is.* I wrote that gravity is a *stressor*—in mechanical terms a force tending to change the shape of, or "de-form," our own and all other bodies—and that our variable adjustment or response to this force is a constant.

Thus, I will accept a criticism of inadequately defining "respond," but not of the substance of the concept.

The Posturality of the Person

AmSAT Journal No. 2, Fall 2012

Of Alexander's language John Dewey said, "… his exposition is made in the simplest English, free of technical words … ."[1] Surely, "the use of self"—in its sphere a profound and unique conception—would seem to be a prime exemplar of that appraisal. Yet this phrase that, serving its proper function, should clearly proclaim the domain of Alexander's technique, has over the years largely failed to do so. "The use of the self" in answer to the query "What's Alexander, anyway?" will likely get you a puzzled "huh?", together with probable loss in the fledgling conversation of initiative if not credibility.

In the case of "use," I submit that this is the situation because, in addition to its inherent ambiguity as either noun or verb, Alexander gave to it an unconventional meaning for human behavior, thereby making of it a technical and esoteric term. And "self" carries a distinct conceptual burden, baggage from philosophy, spiritual disciplines, clinical and popular psychology, as well as a suggestion of personal indulgence. All this is truly unfortunate, because "the use of the self," correctly understood, in five syllables of breathtaking conceptual elegance, obviates the entrenched and specious dualisms of "posture-movement" and "body-mind," and additionally brings to the concept an ethical dimension germane to all voluntary action. But, as G. Spencer Brown has observed in *Laws of Form*, an elegance ("literally, the capacity to

---

[1] In *Constructive Conscious Control of the Individual*, "Introduction" (Centerline Press, 1985), p. xxi.

pick out or elect") in exposition may by its very brevity or condensation be difficult to understand.[1]

Which brings us to "the posturality of the person," not that I for a moment consider it a panacea for the communicational challenges of the Technique. But it does couch the Technique's essential subject matter in terms that are at least unambiguous, as well as relatively unencumbered by the barnacles of association that tend to attach themselves to concepts over time. "Posturality" in its very unaccustomedness perhaps has a capacity, lacking in "use," to pique the curiosity. Strangely enough the term came to me in a dream: I was in a situation where singers were being coached and I, noticing one with obvious postural problems, was trying to work with him. His vocal teacher told me to butt out, that *he* was the musical authority. "But I wasn't dealing with his musicality," I remonstrated, "but with his *posturality*." Thus the genesis of a new concept!

For we find no difficulty at all in referring to a person's mentality, physicality, vitality, spirituality, even normality—why not "posturality"? As Webster tells us, the suffix –*ity* "indicates a state or quality." Recalling my definition, "Posture comprises the flow through space and time of all activity of bodily support and movement in the course of living,"[2] surely the state and especially the quality of the person's *posture*—the only means by which environment can be affected—is worthy of being understood via the suffix that is so readily attached to other traits.

---

[1] (New York: The Julian Press, Inc., 1972), p. 81.
[2] "Posture, Postural Education, and The Alexander Technique," *AmSAT News* (No. 81, Winter 2009), p. 15.

Not, by any means, that I'm drawing these distinctions purely as an academic exercise, but rather to demonstrate that for our present purposes in the Technique, *the nouns "posturality" and "use" may be taken as synonymous.* Doing so has the immediate advantage of linking a large part of our practical work with an already-familiar concept, granted that there remains an educational challenge in reforming the common understanding of posture.

To be sure, there is a connotation in "use" lacking in "posturality," that of an implicit *morality.* For to use something at all—certainly the self—implies not only the manner of this use but also its purpose, always subject as voluntary action to moral judgment. That Alexander was acutely aware of this dimension of his work is clear: "Talk about a man's individuality and character; it's the way he uses himself."[1] But it is also clear from the writings that his overriding concern in the actual teaching was the overall quality of use in postural terms, and not the specific purposes to which the use was put.[2] Thus, in positioning the Technique for a credible 21st-century professionalism—our scope of practice, as it were— "posturality" keeps the focus relatively sharp.

I'm not suggesting here that "the posturality of the person" can be an all-purpose, user-friendly, media-savvy,

---

[1] Edward Maisel, *The Resurrection of the Body* (New York: Dell Publishing Co., 1969), "Notes of Instruction," p. 12.

[2] See, for example, *Man's Supreme Inheritance* (Dutton, 1918) Chap. VII, "Notes and Instances," Part III, "The Theory and Practice of a New Method of Respiratory Education"; *Constructive Conscious Control of the Individual* (Centerline Press, 1985), Chap. IV, "Illustration," Chap. V, "Respiratory Mechanisms"; *The Use of the Self* (Centerline Press, 1984), Chap. I, "Evolution of a Technique," Chap. V, "Diagnosis and Medical Training"; *The Universal Constant in Living* (Dutton, 1941), Chap. II, "The Constant Influence of Manner of Use in Relation to Diagnosis and Disease."

explanatory and/or descriptive phrase for the Technique any more than can "the use of the self": it is just too ponderous, even if synonymous. But, in accepting their conceptual equivalence, we gain the possibility, through becoming more open in our own consciousness, of an explanatory phrase—*postural education*—that is *fully* justified in the practice and theory of the founder, as well as being accessible conceptually to the public we seek to reach. Not to re-hash the arguments I've made for this phrase, I continue to believe that *not* clearly to delineate our work in the public eye and mind is to leave the field negligently open for others[1] that we, through Alexander, have so diligently pioneered, cleared, and worked.

---

[1] For example, a recent Web search on "posture-based chiropractic" yielded about 344,000 hits.

Response to Walton (Larry) White

Unpublished, distributed at the 2011 Annual
Conference and General Meeting, Las Vegas

In the Spring 2011 issue of *AmSAT News*, Larry White takes issue with my advocacy of "therapeutic postural education" as a descriptive phrase for the Technique to be included in our mission statement. Never mind that he is a little late—in 2009 and again in 2010 I announced in *AmSAT News* that I was dropping "therapeutic"—his criticism remains close enough to the mark to require this response.

I have never advocated "postural education" in the sense of comprehensive accuracy about the Technique, but strictly as the most accessibly valid concept to identify the Technique to the public with which we are constantly trying to improve our relations—so that they will find it useful to employ us. I believe that we need to decisively, publicly, and consistently answer the obvious question, "Alexander Technique of *what*?" I can truthfully charac-terize (and I would invite all Alexander teachers to reflect deeply on this in their own experience) the focus of *every* Alexander lesson I've ever had—including ones with Frank Pierce Jones, Walter Carrington, Patrick Macdon-ald, Marjorie Barstow, Goddard Binkley, Deborah Caplan, and Judith Leibowitz—as "postural education." But not in the sense of Larry White's apparently limited concep-tion of posture as "standing up straighter" (he gives us no other, only that "most people" think so), but in that of my published definition that *"Posture comprises the flow through space and time of all activity of bodily support and movement in the course of living."*

Larry White is concerned about "correctly informing the public about the nature of our work." He says that what

we are really out to teach is "how to inhibit certain counterproductive habits and direct a change in the head,
neck, and back relationship to produce a more harmonious response." What *I* am really out to teach are principles and practices leading toward a normal *posturality*
(the state or quality of one's posture, as defined above).
What I bring to that endeavor as an Alexander teacher is
a valid and workable theory—in Alexander's words, *a
lengthened stature*—plus the practical experience of—
again his words, "seeing people and trying to help
them"—using his tools of inhibition and direction both
explicitly and implicitly, and—most importantly—being
able to *see* normal posturality in students as they are
presently with me in the lesson and to take them in that
direction. There being no way of correctly informing the
public about all of that in the very limited time available
for a crucial first impression, I have not found, nor has
anyone else formally put forth, a better alternative than
"postural education." "Psychophysical" in the various
associations suggested by Larry White, only obfuscates
the issue, as it not only refers to an already established
branch of psychology—psychophysics—but also points to
method rather than content in our work. I would suggest
that it is in the hope of results that people come to see us,
caring less about our specific methods (unless they're
Alexander teachers!) than about help for their problems.
So, while it is true that "postural education" is not comprehensively descriptive of the Technique, it is sufficiently
true within a very broad range for purposes of communication.

Larry White makes the point that "postural education"
could also be used to describe yoga, and implicitly, other
things out there such as Pilates, Rolfing, and Feldenkrais,
to name the obvious, but also including posture-based
chiropractic and even the posture-explicit method of
Esther Gokhale, whose book on "natural posture solu-

tions" currently has 377$_{2014}$ five-star reviews on amazon.com. There are also many types of shampoo, automobiles, and medications on the market—welcome to capitalism. The question needs be asked and answered, not how Alexander is unique, but rather how it is *superior* to other approaches, superior because it has a valid and workable theory of normal—which is by no means to say *common*—posturality, and teachers who are expert in providing experiences of that normality *in real time*. That is the broad, open path to spreading the message. To "indirectly promote curiosity and an interest in learning more," as Larry White suggests, may perhaps be appreciated in ideological terms, but risks being swamped by the tsunami of information that is the reality of today.

Letter, *AmSAT Jounal,* Spring 2014

I wish to thank Claire Rechnitzer and *AmSAT Journal* for the review of my book, *The Posturality of the Person: A Guide to Postural Education and Therapy,* published in Issue No. 4. Many aspects of the book were discussed accurately (and gratifyingly, I must add), but there is a further, and actually main, aspect, that I would like to bring out for the attention and consideration of colleagues.

Namely, it was my intention, as I said in the Introduction, to present "a comprehensive, comprehensible, and workable theory of *normal posturality.*" This was the overriding purpose of my Chapter 2, "Conceptual Foundations," the "22 logically ordered concepts" mentioned in the review [see "Posture, Postural Education, and the Alexander Technique," p. 265]. Taken together, these foundational statements delineate the necessary concepts and conditions for *any* full and valid approach to postural education. Relative to any approach other than ours, the Conceptual Foundations provide a *prescription for,* but for the Alexander Technique they already constitute a *description of,* if in perhaps unfamiliar terms, such an approach. For example, what Alexander called "reliable sensory appreciation" becomes "accurate proprioceptive perception" (§15), a psycho-physically more specific description of the processes most dominant in postural education. Indeed, the book's very title—*The Posturality of the Person*—is but a more specific and descriptive way of saying *The Use of the Self.*

It has long been my belief that we engage in an elegant and effective practice without a coherent theory— "theory" here meaning a formal *and consensual* statement of principles and procedures. Of course, reams have been written on the Technique, beginning with the founder, and overflowing explanations, experiences, and insights given about it. But, except for my Conceptual Foundations, I know of nowhere—and if anyone else does, please inform me—that can be found a clear, concise, and yet comprehensive statement of what we believe and practice, *as professionals.*

Why am I so occupied (some would say, obsessed) with "theory"? Simply because theory as verbal expression is the only means that we have, short of hands-on contact or other sensory demonstration, for communicating to the unknowing world, and also to ourselves, what it is that we do, and why, and how. If we cannot, or will not, thus consensually communicate, then we overreach in calling ourselves a profession, and will likely continue to experience the relative neglect accorded our beloved work these hundred-odd years.

How We Learn the Alexander Technique

AmSAT Journal, In Press
[Published No. 7, Spring 2015]

I want to identify an aspect of the process by which the educational content of the Alexander Technique is taken up and applied outside the lesson, where most of the *learning,* as contrasted with the *instruction*, must necessarily take place. I will suggest that this learning occurs largely as a function of an acquired Cognitive-Proprioceptive Model (CPM), potentially one that is progressively more comprehensive and accurate. Perhaps the term cognitive-proprioceptive promptly suggests itself as a sort of pointy-headed version of FMA's psycho-physical, but there is an important distinction: Psycho-physical is of very broad reference, implying, in the vocabulary of psychology, the whole of the affective (emotional), cognitive, and motor domains of human functioning. Cognitive-proprioceptive, on the other hand, is quite specific, referring to thinking in its usual connotation (including imagination and memory), as well as to the neurological sensing of support and movement information from within the body. The latter terminology seems much closer to the actual scope and practice of our work, and therefore more appropriate to the theory of that work, regardless of one's personal view of the Technique relative to the totality of the human condition.

I begin by describing some aspects of a typical Alexander Technique lesson from the viewpoint of an observer without particular foreknowledge, say from Mars. Two adults are fully clothed, in a room containing a straight chair, a massage-type table, and a mirror. One does most, but not all, of the speaking, and from time to time places hands on the other's body, often in the region of head and neck and also on the torso (but excluding the breasts, to be sure)—this one will be referred to as the "speaker/toucher." A portion of the observation period, perhaps 15 minutes, is spent with the speaker/toucher apparently and repeatedly assisting the other—the "touchee"—to sit down on and rise from the chair, using both verbal and manual cues and sometimes the mirror in this process. In another phase, the speaker/toucher adjusts the position of the touchee's body while the latter reclines on the table. Some of the words and phrases heard during both phases of the period, which lasts a half hour or more, are "inhibition," "direction," "primary control," "head," "neck," "back," "hip-joints," and "torso." Physical or verbal manifestations of affect (pleasure, confusion, etc.) might also be observed. The session comes to a close with the speaker/toucher assisting the touchee to get up from the table, and then to walk about the room. Finally, the speaker/toucher (hereinafter, "teacher") receives compensation in some form from the touchee (hereinafter, "student"), another meeting-time is arranged, and the student leaves.

I have cast this scenario in such stark terms to highlight how the very rich meaning of the Alexander Technique boils down for the student to certain perceptions, concepts, and affective responses that occur during the lesson. What the student takes away, however, is not these perceptions and concepts per se, but rather the memory of them. It is through relying upon these memories, always selective and imperfect, that the student inwardly transforms and works with the lesson experience. This inner working-through of received material is essentially a process of modeling, of making one thing represent ("re-present") in a lesser way something that is greater. In daily life, students hopefully summon this model in times of remembering and awareness, sometimes more and sometimes less explicitly, as a guide for their responses and actions in real time.

What paradoxically characterizes one's CPM at any given time is, on the one hand, its distinct presence, yet on the other, its indistinct composition. As I said in "Defining Primary Control" (*AmSAT News* No. 64, Summer 2004) and elsewhere, idea and experience ineffably meet and blend in each unique "empersonment" (that's you, bub) of the Technique. And, as with any model, the quality of the result depends upon the quality of the maker's motivation, talent, and materials. Motivation and talent belong necessarily to the maker—the student—and will always remain more-or-less given and variable among individuals. Materials, on the other hand, real enough during the lesson, become "virtual" in the form of memories afterwards. This constitutes the central problem for Alexander Technique teachers: providing the materials in such form and content as to be remembered most accurately (and positively, to be sure) by the student.

Appendix I

Whither NASTAT?

I've included this essay in an Appendix because it doesn't really fit in any of the other "books" comprising the present work, and yet it really couldn't be left out. While for me not the most important piece I ever wrote,* it was certainly the most controversial, as may be seen by reader responses in subsequent issues of NASTAT NEWS. Never published there, it was circulated among the membership as part of my campaign for NASTAT Chair in 1994, which even to now$_{2014}$—twenty years later—was the last contested election for that office. That I lost the election clearly was not because my platform was equivocal. "Whither" thus belongs to a period of considerable ferment in the American Alexander Scene, a period now—to many newer teachers at least—of almost quaintly "historical" interest, whose salient issues will unlikely and unfortunately ever be more constructively resolved.

In my article "An Overview of Alexander Politics,"** I referred to the formation of NASTAT as, in effect, "a political alliance between STAT and ACAT," and also said "the fact is that the establishment of NASTAT left unachieved the full unification of the American Alexander profession." I now propose to expand upon those themes in order to articulate a vision for the future direction of this Society.

---

* A place I would now assign to "Posture, Postural Education, and the Alexander Technique" (see p. 265), which, as a coherent theory of *normal posturality*, was the progenitor of my first book *The Posturality of the Person: A Guide to Postural Education & Therapy* (Atlanta: Posturality Press, 2103).

** *NASTAT News*, see pp. 107, 109, 114, and 117.

Sometime in 1986 or early 87, into my fourth year as Chairman of ACAT-NY, I sat around a big table in New York with other ACAT representatives and members of not-yet NASTAT's steering committee. We were meeting to address ACAT's various concerns and interests in the new organization, among which were who in the country's diversely-credentialed and/or active population of Alexander teachers would be eligible for charter membership. Realizing the challenges to the Technique's orderly development in the US that had been posed by the country's vast geography, and with the concept of a national organization that had always meant for me the essential uniting of the profession, at one point early in the meeting I floated the idea that perhaps, as a distinctly American endeavor, means should be found to include teachers who had trained in circumstances other than the traditional. I suggested that, in terms of addressing the issue of professional standards, a continuing education requirement be implemented from the outset, so that those so included would be able to expand their skills on a gradual basis, to qualify on the installment plan, as it were. To which a very senior ACAT colleague responded, in effect, "If that means that I would be on the same level as _____ (naming a particularly visible and active teacher of that category), count me out." From that point forward I realized that a more inclusive society would not be possible, and took the position personally, of simply waiting and seeing.

NASTAT of course was duly formed, and has been, as I pointed out in "Overview," relatively successful. Long-frustrated American teachers, including myself, certified by one route or another from the original "lowly" ACAT source have gained recognition and parity on a worldwide basis. Teachers credentialed through STAT now freely pursue their happiness here, their Alexandrian destinies no longer under the aegis of London. Indeed, NASTAT was, and is, the "longed-for union of the mainstream English and American Alexander movements, almost matrimonial in its import." Let me be clear that, while I have regretted that NASTAT could not have been more inclusive from the outset, I have also realized that under the conditions that had developed historically, what was done virtually could not have been otherwise. The long unofficial stalemate between STAT and ACAT relative to mutual recognition needed in all practical terms to be resolved by a species of decisive action which precluded the organic evolution of a national organization more truly representative in scope and spirit of the American Alexander experience.

The impact on the American Alexander profession of this speedily-arranged accommodation between STAT and ACAT has been definitely mixed: on the one hand, the majority of American teachers now have an organizational home, either actually or potentially, and important work toward professionalism is both accomplished and in progress; on the other hand, a significant minority of teachers—those certified or otherwise deriving their teaching credential via Marjorie Barstow, Catherine Wielopolska, and Frank Pierce Jones—remain effectively excluded from full recognition and participation. While NASTAT has made provision for these and other "unaffiliated teachers" to qualify for NASTAT membership through various routes, and while some have indeed successfully negotiated the process and actually joined, the fact is that most of these teachers, a number probably approaching fifty, have not yet after seven years been moved to pay NASTAT's current high price of admission—in temporal, monetary, and/or emotional terms—established from the outset. This represents a loss to NASTAT as an organization, and a blow to the possibility of professional unity in the US.

NASTAT's high admission was, of course, established in the name of "standards," together with the prevailing view that for teachers other than ACAT-certified (including ACAT West), the STAT standard of 1600 hours must essentially be met as a precondition of membership. Let us look more carefully at this issue. In the first place, let us recognize that most if not all of the ACAT-certified teachers eligible for charter membership in NASTAT had been trained at, conservatively, "somewhat" less than 1600 hours. I myself had a little over 900, and many had even less. This is not at all said in argument for a lower quantitative standard or again to open debate on that issue, but simply to remind that most of NASTAT's charter membership was "grandfathered" in that respect.

In the second, and far more important place, we should realize that in terms of professional, in contrast to membership standards, the threat at this point in time and in this country comes not from the fact that not all practicing members of the profession have not yet met the standard—as demonstrated above—but from the continued non-unity of the profession, where each passing day that differing standards are profferred results in the confusion, and thus the *de facto* lowering of standards in the public eye. Thus, at the point where we American Alexandrians now stand professionally—at the true inauguration of our profession, despite the many years of its practice—the issue is not nearly so much that of meeting a standard, but of accepting one. For once a standard is accepted in principle, its realization in fact is for all practical purposes a matter of simple convergence in time; the same cannot be said of differing sets of standards, where divergence is the natural outcome of competition.

"A special concern is the perpetuation of disunion through the continued operation of training programs by independent teachers": the numbers of non-NASTAT teachers will not gradually fade away through attrition, they will increase. And, through the activities of an emerging organization, Alexander Technique International, these teachers will find a ready forum. Lincoln, though not an abolitionist at the outset, saw clearly enough that the Union could not endure permanently half-slave and half-free: that is why he fought the Civil War. On our own scale, it behooves us to recognize like forces of divergence in our profession, and to take steps radically to change their direction: "No one, in NASTAT or out, challenges a salutary degree of diversity, or the good intentions of all those serving the Alexander calling as teachers. But for such a tiny profession, in this era of increasing litigation and regulation, particularly in the health and alternative health arenas, getting all Alexander teachers to pull together in terms of public perception and policy must be seen as a very high priority."

Before getting down to specifics, I want to comment upon the emotional dimension of NASTAT's high admission price. ACAT in New York was this country's first training program. It began in 1967, almost by default, since none of the recognized teachers here who might have done so (Marjorie Barstow, Lulie Westfeldt, Alma Frank, Frank Pierce Jones) actually took the step of establishing a training program. As its founders were neither members of STAT nor certified by Alexander, a distinct air of illegitimacy always surrounded ACAT, not to be fully dispelled for twenty years until its recognition by STAT via NASTAT in 1987. I breathed this air, fully aware of its enervating effect on both personal and institutional spirits, through thirteen years of active involvement at ACAT, first as trainee, and subsequently as board and faculty member. No one involved at ACAT during this period would deny the reality—however impossible to document—of this atmosphere, and yet we all also believed, in Judy Leibowitz's words, "We're doing the Alexander Technique here." We just kept on doing it. Being recognized by STAT was certainly gratifying after twenty years, but it wasn't really necessary in terms of the actual work accomplished and continuing at ACAT.

Of course, the teachers who have trained or otherwise qualified through their work with Marjorie, Kitty, and Frank feel exactly the same: they're doing the Alexander Technique here, too. They are serious and committed, they are qualified in their own terms, and they are heavily invested in their careers, just as we were, and are, at ACAT. Authority at some level of competence has acknowledged their ability, and the public certainly doesn't question their right to put themselves forth as Alexander teachers, or to train new Alexander teachers, for that matter. They do not particularly need NASTAT, and I for one, while maintaining to some extent reservations about their method of training in general, and individual competencies in particular (reservations extending to the NASTAT community as well), can certainly empathize with a sense of integrity that simply will not allow any voluntary submission to or examination by what in its eyes can only seem an external and competing authority. It was thus sad for me, around the big table in New York, even in understanding the history and feelings evoking the response, to hear my colleague brand a teacher of now-lesser stature with the same mark that that colleague had likewise carried for so long.

For, as a profession, we no longer have the twenty years, or even five years, in which to wait. The exclusionary bias of the NASTAT founders, however understandable in terms of the prevailing politics, has nonetheless driven the teachers in question in search of their own avenue of professional identity and legitimacy, and they will find it. NASTAT may indeed choose to retain its assumed role as defender of the faith and the 1600 hour standard, but history may judge it harshly if at some future point two Alexander societies are competing for the same slice of some yet-unknown legislative, judicial, or other pie, to say nothing of the greater loss of professional growth through collegiality and mutual exchange. It is thus my conviction that, here in the United States, achieving professional unity by transcending once for all the bleak sectarianship that has grown up among us is NASTAT's most pressing priority.

To this end then, the healing and unification of the Alexander Technique community and profession in this country, I propose to and for NASTAT the following broad course of action. This I state dogmatically, without great explanation beyond what has already said, because those in a position to understand, whether or not they agree, will already know why; others will require far more explanation than is here feasible, and which will doubtless be forthcoming in debate.

1. The conferring, as soon as possible, of honorary membership upon Marjorie Barstow.
2. The admission to full membership, upon application, of the 26 individuals named by Marjorie Barstow as having fulfilled under her tutelage the 1600 hour requirement, provided only that they accept the standards of NASTAT, including those relative to training, and agree to implement them immediately.
3. The same for any teacher certified by Catherine Wielopolska.
4. The same for Lester J. (Tommy) Thompson, who has demonstrated a clear ability to carry on the teaching of Frank Pierce Jones, and who has already been approved for membership in NASTAT through the waiver review process.
5. The reopening of the waiver review process for any teacher certified by a training program conducted by any of the above-named teachers, or by other teachers of similar qualifications.
6. The implementation of a suitable continuing education requirement for all NASTAT members.

There are, to be sure, as well as many unspecified details, clear and present dangers in this course of action. In the first place, some present members of NASTAT, in total disagreement with the philosophy that would thus be implemented, might resign. In the second place, and for the same reasons, there might be serious repercussions from the affiliated national societies, extending to the repudiation of NASTAT. In the third place, unaffiliated teachers who have already joined NASTAT through the waiver or certification review processes might cry foul. And finally, even if made possible, many or most of the teachers in question might not choose to join anyway, making the whole enterprise a fiasco while tearing NASTAT apart.

In full view and cognizance of these dangers, let us alternatively envision another outcome. Let us see a great majority of the NASTAT membership realizing the long-term blessing of professional unity, and being willing to sacrifice and/or defer apparent gains in the service of that larger goal. Let us see the affiliated societies recognizing and appreciating the unique challenges that have attended the development of the Technique on this continent, and therefore accepting a responsible program for the integration of America's heretofore unaffiliated teachers into the international Alexander community. Let us see the unaffiliated teachers who have already joined NASTAT understanding their effort as an investment already returned in terms of greater skills, knowledge, and self-confidence. And finally, let us see the remaining unaffiliated teachers themselves finding that a welcoming opportunity to join NASTAT and the worldwide Alexander community would move most of them in fact to do so.

We are thus brought full circle to the question that stands at the head of this article. For NASTAT does in fact now face a crossroads, and must in fact now make a choice, even if that choice be for business as usual. It is certainly true that persons of good will may disagree, and that all of us must at times base our decisions upon projections that remain agonizing uncertainties. It is also true that there is little that cannot be accomplished if people of good-will will combine their energies in common cause. This is the historic moment. Each of us must now search and decide within ourselves which for NASTAT is the path with heart.

Finis
March 20, 1994

Appendix II

Vol. II, No. 3 Spring/Summer 1983

Barbara Grant, The Alexander Technique as a Way of
Centering
Robert Rickover, Making a Living as an Alexander
Teacher
edward john mattutat, A Commitment to Actuality
S. Knebelman, Thoughts About the Work

Vol. III, No. 1 Autumn 1983

Helen Higa, Learning to Teach
Charles A. Noble, Habit and Compulsion
Ron Dennis, Reflections on the Alexander Method
(Reprint)

Vol. III, No. 2 Winter 1984

Walter Carrington, Guest Editorial
Stanley Knebelman, The Alexander Technique in
Diagnosis and Treatment of Craniomandibular
Disorders
Robert M. Rickover, An Unspoken Mystery of the
Alexander Technique
Kim Jessor, Catch a Wave: Conscious/Unconscious
Experiences with the Alexander Technique

Vol. III, No. 3 Spring/Summer 1984

Chris Stevens, Towards A Physiology of the Alexander
Technique
Deborah Caplan, Skeletal Appreciations Inspired by
Alexander
Roger Tengwall, The Kouroi: A Physico-Cultural
Analysis of Archaic Greek Sculpture

Vol. IV, No. 1 Autumn 1984

Adam Nott, Guest Editorial: Towards An American
  Society of Teachers
Angela Caine, Fear of Singing
Robert M. Rickover, Seeing and Moving: The Relation-
  ship Between Eye Use and the Alexander Technique

Vol. IV, No. 2 Winter 1985

Walter Carrington, How It Works: A Review of Ann
  Mathews' "Implications for Education in the Work
  of F, M. Alexander: An Experimental Project in a
  Public Classroom"
Meade Andrews, The Alexander Technique: Revitaliz-
  ing the Dancer's Self-Image
Kathleen Lawrence, Directing Your Childbirth
Robert M. Rickover, Two Reviews by Rickover: *The
  Book of the Back* by Brian Inglis and *The Cause of
  Lumbar Back Pain and the Solution* by John Gorman

Vol. IV, No. 3 Spring/Summer 1985

Ron Dennis, New Directions at ACAT-NY
John J. Ensminger, Legal Regulation of the Alexander
  Technique: Current Prospects
Ann Mathews, Implications for Education in the Work
  of F. M. Alexander: An Experimental Project in a
  Public School Classroom (Excerpts)
John Naylor, Can Symptoms Have A Value?

About the Author

The Alexander Technique has been Ron Dennis' second career, the first being in music teaching and performance, notably as Principal Clarinet of The Saint Paul Chamber Orchestra from 1969–1977. It was in this period that he had the first of many Alexander lessons with Goddard Binkley beginning in November 1972. During this time he also met and had a lesson with Frank Pierce Jones, as well as spending a week with Marjorie Barstow in 1975.

Becoming gradually convinced that his calling was in Alexander, he departed the orchestra in 1977—at first on leave and then permanently—to train under Judith Leibowitz at the American Center for the Alexander Technique in New York City, where he was certified in December 1979. The next decade was spent in close affiliation with the Center as Board Member, Board Chair, Assistant and Senior Faculty, and, beginning in 1987, as Executive Director. In this latter capacity, he guided the Center's Training Program to full accreditation under the Accrediting Council for Continuing Education and Training, and also to New York State accreditation, which statuses made trainees eligible for federal student aid as well as foreign student visas.

From 1980 onwards he taught privately and also offered group lessons—among the first offered publicly in New York—at the Hebrew Arts School (now the Elaine Kaufman Cultural Arts Center), the Swedish (massage) Institute, and Teachers College Columbia University, where he took his doctorate in 1987 with the dissertation *Musical Performance and Respiratory Function in Wind Players: Effects of the Alexander Technique of Musculoskeletal Education.* He also established, edited, and over four years brought out 13 issues of *The Alexandrian*, the first Alexander periodical in this country, published by the American Center. He and the late Lorna Faraldi were the first Alexander teachers appointed to teach in the Music Division of The Juilliard School, where he served from 1982–1990.

Since moving to Atlanta in 1990, he has devoted his professional time to private practice and writing, as well as being active in AmSAT, the American Society for the Alexander Technique. His research paper of 1999 on balance in normal older women (see p. 224), the first controlled study with "Alexander Technique" in the title to enter the *Index Medicus*, placed the Technique in the global world of scientific research.

Index

Names of Persons

K

Kallen, H. M., 294
Kapandji, I. A., 200, 210, 212
Keele, S. W., 194, 197
Kelso, Scott, 197
Kierkegaard, 5, 30
King, Gene, 95
Kjeldsen, Tim, 157–58
Klein, Laura, 219
Knebelman, Stanley, 296
Kodish, Bruce, 9, 15, 19–20, 43, 252, 254
Kodish, Susan Presby, 19, 252
Kohli, Daniel R., 61, 161, 165
Korzybski, Alfred, 19, 44, 252
Kuhns J. G., MD, 224, 235
Kuperman, Yehuda, 105

L

Langer, Ellen J., 91–93, 125, 233
Langstroth, David, 10, 16, 18, 20, 33, 49, 251
Lawrence, Kathleen, 297
Leibowitz, Judith, 106, 110, 276, 294, 298
Lewis, Pamela Payne, 294
Luening, Otto, 294

M

Macdonald, Patrick, 24, 43, 105, 115, 246, 276
Magnus, Rudolph, 16, 22, 46, 174, 245

Maisel, Edward, 84, 176, 240, 274
Mandal, A. C., 219–20
Mathews, Ann, 297
Mathews, Troup, 212, 294, 297
mattutat, edward john, 296
Meulendijks, Frank, 26
Mueller, Phyllis, 149
Murray, Alexander, 23–24, 27, 62, 295
Muson, Howard, 95, 98

N

Naylor, John, 297
Nevins, Frederick K., 295
Niblett, Bryan, 54, 74
Nicholls, John, 74, 242, 255
Noble, Charles A., 296
Nott, Adam, 297

O

Olney, James, 27–28
Osgood, Robert B., MD, 140, 235
Ottiwell, Frank, 294

P

Palombo, Stanley R., MD, 62
Pinkas, Giora, 24
Polanyi, Michael, 64. 65
Pound, Ezra, 3, 63
Priest, Julia, 130
Protzel, Michael, 242, 254, 270

Subjects

V

W

www.ingramcontent.com/pod-product-compliance
Lightning Source LLC
Chambersburg PA
CBHW051820040426
42447CB00006B/290